Arduino Adventures

Escape from Gemini Station

James Floyd Kelly
Harold Timmis

apress®

Arduino Adventures: Escape from Gemini Station

ISBN-13 (pbk): 978-1-4302-4605-3

ISBN-13 (electronic): 978-1-4302-4606-0

President and Publisher: Paul Manning
Lead Editor: Jonathan Gennick
Technical Reviewers: Jeff Gennick and Andreas Wischer
Editorial Board: Steve Anglin, Ewan Buckingham, Gary Cornell, Louise Corrigan, Morgan Ertel,
    Jonathan Gennick, Jonathan Hassell, Robert Hutchinson, Michelle Lowman, James Markham,
    Matthew Moodie, Jeff Olson, Jeffrey Pepper, Douglas Pundick, Ben Renow-Clarke, Dominic Shakeshaft,
    Gwenan Spearing, Matt Wade, Tom Welsh
Coordinating Editor: Kevin Shea
Copy Editor: Sharon Terdeman
Compositor: SPi Global
Indexer: SPi Global
Artist: SPi Global
Cover Designer: Anna Ishchenko

Distributed to the book trade worldwide by Springer Science+Business Media New York, 233 Spring Street, 6th Floor, New York, NY 10013. Phone 1-800-SPRINGER, fax (201) 348-4505, e-mail orders-ny@springer-sbm.com, or visit www.springeronline.com.

For information on translations, please e-mail rights@apress.com, or visit www.apress.com.

Apress and friends of ED books may be purchased in bulk for academic, corporate, or promotional use. eBook versions and licenses are also available for most titles. For more information, reference our Special Bulk Sales–eBook Licensing web page at www.apress.com/bulk-sales.

Any source code or other supplementary materials referenced by the author in this text is available to readers at www.apress.com. For detailed information about how to locate your book's source code, go to www.apress.com/source-code.

To all those who aspire to learn, and teach, for the betterment of society

—Harold Timmis

This book is for Decker and Sawyer – my two little inspirations.

—James Floyd Kelly

Contents at a Glance

About the Authors xiii

About the Technical Reviewers xv

Acknowledgments xvii

Introduction xix

■Chapter 1: Trouble at Gemini Station 1

■Chapter 2: Challenge 1: Fun Stuff to Know 9

■Chapter 3: Challenge 1: Examining the Hardware 19

■Chapter 4: Challenge 1: Examining the Software 31

■Chapter 5: Damage Assessment 41

■Chapter 6: Challenge 2: Fun Stuff to Know 47

■Chapter 7: Challenge 2: Examining the Hardware 53

■Chapter 8: Challenge 2: Examining the Software 65

■Chapter 9: Feeling The Heat 71

■Chapter 10: Challenge 3: Fun Stuff to Know 77

■Chapter 11: Challenge 3: Examining the Hardware 83

■Chapter 12: Challenge 3: Examining the Software 95

■Chapter 13: Uninvited Guest 103

■Chapter 14: Challenge 4: Fun Stuff to Know 109

■Chapter 15: Challenge 4: Examining the Hardware 115

■Chapter 16: Challenge 4: Examining the Software 131

■Chapter 17: Hide and Seek 141

■Chapter 18: Challenge 5: Fun Stuff to Know 147

■Chapter 19: Challenge 5: Examining the Hardware 151

■Chapter 20: Challenge 5: Examining the Software 167

■Chapter 21: Carousel Ride 173

■Chapter 22: Challenge 6: Fun Stuff to Know 179

■Chapter 23: Challenge 6: Examining the Hardware 183

■Chapter 24: Challenge 6: Examining the Software 201

■Chapter 25: Push the Button 211

■Chapter 26: Challenge 7: Fun Stuff to Know 215

■Chapter 27: Challenge 7: Examining the Hardware 219

■Chapter 28: Challenge 7: Examining Software 233

■Chapter 29: Off the Station 241

■Chapter 30: Challenge 8: Fun Stuff to Know 247

■Chapter 31: Challenge 8: Examining the Hardware 253

■Chapter 32: Challenge 8: Examining Software 271

■Chapter 33: Epilogue 289

■Appendix A: Parts List 293

Index 303

Contents

About the Authors...xiii

About the Technical Reviewers xv

Acknowledgments...xvii

Introduction xix

■Chapter 1: Trouble at Gemini Station...1

Trouble Begins..1

On the Level, or Not?...2

Andrew 5.0..4

Boom!..4

Escape, or Not 6

A Plan 6

■Chapter 2: Challenge 1: Fun Stuff to Know...9

What Is an Arduino? 10

Giving an Arduino a Job to Do 12

Installing the Software 14

Things to Watch for on Windows 14

The Development Environment...16

Ready to Build Something? 18

Chapter 3: Challenge 1: Examining the Hardware 19

Locating the Parts You'll Need 19

Potentiometer 20

Solderless Breadboard 22

The Arduino Uno 23

Wire 25

Let's Build Gizmo #1 25

What's Next? 30

Chapter 4: Challenge 1: Examining the Software 31

The Arduino IDE 31

The Challenge #1 Sketch 33

Beginning the Sketch 34

Configuring the Serial Port 35

Listening on the Serial Port 35

Translating the Input into Digits 37

Displaying the Result 38

Solving Challenge #1 39

Chapter 5: Damage Assessment 41

The Face of Andrew 41

An Embarrassed Cade 43

The Unlocking 44

Chapter 6: Challenge 2: Fun Stuff to Know 47

Let's Look at a Battery 48

And Now a Circuit 50

Current Flow 51

Ready to Build Something? 52

Chapter 7: Challenge 2: Examining the Hardware 53

The Push Button 53

The Light Emitting Diode 54

The Resistor 55

Let's Build Gizmo #2...56

What's Next? 64

■Chapter 8: Challenge 2: Examining the Software 65

Functions Explained 65

The Challenge 2 Sketch...66

Solve Challenge #2 68

■Chapter 9: Feeling The Heat...71

On a Pedestal 72

Chutes and Ladders 73

Green-eyed Hatches 74

■Chapter 10: Challenge 3: Fun Stuff to Know...................................77

Looking at the Temperature Sensor 77

Ready to Build Something? 81

■Chapter 11: Challenge 3: Examining the Hardware 83

What Is a Sensor? 83

Let's Build Gizmo 3!..85

■Chapter 12: Challenge 3: Examining the Software 95

The Conditional If-Else Statement...96

The Challenge #3 Sketch...97

Solve Challenge #3 101

■Chapter 13: Uninvited Guest..103

Upward 103

Spooky?...104

Urgency! 105

Danger!..106

Bucket 107

Chapter 14: Challenge 4: Fun Stuff to Know 109

Looking at the Bucket Mover 110

Understanding the ICs 111

Ready to Build Something? 113

Chapter 15: Challenge 4: Examining the Hardware 115

New Hardware 115

Let's Build Gadget #4 118

Chapter 16: Challenge 4: Examining the Software 131

The Challenge 4 Sketch 132

Breaking It Down 134

Solve Challenge 4 138

Chapter 17: Hide and Seek 141

The Crossing 141

Five Minutes! 142

Run! 144

Walk 145

Chapter 18: Challenge 5: Fun Stuff to Know 147

Let's Look at the Challenge 5 Gizmo 148

Ready to Build Something? 150

Chapter 19: Challenge 5: Examining the Hardware 151

A Closer Look at the PIR Sensor 152

Let's Build The Challenge 5 Gizmo 154

Chapter 20: Challenge 5: Examining the Software 167

Thinking Through the Solution 167

Understanding the Tone Function 168

The Challenge #5 Sketch 169

Solve Challenge #5 172

■Chapter 21: Carousel Ride 173

Close Call..173

Nothing To See Here 174

An Engineering Problem 175

■Chapter 22: Challenge 6: Fun Stuff to Know 179

Let's Look at the Challenge 6 Gizmo 179

Ready to Build Something? 182

■Chapter 23: Challenge 6: Examining the Hardware 183

A Closer Look at a Servo Motor 184

Let's Build the Challenge 6 Gizmo 186

■Chapter 24: Challenge 6: Examining the Software 201

Servo Library Explained 202

The Challenge #6 Sketch..203

Solve Challenge #6..207

■Chapter 25: Push the Button 211

Backup Plan 211

Control Center 212

Crazy Plan 212

The Flashlight..214

■Chapter 26: Challenge 7: Fun Stuff to Know 215

Let's Look at the Challenge 7 Gizmo 216

Ready to Build Something? 218

■Chapter 27: Challenge 7: Examining the Hardware 219

A Closer Look at a Photoresistor 220

Let's Build the Challenge 7 Gizmo 221

■Chapter 28: Challenge 7: Examining Software 233

The Challenge #7 Sketch..233

Solve Challenge #7..237

About the Technical Reviewers

Jeff Gennick is an avid gamer and all-around technology enthusiast. He is a high school junior from Munising, in Michigan's Upper Peninsula. Jeff lives six blocks from Lake Superior, in a snow belt though he is decidedly not a snow person and prefers to spend a cold winter's evening huddled around a hot, Steam-powered game on the gaming rig he spec'd, paid for, and assembled himself. Jeff enjoys technology and sometimes helps his father test the projects in hands-on books, such as the one you're holding now.

Andreas Wischer lives in Paderborn, Germany. While reading about Gemini Station in this book he found astonishing similarities to the world's biggest computer museum located in his home town. Andreas holds a degree in electronics and has worked as a software consultant throughout Europe for more than 10 years. He currently works as an IT professional for a big electronic supplier.

Acknowledgments

First, my heartfelt thanks go to my wonderful wife, Alexandria. Without her support, I could not have written this book. I would also like to thank my family and friends who supported me on this adventure: Mom, Dad, George, Amanda, you guys always help me believe in myself. And a special thank you to my Aunt Sue, who inspired me to write for the rest of my life.

I am also grateful to the Arduino team for developing the incredible piece of hardware known as the Arduino, and to all of the venders that distribute such high-quality components—SparkFun, RadioShack, Adafruit, and MakerSHED.

This book would have never have sounded half as impressive without the great editing skills of Jonathan Gennick, Kevin Shea, and the entire Apress team.

Finally, a very special thanks to our technical reviewers, Jeff Gennick and Andreas Wischer, who did a great job giving Jim and me feedback on this book.

Harold Timmis

Getting this book written, edited, and in your hands required a lot of hard work. I'd like to offer a very big thank you to Kevin Shea at Apress for his patience, hard work, and tenacity in keeping his two authors on track. If you like this book, Kevin had a big part to play in that.

Another thanks goes to Jonathan Gennick at Apress. I've been writing for Jonathan for quite a few years now and I consider him a good friend. Most readers are unaware of the hard work that goes on in just getting a book approved; Jonathan believed in our idea and made it happen.

This book also had some great technical reviewers, Jeff and Andreas. They caught our errors and helped make this book that much better. Any errors you may find are those of the authors. Just be sure to check our web site, arduinoadventurer.com, for any updates or fixes to problems we discover later. A special thanks goes to Jeff, who has been with us since the first few chapters and provided some great feedback that helped us improve the book from the start. His suggestions on how we could better explain wiring up the hardware are much appreciated.

Of course, my family has been completely supportive as I've worked on this book. My wife, Ashley, has always encouraged my career, and my two boys are my daily inspiration as I see their wide eyes taking in all the cool gadgets in my office. It's hard not to be excited about a book when the end result is something that will almost certainly benefit my sons once they're a bit older.

James Floyd Kelly

Introduction

Fun. We (your authors) wanted a word to describe our ultimate goal for this book, as well as a word we hope you (our reader) will use to describe it, and that's the one we chose. There are others goals, of course, but in the end, when you've finished the book, we're hoping you'll have enjoyed the activities described in these pages.

Many books use the Introduction to explain exactly what the book is about, what the reader will learn, what the reader needs (a skill or maybe an item or piece of software), and what the reader will be left with when that last page is completed. And this Introduction will do those things, but ... hopefully it'll make you excited to get started.

So, welcome to Arduino Adventures. We won't make you spend too much time on this Introduction—just give us a few pages and let us tell you how this book works. You'll find a bunch of useful information that will help make the rest of the book more enjoyable.

What Is Arduino Adventures?

That's an easy question to answer! First, the book is about the Arduino. Hmm ... okay, well, that sort of assumes you know what the Arduino is, right? Don't worry, we'll get to that. For now, just take a look at Figure I-1. You're going to use that little electronic device to make some fun and interesting gizmos. Think of it as a teeny-tiny computer (of sorts) that can do some amazing things when you add power and a few other tiny components to it. It's called a microcontroller, and by the time you finish this book, you'll know how to do quite a few things with it.

Figure I-1. *The Arduino Uno microcontroller*

As for the Adventures part of the title, that we can answer right away. You're going to learn how to use the Arduino microcontroller by putting yourself in the shoes of the hero and heroine whose fictional story is told throughout the book. You see, we could have just written a book that tells you to take the particulmaxinator and plug it into the fibulonical port and then tells you to upload the program called MaxFibV2 ... snore! Did your forehead just smack the table? Boring, right? And not the best way to learn.

We're guessing you'll enjoy learning about the Arduino a bit more if you feel involved in the activities. So the storyline is used to present a particular challenge that can only be solved using the Arduino. How many challenges? Eight of them! You'll read a bit of the story, discover the problem our hero and heroine are facing, and then wire up the Arduino and some other components to build a working solution to the problem. That, in a nutshell, is what Arduino Adventures is all about—using a fun story with unique challenges to help you gain a real understanding of how to use the Arduino microcontroller—by actually using your hands to create things. Trust us—it'll be fun!

Will I Be an Arduino Guru When I'm Done?

Ummm ... no. With a limit of 400 pages placed on your new favorite authors, we'll certainly try to give you as much training as we can, but there's only so much we can show you. But don't stress! As you progress through the book, we're going to introduce you to web sites where you can go to learn more about the Arduino. We're going to tell you which books to seek out so you can continue expanding your Arduino skills. And we're going to offer plenty of tips and advice on how to avoid reinventing the wheel—you're going to be pleasantly surprised to find that a lot of work has already been done for you, with shortcuts and tutorials available to do just about anything you can imagine with the Arduino.

When you finish this book, you will have moved from Arduino Novice to Arduino Explorer. You'll have enough of an understanding of the Arduino to feel comfortable working with it, programming it, and tinkering with it to create your own special projects.

What we want you to walk away with when you finish this book is a sense of confidence that you know what the Arduino is, what it can do (and what it can't do), and how to get your own answers and solutions using all the resources that are currently available for Arduino Novices, Arduino Explorers, and Arduino Gurus. If your goal is to become an Arduino Guru, this book will get you moving in the right direction quickly.

What Skills Do I Need?

While we would love to make no assumptions about the basic skills our readers will bring with them and provide a comprehensive, start-to-finish book on everything you'd ever need to know to use the Arduino … it's just impossible. First, a book like that would be around 1,500 pages and weigh about 45 pounds (20 kilos for our metric friends)—and that's not a book we'd want to carry around. And sure … you could always get the digital ebook version, but honestly we don't have the time to write a 1,500 page book. So we're going to have to make some basic assumptions about what our readers possess, such as:

Basic computer skills with either Microsoft Windows or Mac OS. This includes things like being able to use a mouse (or touchpad), knowing how to save files in folders, and a good comfort level with one of the best tools around, the Internet. Chances are good that a large percentage of our readers were handed a laptop or smart phone almost as soon as they were born, so technology is unlikely to faze them in the least. If, however, you are lacking in some basic computer and Internet skills, please just ask your children or grandchildren to assist you—they're really good with this stuff.

A brain. For some reason, people who want to learn about the Arduino tend to do better when they have a real brain, not a foam one that you squeeze when you get stressed or use to play fetch with the dog. If it's been verified that a brain does exist inside your skull, you're going to do well. If you don't have a brain, please put the book down and have someone drive you to the hospital—you'll need to have some tests run. Sorry.

A parent, teacher or good friend. Not only do these people make good partners for working on the challenges in this book, but they're also really useful when it comes time to show off what you've done. Bonus points will be awarded if a look of surprise is visible on their faces. Double bonus points are awarded if they shake their heads and have no idea what they're looking at and ask you to explain. Seriously … you know you've made something cool when people look at you like you're a mega-genius or something.

How is the Book Organized?

As we mentioned, there are eight challenges in all. This means the story will be broken into eight parts (okay, nine if you include the story's conclusion). But the fictional story isn't going to offer you the information you need to solve the eight challenges. Nope! To solve those challenges, you'll be getting some additional instruction that, again, we hope you'll find easy and fun to read.

The book is broken into eight parts. Each part starts with a chapter containing a piece of the overall story. Following the fiction chapter is a theory chapter that offers information on the skills and components needed to complete the challenge. Each theory chapter is followed by a hardware chapter that shows how to build the Arduino-controlled solution to the challenge. A software chapter concludes each challenge with details on how to make the solution work using what's called a sketch. Don't worry, we know these may be new words to many of you, so for now just know that all Arduino-controlled devices require both a hardware and software component. You'll gain experience in both areas as the book progresses. Also, at the end of each software chapter you'll find extra problems to solve to help you become a better Arduino tinkerer.

So, here's a summary of how the book flows:

Fiction Chapter – You'll read the story and discover the challenge that must be overcome using something you're going to build using an Arduino microcontroller. Yes, the story is fiction, but the challenge is 100% real—and by buying this book you PROMISE to not move forward to the next challenge until you've successfully completed the current challenge. Agreed?

Theory Chapter – You'll get a basic education on the hardware that will be used to solve a challenge, as well as some more detailed explanations on relevant topics involving electronics and programming. This is the kind of chapter that would typically put us to sleep, too, so we promise to try and make it somewhat entertaining so your eyes don't glaze over and you start snoring.

Hardware Chapter – When you finish this chapter, you'll have a solution to the challenge introduced in the fiction chapter. It'll look cool ... we promise—lots of wires and cool-looking extras you can show off to your friends and family. You'll also be introduced to other electronics components that we might not use in the book but that we think you'll find cool and fun to know about for your own projects.

Software Chapter – That gizmo you put together in the hardware chapter isn't finished yet. In this chapter you'll be given basic instructions on how to make the gizmo work using simple programs we'll provide. But we're not just going to give you a program—we'll also explain how and why it works so you'll be able to experiment and modify it if you like.

Do I Need to Understand Electronics?

Not at all. That's not to say any electronics knowledge you do have won't come in handy, but we'll be introducing you to the concepts you need to know about in the book, so no electronics experience is necessary. Still, just as you won't be an Arduino Guru when you finish this book, you won't be an Electronics Guru either. But we'll make sure to point you to resources that will help you move in that direction if that's your desire.

The challenges presented in this book involve a variety of electronics components, but we'll go over all of them as needed and give you the information you need to finish a challenge and understand how it works.

Do I Need to Know How to Solder?

In case you don't know, soldering is a method used to more permanently connect electronic components and wires. Heat is used to melt a mixture of various metals that quickly cools and solidifies. You can use this mixture (called solder) to make two wires stick together or make an electronic component maintain its connection with other components.

But … no soldering is required. If you know how to solder, great! But you won't need to do so for the challenges in this book. And if you don't know how to solder, we'll point you later on to some good tutorials that show you what's involved. If you do decide to go deeper into electronics and Arduino tinkering, it's a skill you'll definitely want to learn.

What Do I Need Besides This Book?

Appendix A includes a complete list of all items you'll need to complete all eight challenges. You'll also find part numbers for the various vendors we recommend. If you prefer to get the items a little at a time, you'll want to read the theory chapter for each chapter to discover the specific items required for each particular challenge. We want to be upfront and let you know that if you purchase all of the required components for this book individually, you'll end up spending around $175.00. But be sure to check out the book's web site because we'll be telling you how to save money by buying pre-bundled packages that contain the components at reduced prices. We're pushing you to the web site because this information will likely change frequently, so whatever we put in this book may well be out of date (and higher priced) by the time you read this. So, again … check the web site for the latest information on pricing and parts required!

The one item that's required for all challenges, however, is the Arduino Uno. You'll find a number of vendors that sell the Arduino, but you'll be happy to know that Radioshack is currently an Arduino retailer. This means if you've got a Radioshack in your town, it probably carries the microcontroller. If you prefer to purchase online, you may find an occasional sale that has Arduinos at a reduced price. But the Arduino is already a very inexpensive microcontroller (typically between $20 and $30), so just buy one at the best price you can find. Just one! You won't need multiple Arduinos for the challenges in this book.

You'll also want Internet access as you'll use it to download full-color wiring diagrams for the challenges on the book's web site, www.arduinoadventurer.com. And although it's not required, you'll find when you get to the first challenge that you can download some PDFs that will make some of the challenges a bit more fun. We call them Challenge Cards, and if you decide to use them, you'll want to print them out on 8.5x11 card stock (more sturdy than standard paper).

We'll also be sending you to an occasional Arduino-related site. We're not doing that in order to save on typing—we just want to show you how to search for and find particular solutions that already exist online.

The Arduino can be powered by either batteries or AC (wall) power. For this book, however, we'll be using battery power and a USB cable. This means you'll want to purchase a number of batteries depending on how you wish to provide power to your Arduino and a USB A male to USB B male cable is used in some of the challenges to power the Arduino as well. Appendix A provides you with a few options for power; choose the one you like best.

Finally, you'll need some specialty electronics items that most likely you won't find locally (at a Radioshack, for example). While we'll do our best to keep costs down, realize that learning to use the Arduino requires you to purchase a few unique items to make the Arduino work and the challenges successful.

What Do I Need For the First Challenge?

Well, for Chapter 1 you're going to need to know how to read. If you've made it this far into the Introduction, then it's safe to say you'll be okay and can move forward.

You're also going to want to make a shopping list for the components used in the first challenge. We've made this easy for you and placed the first challenge's list of required components at the beginning of Chapter 3. For all remaining challenges, consult Appendix A for the rest of the components you'll need.

Finally, you're going to need to a pep talk. So here it is:

You're going to have fun. And you're going to learn some really cool things that are going to amaze your family, friends, teachers, and pets. (Yes, even dogs and cats appreciate a well-designed gizmo.)

You can do this. There is nothing in this book that is beyond your skills. If you get confused or lost, it's a book—you can easily go back and reread any sections you like. And we'll also be sharing with you some great online resources where you can go and ask questions. You're fully qualified to accept the challenges in this book, so don't get discouraged.

We (your authors) want you to enjoy this experience. Arduino Adventures was written specifically for people like you. We promise that when you finish this book, you'll have a LOT of reasons to smile and be proud.

So … let's get to it. Your first Arduino challenge awaits. All you need to do is turn the page …

Chapter 1

Trouble at Gemini Station

"Do you just look for ways to get us into trouble, Cade?" asked Elle. She looked back over her shoulder to make certain no one else had followed them down the dark hallway.

"Are you telling me you actually wanted to stay with the tour group?" Cade flashed the same grin he always used when he tried to convince Elle he could do no wrong.

Trouble Begins

Sneaking away from the rest of the class just as the tour of Gemini Station began was pure Cade. The two students were both convinced that listening to lectures on the history of computing and electronics during the pre-gateway period would have them yawning and looking for a quiet corner to sleep. Mrs. Hondulora and the the other two instructors had made the mistake of being at the head of the line, allowing Cade and Elle to drop their location beacons in the backpacks of two other students who weren't paying attention before sneaking away.

"No, but you just know Mrs. H. is gonna pull a pop quiz on us next week about some little bit of trivia we're going to miss," replied Elle. "My grades aren't bad, but if I fail a quiz my mom and dad'll put me on a drop-ship to the outer ring."

"You've got the best grades in the class, Elle. Give it a rest," said Cade. "Hey, here we go."

Elle followed Cade's gaze to a digital display mounted at the edge of the intersection. Colored lines on the floor were finally given meaning as the pair read instructions color-coded to indicate which line to follow for various exhibits.

"Pre-2050 Video Game Technology," said Cade. "Red line. That could be interesting."

Elle shook her head. "No, the blue line. Hologram Storage Solutions 2020–2085. I've always been curious to know how they solved the distortion problem."

Cade frowned and slowly turned his head to look at Elle. "You're kidding, right."

Elle tried to hold back the grin, but it lasted only a few seconds. "Almost had you."

"Well, we've got five or six hours to burn and an entire station turned into a technology museum, so I thought you might be serious. You really do get into this stuff more than anyone else I know," said Cade.

"How about that third option?" asked Elle. "Yellow line."

Cade looked back at the display. "History of Processors 1960–2015. Yeah, you've picked another winner, Elle."

Cade dodged just in time to avoid Elle's hand aimed for the back of his head. "We're running out of options," she replied. "We can always just go back and see what the group is doing."

Another grin crossed Cade's face.

"I don't like that smile," said Elle.

"How many levels did Mrs. H. say were on this station?"

Elle shook her head. "No way, Cade. That'll get us banned from field trips for the rest of the school year."

"Come on, Elle. How many?"

On the Level, or Not?

Elle bit her lip and thought back to the small presentation the students had watched prior to the trip. The space station had been decommissioned back in 2091. The twenty-three levels that made up the cigar-shaped station circling M-392 were originally used for deep-space research and provisioning of outbound ships, but the station had been literally cut in two to form Gemini Station and Taurus Station. The latter had been towed to the opposite side of M-392 so both stations were in geosynchronous orbits above the two largest settlements, Gemini for mining and Taurus for energy production to power the gateway for this system. Elle had to concentrate to recall the number of levels on Gemini Station, but then one of her memory tricks fired and she saw twelve rocks arranged to form the letter G.

"Twelve for Gemini. Eleven for Taurus."

Cade sighed and pointed at Elle's forehead. "It's really creepy how much information you store up there, you know that? I'll bet you a week's worth of 'Net access tokens that you probably have the entire station's layout memorized, don't you? Come on. . . admit it."

"The map was in the data pack. It might be on a test or something," Elle replied, her face red.

"Yeah. A test or something."

"Shutup."

"So, twelve levels. The shuttle dock is what, level twelve?"

"Eleven. Command and Control is level twelve," said Elle. "Think of it as a tube standing upright. Level twelve at the top. . ."

"And we took the elevators all the way down to the bottom. This big number one painted on all the walls seems to be important," asked Cade. "I'm guessing restrooms?"

"Funny," said Elle. "But the answer is still no. I'm not getting too far from the group, Cade."

Cade took a deep breath and exhaled. "Fine. You stay here. But if you're not going to go with me, at least do me a favor and tell me what else there is on this station that might be interesting and where it's located?"

Elle knew that if she didn't offer up more details, Cade would just continue to bug her. And he could be annoyingly persistent. She frowned for a brief moment and then nodded. "Alright. What are you wanting to see?"

Cade looked back down the hallway they had just crossed to the set of double elevator doors. "What's on level two?"

Elle once again called up the data pack from memory. She had read the museum summaries of each level numerous times, and the holographic tour of the main tourist levels were a bit dull but she'd run it at triple-speed, listening to the AI's high-pitched helium voice and trying not to laugh.

"Let's see. . . level two was food court, gift shop, and a couple of holo-rooms. Basic stuff, really. Interactive historical views of various breakthroughs in technology. Supposedly you can have lunch and chat with some of the titans of tech. Hey, that might be fun to go and talk to those original Google guys. . ."

"Stop. No, thank you," said Cade. "What about level three?"

"Um. . . let me see. More exhibit space. Microcontroller antiques. The Andrew 5.0 Experience. Some early tablet technology," said Elle.

"Wait. . . Andrew 5.0?"

"Yeah," said Elle. "The first AI. You like that kind of thing?"

"Absolutely!" Cade smirked and looked down the hallway, hoping his voice hadn't carried and alerted the teachers to their absence. "Come on, Elle. You've got to come with me."

"Not a chance," she replied. "I think I'm going back to the group. Maybe they won't notice me trying to blend in."

"I'll never find my way around up there by myself," said Cade. "Please, please, please?"

"Lame," said Elle. "There are signs everywhere, moron. Like that one." She pointed at the one directly over Cade's head.

"If you come with me, I'll do all your formatting work for a week."

Elle cringed. Of all the things she hated to do, formatting her written assignments to fit Mrs. H.'s picky standards was at the top of the list. And Cade knew it.

"A month," she replied.

"What? No way!"

"See ya," Elle said and turned to walk away.

"Alright," said Cade. "One month. But you're going to have to get me to more places than the Andrew 5.0 location."

"This is not going to end well for me," said Elle.

Cade laughed. "Yes! Okay, come on. The elevators look clear."

Andrew 5.0

The elevator doors opened. "Level Three," said a polite voice. "Be sure to visit the Andrew 5.0 Experience to hear the history of artificial intelligence from a splinter node of the original Andrew 5.0!"

Cade poked his head out the door, looking left and then right. "All clear."

Elle pushed him aside and walked quickly out of the elevator. "You don't have to be all sneaky, Cade. We're the only ones on the station today. Come on, let's hurry."

Cade walked fast to catch up. "Are you sure?"

"Yep. The entire station is automated. Didn't you notice that our two shuttles were the only ones docked?"

"Uh, yeah. That's right. Two shuttles." Cade tried, and failed, to sound informed.

"We were supposed to share the tour with a group of Japanese students gating in from Earth, but I heard that a bunch of them came down with a bug. And Gemini is pretty strict about its quarantine rules."

"Yuck," said Cade, turning left at a display of old LCD screens. He stopped to look. "This is how kids used to have to read? With a screen?"

"Would you come on?" hissed Elle.

"I'm coming," said Cade. "Calm down."

Elle pointed down a hallway. "This way. I assume you want to visit Andrew 5.0 first?"

Cade nodded. "Yeah, let's go there first."

Elle continued speed-walking, making a right turn at a large display of rectangular boxes. A sign read "PC Case Mods 2010-2015" and Cade was tempted to stop for a quick peek, but a stern look from Elle convinced him to keep moving.

"What's so interesting about Andrew 5.0?" Elle asked.

"Family history," said Cade. "My great-great-grandfather was on the original programming team when Andrew achieved sentience."

"Really? That's cool."

"Yeah, I'm curious to know if he remembers him."

"Well, he should," replied Elle. "It's just a splinter node, but since we're on a station dedicated to technology history, I'll bet this node has kept that stuff in local memory."

"I hope so," said Cade.

Boom!

Elle stopped and looked up at a sign. "Microcontroller Hands-On Exhibit in that room over there. The Andrew 5.0 Experience is on the other side. Let's cut through and save some time."

"Sounds good."

The door opened as Elle approached and the interior LED lights instantly awakened. Cade followed Elle as they walked by dozens of tables. Large black toolboxes and strange equipment lay scattered across the tables. Clear bins contained hundreds, maybe thousands, of small electronics components that were colorful and completely alien to Elle and Cade.

"This room actually looks fun," said Elle. "Wish we had time to play."

"With this stuff?" asked Cade. "Really? This tech was outdated when your grandmother was a baby."

"Maybe, but I've always liked learning about how people in the early days did things."

"I tell you what, Elle," said Cade. "If we have time, maybe we can come ba. . ."

BOOM!

The floor shook hard enough to knock Elle and Cade off their feet.

BZZZZZT!

BZZZZZZZZZT!!!

The lights flickered off, then on, then off again. There was a small electrical pop, followed by a whining sound that dwindled in the distance.

And then the alarm began to wail.

"Cade! Cade!"

"I'm okay," Cade replied. "Are you alright?"

Emergency lights had turned on, not quite as bright as the standard LED lighting, but enough that they could see that the floor was covered with dented toolboxes and small pieces of metal. A few tables had overturned, and a red light on the wall was flashing.

"Yeah. Yeah. . . I'm fine. What was that?" yelled Elle.

Cade stood up and helped Elle to her feet. "We need to get back to the group. That felt like an explosion."

Elle's eyes widened. "Are you sure? Maybe it was something else."

"Anything else is just as bad," said Cade. "It was enough to knock us off our feet, Elle. Let's go."

Elle followed Cade toward the entry door and then bumped into him as he stopped short. The door didn't open. Cade waved his hands in the air, hoping to set off whatever motion sensor was supposed to trigger the door, but there was no response.

"No good," said Elle. "Try the keypad."

Cade pointed at the bits of melted plastic hanging from the small white rectangle mounted to the right of the door. "You mean that bit of junk?"

"Oh, this is not good," said Elle.

Cade turned to look to the other side of the room that led to the Andrew 5.0 Experience. A matching burned and melted control panel hung by a few wires from the wall. "Other keypad is damaged, too."

"Do you know how big a power surge it would take to do that?" asked Elle.

"We need to get out of this room, Elle," said Cade. "Look for another exit."

Escape, or Not

"All visitors, please make your way to the emergency escape pods located on levels one, six, and ten. For other levels, ladder access tubes for visitors to reach levels one, six, and ten are now open. Please follow the blue and yellow flashing lights to the nearest ladders and escape pods. Visitors on levels eleven and twelve should proceed to the level eleven docks. Repeating. . ."

"No exits on that side," Cade reported as he joined Elle at the main entrance that was now blocked. "The ceiling is fifteen or twenty feet up and I'm not finding any ladders or other way to climb up there."

"The floor is tiled, but none of the tools I found will let me pull them up," said Elle.

"Do you know anything about electronics?" asked Cade. "Maybe we can fix the keypad?"

Elle leaned in closer to stare into the burned circuitry that made up the keypad. "I wouldn't know where to start."

"Me either," replied Cade.

"We could try yelling for help. Maybe someone will hear us."

Cade and Elle began yelling and pounding on the door.

"HELP!"

"Let us out!"

"Anyone out there? Please help us!"

The banging slowed as the two students tired. And that's when they heard a faint voice from the opposite side of the room.

"What is the problem?"

Elle and Cade ran to the opposite door in the room.

"Hello? Hello? Can you help us? Who are you?" asked Elle, putting her ear to the door.

"Hello. I am Andrew. What is your name?"

A Plan

Five minutes later, Cade and Elle finished explaining the situation to Andrew 5.0. Andrew couldn't provide any explanation for the alarm and evacuation, but he did verify a significant amount of damage being reported on the station via an internal damage-control network he was able to monitor.

"Are you able to communicate with the station AI?" asked Cade. "Can you let someone know we're locked in this room?"

"I am sorry, but I am unable to communicate outside of my current location. I can pick up certain reports traveling over the station's communication grid, but my programming was modified to limit my capabilities, including interfacing with other AIs."

"Is there anyone on this level besides us?" asked Elle. "Is there any chance an emergency team will be sent to check out the station?"

"Unknown, Elle," replied Andrew. "There are probably protocols in place for emergencies."

"So we just sit tight and wait," said Cade.

"But we don't know what's happened,' said Elle. "What if the station is venting oxygen? Or what if there's a fire?"

"Way to stay positive, Elle."

"Sorry. I'm just saying we need to get out of here. We can't assume anyone is coming to get us. We did drop our personal beacons into other people's backpacks."

Cade's face reddened. "That was a bad idea. Sorry."

"Hey, I went along. I'm not blaming you. But it means we're on our own. No one knows we're here." Elle put her hand on Cade's shoulder.

Cade nodded. "Well, not to sound cocky, but we are the two smartest kids in the class. We should be able to figure out how to escape a locked room, right?"

Elle laughed. "And we've got an AI in the next room."

"That's right! We're unstoppable! Andrew, we need to figure out how to get out of this room. Any ideas?"

Andrew had remained quiet but responded instantly. "You said the two keypads are damaged. Can you tell me if the circuit board behind the panel is also damaged?"

"The green board?" asked Cade.

"Yes."

"Yeah, it's toast. I see black burn marks across it."

"Above the circuit board is a small sealed metal case with four or five wires going into it. Are the wires still intact?"

Elle poked at the wires going into the small metal box. Each of them stayed in place. "Yeah, they're fine. I think."

"Good. We'll need to spoof the entry code, but you can easily do that with a variable resistor and a small power source. Of course, you'll need to do some custom programming so that will require some processing capabilities. Do either of you have an Intellitab with you?"

Cade turned and stared at Elle. "Is he kidding?"

Elle frowned. "Andrew, we don't have our tabs with us today. Sorry."

There was a slight pause.

"Andrew?" asked Elle.

"I was just consulting my database inventory of the station. You are in the Microcontroller Hands-On Activity Lab Room. We'll just use what's available."

Once again, Cade shook his head and stared wide-eyed at Elle. "Seriously. . . is he kidding?"

Elle held up her hand.

"Andrew, this stuff is ancient. Old-style electronics and stuff we don't even recognize."

Andrew's voice changed, becoming slower and sounding much more patient. "Elle. Cade. It will be a challenge, but I can help you get that door open using some of the components in the room. You'll have to listen to me carefully, but if you follow my instructions, you'll be able to open the door. Are you ready?"

Cade exhaled and nodded his head slowly. "Sure, I don't think we have any other options."

Elle grinned. "Looks like we're going to get some hands-on time whether we like it or not. Okay, Andrew, tell us what we need to do."

"First, I need you to locate something called an Arduino microcontroller. My inventory tells me there are hundreds of them in a cabinet in the room in labeled boxes. Find one now."

Chapter 2

Challenge 1: Fun Stuff to Know

We thought about calling this Challenge 1: An Arduino Applied Exercise, but that sounded too much like going to the gym. Our second attempt was Chapter 1: Theoretical Concepts, but it caused both of your authors to fall fast asleep. So we had a short discussion about what exactly we hoped you'd get out of this chapter and it came down to this—the fun stuff.

As we mentioned in the Introduction, we aren't going to be able to teach you everything there is to know about electronics, programming, and the Arduino in general. But what we can do is point you in the right direction to other resources that will help fill in the gaps between what we can teach you in this book and what you'll want to learn elsewhere to become an Arduino guru.

So, this is what we decided. First, we're not going to flood you with tons of information about the Arduino all at once. We'll spread it out over the entire book so by the time you complete all the challenges, you'll have a good understanding of what the Arduino is, what it can do, and how it works. Along the way you'll pick up some good programming skills that will only improve over time as you branch out and go crazy designing your own Arduino gizmos.

We're inviting our favorite artificial intelligence, Andrew 5.0, to help along the way by offering additional advice, tips, and references. Don't think of it as homework … but yeah … it's homework. But we promise it'll be *interesting* homework!

So, here's the deal. After each fiction chapter that moves the story of Cade and Elle along, we're going to give you a Fun Stuff to Know chapter. You're going to learn stuff, so don't let that scare you away, okay? The goal of this book isn't to overwhelm you with technobabble and complicated discussions, and we'll do our best to keep the fun stuff really fun. So, grab a chair and a drink and maybe your favorite snack and let's get started helping Cade and Elle get out of that locked room and introduce them to the Arduino. Sound fun? We agree … let's go.

What Is an Arduino?

Just because you have this book doesn't automatically mean you know what an Arduino is, so we're going to get that over with right away. The easiest way to explain is to show you what an Arduino looks like. Take a look at Figure 2-1 and you'll see an actual-size Arduino Uno.

Figure 2-1. The Arduino Uno microcontroller

That *Uno* part is the name given to this particular version. You've probably heard of the iPhone 3, 4, and 4s and Windows XP, Windows Vista, and Windows 7 (and soon Windows 8). These are simply various versions of products people use and the Arduino is no different. Well, that's not completely true. The Arduinos are typically given names instead of numbers (as well as revision numbers; the current version of the Uno is Revision 3, or Rev 3 for short), so what you need to know is that we'll be using the *Arduino Uno* version *Rev 3* for all challenges in the book.

> **Note**   You'll want to purchase an Arduino Uno before beginning the actual challenges, so consult Appendix A for a list of sources where you can purchase the Arduino Uno as well as the other components you'll need to complete the book.

At the time that we're writing this book, the Arduino Uno is the latest version. Without getting too technical, the Arduino Uno and its predecessors are called microcontrollers, which is just a fancy word for a really tiny computer. And that's exactly what it is! A computer. And just like the computers you're familiar with, the Arduino can have things plugged into it: power supplies, motors, and sensors—all sorts of components. But the Arduino can also do other things, such as calculate 4,234,876 x 5,981 or figure out how many days are left until school is over for the summer.

ANDREW 5.0

Gentlemen, I'd like to interrupt here for a moment just to let your readers know that if they have an older version of the Arduino, it might be possible to use it instead of the Arduino Uno. They might have to do a little research to make a non-Uno version work properly, by finding out what's the same and what's different between models. If you'd like to see other versions and learn about their differences, visit http://arduino.cc/en/Main/Hardware. There's quite a lot of information on this web site, so don't feel you have to understand it all right away. As you continue through the book, many of the technical aspects of the Arduino Uno and its predecessors will begin to make more sense.

Andrew is correct. Older versions of the Arduino might work for the challenges you'll find in this book, but obtaining an Arduino Uno is going to be the easiest way to avoid frustration when working through the challenges. From this point forward, however, we'll just use the term Arduino instead of Arduino Uno. It's kind of like saying "My computer runs Windows" instead of "My computer runs the Windows 7 Professional 64-bit operating system." You won't sound so goofy and long-winded.

The Arduino has a bunch of interesting things attached to it, but we're not going to go over all of them in this chapter. Instead, we'd like to point out a few key items you'll be using for the first challenge. Figure 2-2 shows the Arduino with some fancy arrows pointing out a few important locations. Check them out now, we'll wait.

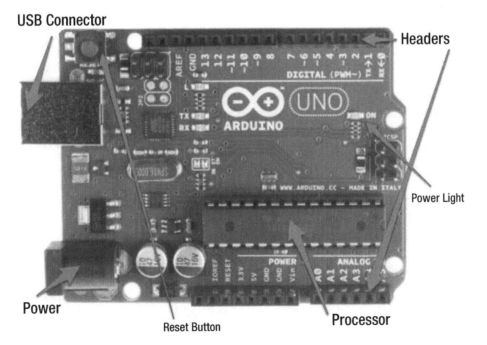

Figure 2-2. The Arduino again ... but this time with fun arrows!

The Arduino can be powered using batteries or AC power, also known as an AC adapter. Or, if you really want to be funny, call it a wall-wart. We do.

The point is that the Arduino requires power, so you'll either need to plug it in with a wall-wart or use a battery harness like the one shown in Figure 2-3 to hold one 9V battery. We'll show you in Chapter 3 how to provide power to your Arduino if you choose to use a battery harness. (We actually recommend the battery harness because it makes your Arduino portable. Cade and Elle will be using this method in the book.)

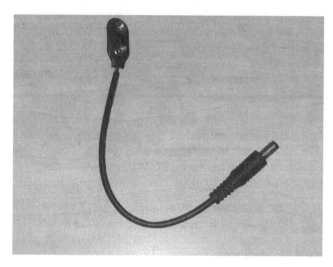

Figure 2-3. A battery harness can provide portable power to an Arduino

See those things called headers? (Refer back to Figure 2-2 if you need a reminder.) Those little black rectangles have holes in them. You'll be inserting wires and other items into those holes later in the book—this is how you attach motors or sensors or other components to the Arduino. For right now, don't worry about all the little numbers and words printed next to the headers. We'll explain everything when the time comes; for now we just want you to notice that not all the holes are the same. Some have numbers, some have words, and some are completely confusing until you know what they're used for. Rest assured we'll explain it all by the end of the book.

There are many more parts of the Arduino that you'll learn in time, but the last one we want to point out now is that big rectangle mounted almost in the center. That's the brains of the Arduino and it's called a processor—specifically, an Atmel AVR processor. That little thing is what will be running the show once you've got your challenge gizmo created and ready to test. And how exactly does the processor run the show? Glad you asked.

Giving an Arduino a Job to Do

An Arduino won't do a lot by itself. Yes, it can perform math calculations and it keeps pretty good time with its internal clock, but the microcontroller by itself is really just a pretty cool-looking paperweight. (And it's not that heavy, really, so it's not going to function as a paperweight all that well.)

What makes an Arduino fun to use is plugging in all sorts of electronic components that do stuff. Motors. LEDs. Sensors that can detect a dog barking (sound) or an intruder entering your room (ultrasonic). Things called resistors, capacitors, transistors, and much more. It doesn't matter if you don't know what all those things are or how they work yet … just be aware that when they're connected to the Arduino, they're ready to do a job. By itself, of course, the Arduino doesn't know how to control those components and tell them what to do. For that, it needs some instructions … from you. These instructions come in the form of written words and numbers that you type up, similar to that essay you wrote for class titled "A History of Colonial Gardening Techniques" but much more interesting and fun.

The Arduino gets these instructions and stores them in its memory. The set of instructions is often called a program, but Arduino users also call them sketches. No, an Arduino sketch doesn't require you to provide your best hand drawing of two deer running in the forest. A sketch is simply the name given to a list of written instructions that tell the Arduino what to do, how to do it, and how to play well with all the stuff connected to it. Why did they choose "sketches" instead of "programs"? We're not really sure, but we do like the sound of it: "I just loaded a sketch into my Arduino."

ANDREW 5.0

I think an example might help your readers understand what a sketch looks like. Listing 2-1 shows a simple sketch that makes a single white LED that has been connected to an Arduino blink on and off.

Listing 2-1. An Arduino Sketch That Makes an LED Blink

```
/*
  Blink
  Turns on an LED on for one second, then off for one second, repeatedly.

  This example code is in the public domain.
*/

// Pin 13 has an LED connected on most Arduino boards.
// give it a name:
int led = 13;

// the setup routine runs once when you press reset:
void setup() {
  // initialize the digital pin as an output.
  pinMode(led, OUTPUT);
}

// the loop routine runs over and over again forever:
void loop() {
  digitalWrite(led, HIGH);   // turn the LED on (HIGH is the voltage level)
  delay(1000);               // wait for a second
  digitalWrite(led, LOW);    // turn the LED off by making the voltage LOW
  delay(1000);               // wait for a second

}
```

You can also find this sketch at arduino.cc/en/Tutorial/Blink.

Just like you probably don't speak ancient Greek, you're not expected right now to totally understand what this sketch is saying. That will come in time. Just note that this sketch uses some English words that you'll recognize. We'll provide the sketches you'll need to complete the challenges, but you'll also learn how they work and how to create your own as you work your way through the book. Writing sketches is fun, and this is what really gives you the power to create your own Arduino-controller gizmos that can do whatever you can dream up.

To create sketches, you have to download and install something called the Arduino IDE. The IDE part stands for Integrated Development Environment. Yeah, we feel the same way. Just call it the IDE and know that it's the software tool you'll use to write sketches and upload them to the Arduino.

Installing the Software

We don't know whether you'll be using a Windows, Linux or Mac computer to create your sketches, but you'll be happy to know that the IDE is available for all three operating systems. You can download the Arduino IDE by opening a web browser and visiting www.arduino.cc, then clicking the Download button on the green menu bar running across the screen. After you download the appropriate version for your computer, click on the Getting Started button (also on the green bar at www.arduino.cc) and follow the instructions for installing the software for your particular operating system; you'll find instructions for Windows, Mac, and Linux.

> **Caution**   Do take the time to read the install instructions for your operating system. Otherwise, it's all too easy to overlook key details like the need to install drivers under Windows. As with just about anything in life, it's good to read the instructions.

Things to Watch for on Windows

We noticed a few things while installing on Windows that we want to share with you. The Windows install can be intimidating if you're used to simply plugging in a device and having it work. There's no setup program to mindlessly click through. You must install the drivers manually. We hope what follows is helpful. It comes from our install on Windows 7.

> **Tip**   Scan this section first for background. Then read and follow the official install instructions found on arduino.cc. We hope that what you read here will help and give confidence when following the instructions provided on Arduino's website.

When you first plug in the device, Windows will begin searching for a driver. That search will fail. If you click to see the specific error message, you'll probably see something like the dialog in Figure 2-4. Do not worry! Read the install instructions from the Arduino website carefully. The error in Figure 2-4 is an expected error. Simply click Close and follow the remaining instructions carefully.

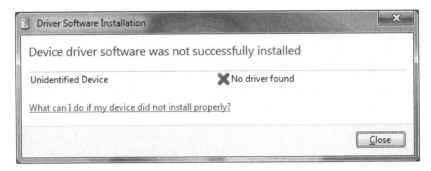

Figure 2-4. The error that really isn't

The current install instructions on arduino.cc have you opening the Device Manager and looking under "Ports (COM & LPT)" for a device called "Arduino UNO (COMxx)". Figure 2-5 shows what you *really* need to look for.

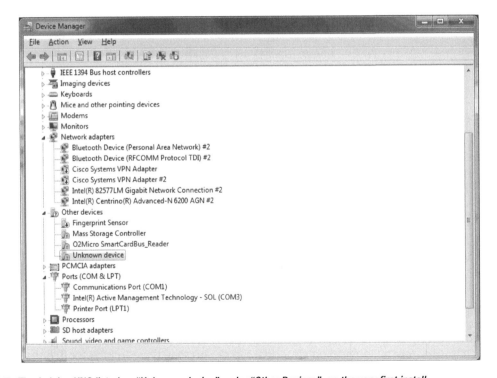

Figure 2-5. The Arduino UNO listed as "Unknown device" under "Other Devices", on the very first install

The very first time you install the device, it shows up as "Unknown device'. If you have doubts about what you are looking at, unplug the USB cable, wait a few seconds, and plug it in again. You will see the "Unknown device" disappear from Device Manager listing, and then reappear again. After you have installed the Arduino's drivers, *then* the device will appear under "Ports (COM & LPT)" as "Arduino UNO (COMxx)". But the very first time around, the device is unknown.

The last thing we noticed in our testing is that the install instructions ask you to navigate to a driver file named ArduinoUNO.inf. In Windows 7, we were able to navigate only to the directory containing the file, and not to the file itself. Figure 2-6 shows where we ended up. Just click to highlight the drivers directory, and then click the OK button. Windows will find the specific file by itself.

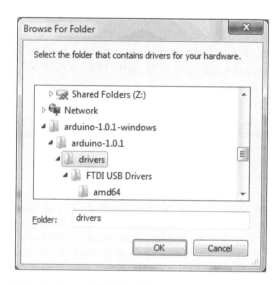

Figure 2-6. The drivers directory containing the Arduino UNO driver file

We hope the heads-up we gave in this section helps during your install. Keep in mind that the instructions on the Arduino website may get corrected between now and when you read the book. Read those instructions carefully. Follow them thoughtfully. Those are the keys to success.

The Development Environment

After installing the software and drivers, open the Arduino IDE by double-clicking the Arduino executable; this icon may be located on your desktop or you may have to look for it in the Applications folder (Mac) or the All Programs/Programs folder (Windows). Figure 2-7 shows what the IDE looks like after it opens.

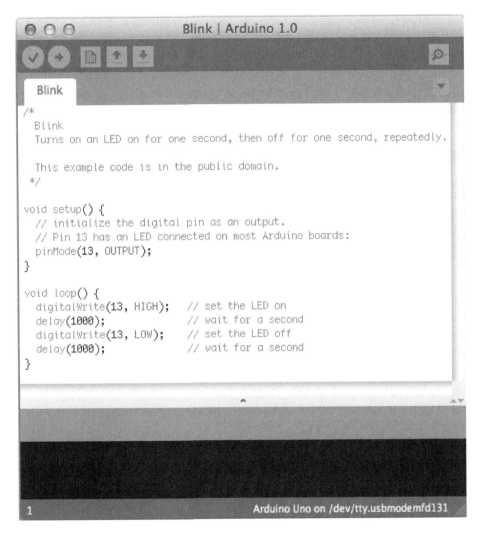

Figure 2-7. The Arduino IDE ready for action!

Note   Installing the IDE is fairly straightforward, but we're going to point you to
http://arduino.cc/en/Guide/MacOSX and http://arduino.cc/en/Guide/Windows
(for Mac and Windows users, respectively). These guides provide additional detailed instructions for
installing the IDE so we can get on with the fun stuff. We're not going to go over every menu, button,
and bell and whistle in the IDE interface, but if you're just dying to know all the features and tools the
Arduino IDE offers, feel free to dig in and read it all now. It's good stuff!

The IDE works just like most programs. You can save a new sketch file and give it a name by using the Save command under the File menu; you can modify an existing sketch and save it under a new name using the Save As command; and you can open existing sketches on your hard drive by using the Open command (under the File menu) and browsing to the location of the sketch you wish to open.

Don't worry—we'll give you plenty of opportunities to use the IDE, create sketches, save them, and more. You'll get enough hands-on experience to know your way around the IDE like a pro.

Ready to Build Something?

We promised to keep the theory short and sweet, didn't we? Working with the Arduino should be fun, and having to learn a whole bunch of programming theory and math equations would really slow you down! We're not suggesting that learning all that stuff isn't important—it is. But we suspect you're dying to get your hands on the Arduino and build something, right? Elle and Cade are stuck in that room and you're probably squirming in your chair wanting to build a gizmo that will help get them out. So let's do it!

Chapter 3 is going to show you how to wire up the Arduino with a few simple components. Along the way, we'll give you some explanation of various parts of the Arduino that we ignored in this chapter. And we'll explain some concepts that are important when it comes to working with electricity. Our goal, again, is to make this fun for you, so we hope you'll forgive us for a bit as we ease you into the challenges and offer up more information as we go.

Take a quick look at Appendix A now and make sure you've got all the items listed for Challenge 1. If so, you're ready to begin your adventure and put that Arduino to good use! (And if you haven't yet picked up all the items in Appendix A for Challenge 1, you can still read ahead and get a glimpse of what you'll be doing once you've collected everything.)

Time to build!

Chapter 3

Challenge 1: Examining the Hardware

And here we are at Chapter 3, ready to get our hands on an Arduino so we can build something. But what will we make? We'd like to tell you you'll be building a highly technical computer system that will control a rescue shuttle that will zoom in and rescue Elle and Cade. But like any skill you pick up in your life, the key to success is starting slow and simple. Our first task will be to figure out what hardware we'll use to build the gizmo that will get Cade and Elle out of the room in which they're trapped. It's not a complicated gizmo, however, as you'll soon see. As a matter of fact, most of the heavy work to get Cade and Elle out of the room will be done in Chapter 4 after you've built the gizmo. Then, and only then, will you learn a bit about the sketch you'll need to create to make your gizmo work properly. All in good time. For now, let's take a look at the short list of hardware you need to build the gizmo that will free Cade and Elle.

Locating the Parts You'll Need

For this first hardware chapter, we're going to go over the list of parts for Challenge #1 in detail. We want to show you how to go about finding the parts you need whether you use an online supplier or a local Radio Shack store. In later chapters we may bring up an occasional new piece of electronics, but we won't cover parts already discussed in earlier chapters.

Be on the lookout for recommendations from Andrew! Our favorite AI has a nice selection of web sites and books and other tips that he'll be providing so you can do some research on the side.

Also in this chapter you'll begin to find what we'll call Homework Assignments. We'll be introducing some basic concepts as you build the various gizmos in the book, and we'll provide you with web sites and possibly some book suggestions should you want to go deeper into a particular subject. (That's the way we authors learn, by the way). We're betting that if you're bitten by the Arduino bug, you'll want to learn as much as possible—and we aim to give you the resources to continue moving forward.

Potentiometer

For Challenge #1, you'll connect a *potentiometer* to the Arduino to use as a sensor. The potentiometer is a small part with a knob you can twist back and forth. You'll twist the knob on the potentiometer to "dial in" and discover the positions the knob must be in to generate values between 0 and 9; these numbers will be used to mimic a code entered in a keypad to unlock a door.

> **Note**   If you don't yet have your potentiometer, that's okay. Read through the rest of the part descriptions that follow. Then check in Appendix A for the parts needed for Challenge #1. Purchase those parts, and circle back to this chapter when you have them in hand.
>
> Ideally you'll always have the required parts for each challenge handy as you read the chapters that immediately follow each fiction chapter.

What we'd like you to do right now is pick up your potentiometer. Got it? Okay, good.

It's tiny, isn't it? Hard to believe something so small can be so useful! Potentiometers come in a variety of shapes and sizes but they all tend to work the same way. They have a moving part that can be turned clockwise or counterclockwise, sometimes by hand and other times using a small screwdriver. The one we'll be using for Challenge #1 will have a knob. The very center of the potentiometer is turned, left or right. Don't try to force it to turn once it stops—this can damage the potentiometer.

The best way to think of the turning of the potentiometer is to look at a water faucet's Hot or Cold handle. If you turn the handle all the way open, you allow water to flow at full speed. Likewise, if you turn it just a little bit, you might get just a few dribbles. The handle controls how much water flows out of the pipes. If you had a tool to measure how many gallons were flowing out of the pipe per minute, you could experiment with different positions of the handle so you could control the flow of water to make it flow as fast or slow as you desire. You'd be in control!

All electronic devices use electricity to function. This electricity can come from batteries or from a source such as a wall adapter (also called an AC adapter). Electricity is simply a flow of electrons and this flow can be controlled using a device like a potentiometer. The potentiometer adds or removes what is called resistance to an electrical circuit. Turning it one way decreases the resistance, allowing a greater flow of electrons (called current, just like water). Turning it the other way increases resistance, reducing the current (or, flow of electrons).

ANDREW 5.0

You might be interested to know that a potentiometer can also be referred to as a *variable resistor*. We haven't gotten to resistors yet, so I'll just tell you that there's a small electronic component called a resistor that slows the flow of electrons in a circuit. During your adventures you'll be using resistors to help protect other electronic components from becoming damaged, which can happen if too much electricity is applied to a component. Resistors help by reducing the flow of electrons through components. Most resistors have a constant value for how much resistance they can provide, but the "variable" part of a variable resistor tells you that the device can be adjusted to different values of resistance.

For much more information on potentiometers, visit Wikipedia (`http://en.wikipedia.org/wiki/Potentiometer`). You may find yourself overwhelmed at the level of information provided there, but know that whenever you have questions about electronics, a particular component, or a term such as resistance, your answers are almost always just a search away.

One final thing we'd like you to notice about your potentiometer are the three small posts on the bottom. Do you see them? Each has a function. The posts on the left and right will be wired into the circuit you're going to build and the one in the center will be used to obtain a reading of the potentiometer's resistance (a number value) that can be displayed on a computer screen. We'll explain this a bit more in Chapter 4.

As Andrew 5.0 told you, resistance is an important factor to consider when assembling a circuit. The gizmos you'll be building in this book all require electricity. But how much? You've probably heard batteries referred to as nine volt (9v) or twelve volt (12v). Voltage is simply a number that refers to how much "force" can be applied by a battery or other power source. Think back to our discussion of water faucets. If you open the faucet all the way, the flow is strongest, right? Well, batteries can supply power to a circuit at slow speed or full speed, and the speed is controlled by the proper addition of resistance to a circuit. When you wish to have control over just how much resistance can be applied in a circuit, you use potentiometers just like the one you're holding in your hand. Figure 3-1 illustrates a few of the different types of potentiometers.

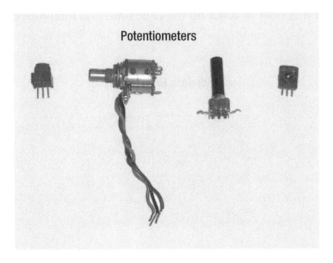

Potentiometers

Figure 3-1. Some examples of potentiometers

Solderless Breadboard

Many of the various electronic components you'll be using in this book have wires and metal posts sticking out of them. These wires and posts are simply how the components are connected to one another. If you want to connect the ends of two different wires together, you have many options:

- *Tape*: You can use electrical tape to keep two wires connected, but this is not the best method. Wires can shift inside of the tape during bending or simply over time and cause a break in the connection, which prevents electricity from flowing through one wire and into the next.

- *Solder*: You can use a special tool called a soldering iron (or solder pencil) and a coil of special metal called solder to connect two wires. In a nutshell, you use the soldering iron to melt the solder over the two wire ends and when the solder cools it makes a strong connection that's hard to break.

- *Solderless breadboard*: You can use this special board, which allows you to connect circuits without having to solder the circuits together. This is what we are going to use.

Go ahead and pick up your solderless breadboard so you can examine it. The most obvious thing you'll notice about it is all those holes! What are they for? These holes are where you'll insert wires and metal posts from various electronic components (such as the ones on the bottom of the potentiometer).

Underneath these holes are small metal plates. Each plate typically connects five holes and makes them "share" a connection. Any wire or post inserted into one of these shared holes will behave as if they are soldered or taped together, forming a single connection.

Figure 3-2 illustrates a solderless breadboard. The breadboard is oriented on its side, with the top facing to your right. You'll notice that the holes grouped in fives can be referenced using a letter (A, B, C, D, and E, or F, G, H, I, and J) as well as a number (1 to 30). There are 30 rows (count by 5s – Row 1, Row 5, Row 10, Row 15... all the way up to Row 30). Each row has five holes. And each of those holes falls under a letter—A, B, C, D. E, F, G, H, I, or J. So if we tell you to insert a wire into D-3, you'll find that hole by locating the D column and then moving down to Row 3.

Figure 3-2. A solderless breadboard

But what about those holes on the left and right sides of the breadboard? (You see them at the top and bottom in Figure 3-2, because the board is rotated sideways). They don't have letters or numbers, do they? Well, those holes have a very special function when building circuits. Look at your breadboard and you should see two columns of holes sandwiched between a blue line and a red line on one side of the breadboard, and a matching blue and red line (and more holes) running down the other side of the breadboard. The holes closest to the red line are used to provide a connection to power (or voltage) from the Arduino or a battery. The holes closest to the blue line are used to connect components to ground (GND). This probably won't make a lot of sense right now, and we don't want to overwhelm you with a lot of technical talk about voltage and ground, so we're going to put off a more detailed discussion on the uses of the voltage and GND columns for a later chapter. But don't worry—a lot of this stuff will begin to make more sense as you progress further into the book.

ANDREW 5.0: HOMEWORK

Solderless breadboards are very useful for experimenting with building your own circuits. Because wires and posts can be removed easily—unlike solder, which must be re-melted to break a connection—you can quickly make changes to a circuit and move components around.

And, by the way, if your breadboard doesn't have the letters and numbers on it, that's easy to fix! Just grab two Sharpie pens, red and blue if possible, and write in the numbers 1, 5, 10, 15… all the way to the end. Write the letters A, B, C, D, and E across the top of the groupings of 5 holes. And finally, draw a blue and red line down both sides of the breadboard to indicate power and ground.

I also want to point you to a few tutorials on the breadboard. To see what a breadboard looks like if the top shell is removed, visit `http://eecs.vanderbilt.edu/courses/ee213/Breadboard.htm`. To watch a video that discusses various aspects of the breadboard, go to `www.youtube.com/watch?v=oiqNaSPTI7w`. Don't worry if some of the discussion doesn't make sense to you just yet. Finally, for everything you could ever want to know about the breadboard, head over to `http://en.wikipedia.org/wiki/Breadboard`.

The Arduino Uno

The Arduino Uno is the brains behind the circuits you'll be building in this book and with it you can perform many functions that would be almost impossible for a first-time electronics hobbyist to accomplish; you create projects by allowing software to control the Arduino. Figure 3-3 shows the Arduino Uno. (As noted in the previous chapter, other Arduino devices such as the Duemilanove will also work).

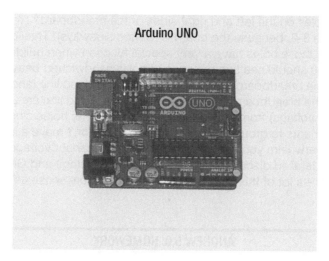

Figure 3-3. *This is the Arduino Uno*

As we said, we're going to explain bits and pieces of the Arduino as the book progresses, allowing you to take in the details a little at a time. By the end of the book, you'll have a better understanding of how the Arduino works and what many of those strange and wonderful things on its surface are and what they do.

One of the first things we'll show you about the Arduino, a bit later in the chapter, is how to give it power. To deliver power to the Arduino, you're going to need a USB cable like the one seen in Figure 3-4, which also show some other components that are required to successfully complete Challenge #1. It's really not a lot of stuff, is it?

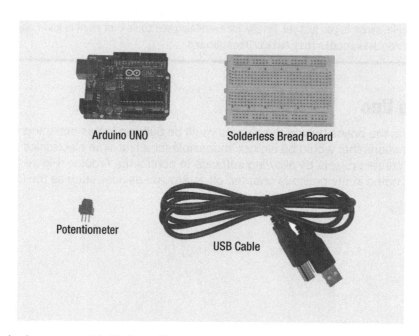

Figure 3-4. *All the hardware you need for Challenge #1*

Wire

In order to connect the electronic components, the Arduino, and the breadboard all together, you're going to need what's called jumper wire. You can make your own by purchasing a few spools of AWG 20 or AWG 22 wire (see Appendix A for part number suggestions; solid works best, but stranded will work if that's all you can find) and trimming the ends with a wire stripper (see Appendix A for suggestions) or you can purchase pre-stripped wires of various lengths. Figure 3-5 shows a single spool of wire as well as pre-stripped jumper wires. (Pre-stripped jumper wires are great; we highly recommend them if you can get some.)

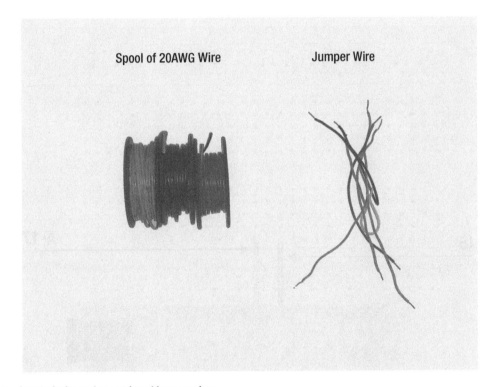

Figure 3-5. Spool of wire and pre-stripped jumper wires

Let's Build Gizmo #1

Woo hoo! Okay, time to start building. If you've got all the hardware shown in Figure 3-4 as well as some wire for connecting components, you're ready to begin. In this section we'll create the circuit in a step-by-step manner. Then, in Chapter 4, you'll learn how you can give your Arduino its instructions.

As challenges go, Challenge #1 may not seem all that exciting. But there's a lot going on here behind the scenes. Now, assemble the items you see in Figure 3-4 and let's get ready to build your Challenge #1 gizmo!

1. Orient your Arduino Uno as shown in Figure 3-6 and look closely at its surface near the top. You should see two small black rectangles that are connected to the blue surface of the Arduino. These are called headers, and

they each have six holes in their top. One of these holes will be labeled 5V (for five volts) and another will be labeled GND (for ground). Now insert one wire into the Arduino's 5V pin header hole and insert another wire into the header pin labeled GND. Take the other end of the 5V wire and insert it into the breadboard at position A-17 as shown in Figure 3-6, then take the other end of the GND wire and insert it into position A-15 on the breadboard (also shown in Figure 3-6). You want one free row of holes on the breadboard between where the two wires are inserted. Figure 3-7 in the next step shows a close-up of the wires inserted into the breadboard.

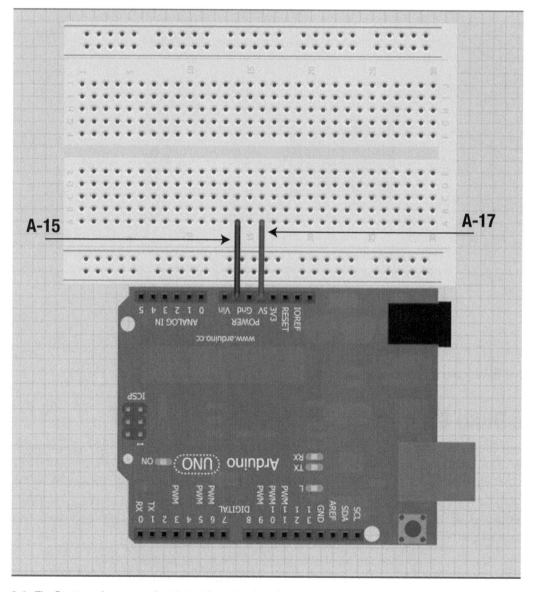

Figure 3-6. *The first two wires connecting the Arduino to the breadboard*

2. Next take the potentiometer and insert it into the breadboard as shown in Figure 3-7. Make certain that the three small posts are positioned so that the middle pin is inserted into the empty row on the breadboard between the rows holding the 5V and GND wires. Push down carefully to make certain the potentiometer is firmly seated in the solderless breadboard

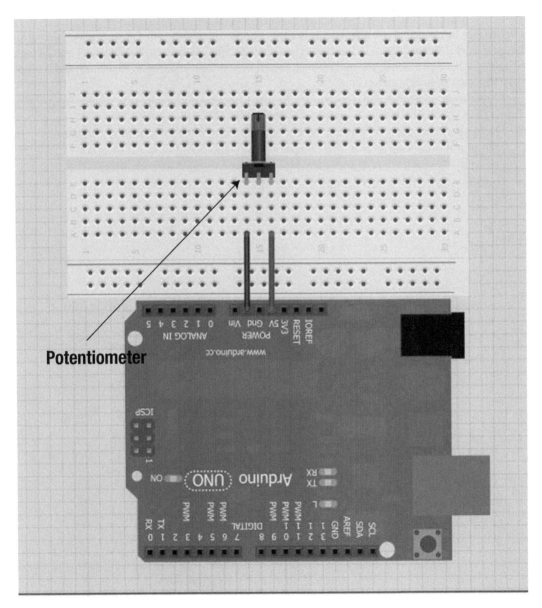

Figure 3-7. Insert potentiometer into the breadboard

ANDREW 5.0

You may have noticed in the figures that the connecting wires are different colors. A black wire is used for GND and a red wire is used for 5V. You don't have to use different colors, but it helps when troubleshooting. Red wire is often used to indicate the wire that will provide power to a circuit, while black is generally used for the ground connection (GND). Green and other colors can then be used for all other connections.

By the way, you may be wondering just what exactly is this thing called ground or GND. For more information, take a look at the Wikipedia entry at http://en.wikipedia.org/wiki/Ground_(electricity). But don't worry if the concept of ground doesn't make a lot of sense yet. You can build circuits even without knowing all the strange and confusing terminology; that knowledge will come in time.

3. Next you'll use another jumper wire (at position A-16) to connect the middle pin of the potentiometer to the header on the Arduino labeled A0 (Analog Input 0). Figure 3-8 shows a close-up of the new (green) wire inserted between the GND and 5V wires that connect to the potentiometer.

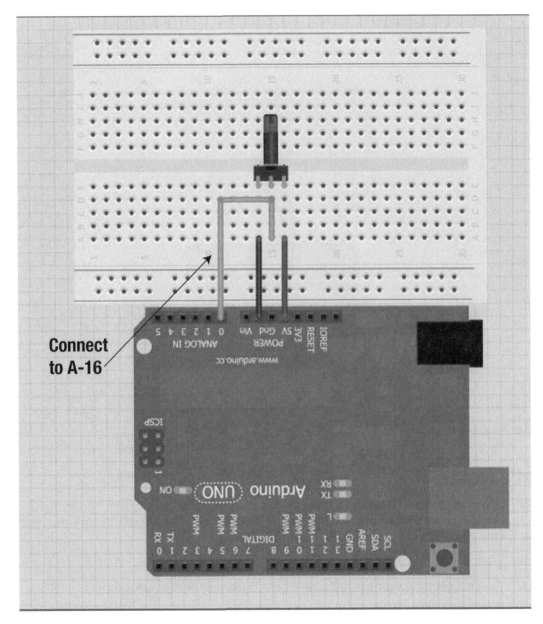

Connect to A-16

Figure 3-8. Connect the middle terminal of the potentiometer to the Arduino's Analog Input 0 (A0)

Figure 3-9 shows the green wire inserted into the Arduino's header (A0). And guess what? That's it! The circuit is complete.

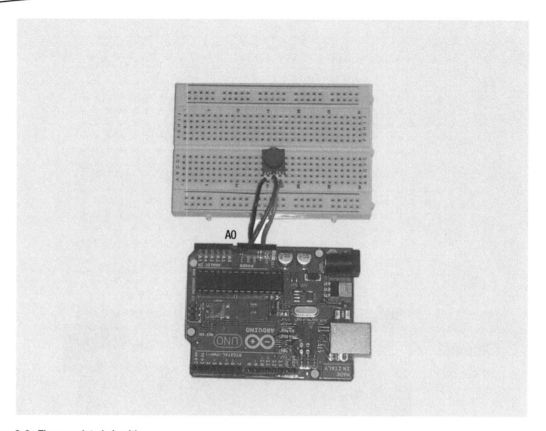

Figure 3-9. The completed circuit!

What's Next?

So now you're staring at this little circuit that makes up your Challenge #1 gizmo. And you're probably asking yourself, "Okay, now what?" (Or you may be asking yourself, "What's the phone number for the pizza shop? I'm hungry after all this tinkering!")

Well, you've got three things left to do:

1. Create a sketch (or program) that will be downloaded to the Arduino.

2. Connect the Arduino to the laptop or computer.

3. Free Cade and Elle from the room by unlocking the door.

In Chapter 4, you'll do all three. You'll learn how to program the Arduino to serve as a Keypad Repair Gizmo, and how to enter the four-digit code needed to unlock the door. You'll use a small slot screwdriver to fine-tune the potentiometer and find different resistance values that correspond to different numbers on the keypad. It's going to be fun, so turn the page and start reading – Elle and Cade are counting on you!

Chapter 4

Challenge 1: Examining the Software

Here we are at Chapter 4, ready to take the gizmo we assembled in Chapter 3 and put it to work to free Elle and Cade. So, what's this chapter all about? Well, you're going to learn some basics about the Arduino IDE and how to use it to create the sketch (program) that will be loaded into the Arduino gizmo to help Elle and Cade get through the door to Andrew. But first you need to learn about the Arduino IDE.

The programming aspect of creating gizmos with Arduino can be daunting. Many people compare learning to program with learning to speak a foreign language, but we'll argue that learning to program your Arduino is definitely not as difficult as trying to learn Japanese or French. As you'll see later in the chapter, you can do quite a lot with your Arduino with only a small bit of programming skill.

One thing we want you to remember as you read through this chapter, however, is that no one expects you to understand everything about the sketches we give you. We'll provide plenty of references so you can go out and learn as much as you like. Our goal here is to just get you playing with the Arduino and seeing how the sketches go hand in hand with the hardware. Along the way, we'll definitely introduce you to some programming information and terminology, so be sure to take note when we do—and enjoy the challenge.

The Arduino IDE

Double-click on the Arduino IDE icon that was added to your desktop. That blank window you see in Figure 4-1 is where all the magic happens. What do we mean by magic? Well, that blank window will be filled with words and numbers and other text that tells the Arduino gizmo you built in Chapter 3 just how it should operate. That window is just like any other software tool you've used—it's got menus and buttons and special pop-up alerts, and all sorts of controls you'll learn over time. The first thing to note are the six buttons just below the File, Edit, and other menus: Verify, Upload, New, Open, Save, and the Serial Monitor button at the far right. For right now, we'll be using only the Verify, Upload, and the Serial Monitor buttons.

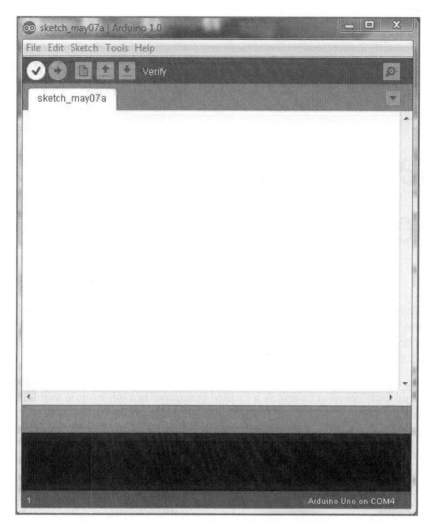

Figure 4-1. The Arduino IDE window

What do these three buttons do? Here's the nitty-gritty:

Verify: This button lets you make sure your software is free of syntax errors. Think of a syntax error as similar to a spelling error. If you've entered a command or bit of the sketch program incorrectly, the Arduino IDE will catch it and tell you so you can correct it.

Upload: This button can both verify and upload a sketch to the Arduino if no spelling or formatting errors are found. To upload, however, you must connect the Arduino to your computer with a USB cable. Once the sketch is uploaded, you can disconnect the USB cable (though it's often convenient to leave the Arduino connected to your PC so you can modify the sketch or use the serial monitor feature).

Serial Monitor: This button lets you open the serial monitor and view the information coming from the serial port on the Arduino. Think of the serial monitor as a tool for "talking" to the Arduino, and you use it to view things of interest. For example, if you had a temperature sensor attached to the Arduino, you could use the serial monitor to watch a live (often called real-time) display of the temperature the sensor is detecting.

Reminder   We told you back in Chapter 2 where to download the IDE and how to install it, but here's that information again, just in case you haven't yet had time to get the Arduino IDE installed.

Mac version `http://arduino.cc/en/Guide/MacOSX`

Windows version `http://arduino.cc/en/Guide/Windows`

There's one more thing to notice about the Arduino IDE shown in Figure 4-1—the large, white, empty area of the screen. This is where you type in the sketch to upload to the Arduino. We'll give you the sketch for Challenge #1 later in this chapter, and you'll use your keyboard to type it in exactly as we give it to you. You may notice certain words or symbols are shown in special colors—this is how the Arduino IDE makes it easy for you to "read" your sketch. We'll talk more about this shortly.

The other area of the screen to note is the black rectangle at the bottom of the window. When you are uploading a sketch to your Arduino, you'll see all sorts of strangeness appear in this area. All those odd words and phrases are perfectly normal. This area of the screen is most often useful to you when you're trying to "debug" a sketch—that is, when you're trying to find any errors in your program. Sometimes this part of the screen will tell you exactly where in your sketch an error is located– very helpful!

Now that you know a bit about the Arduino IDE, you can create the program to help Elle and Cade.

The Challenge #1 Sketch

And here you are—ready to give life to the gizmo you wired up back in Chapter 3. Once you've got the Arduino wired up, go ahead and open up the Arduino IDE. Place the cursor in the white space and type in the sketch shown in Listing 4-1 below. After you've typed it in, we'll go over a few sections of the sketch in more detail.

Listing 4-1. Arduino Software for the first Project

```
void setup() {
  // setup serial port
  Serial.begin(9600);
}
```

```
void loop() {
  // set sensorValue to the reading on analog input 0
  int sensorValue = analogRead(A0);
  // set the mappedSensorValue to the value of the map() function
  int mappedSensorValue = map(sensorValue, 0, 1023, 0, 9);
  // send mappedSensorValue to the serial port.
  Serial.println(mappedSensorValue, DEC);
}
```

> **Note**   You can also download a text file that contains the sketch from the `http://arduinoadventurer.com` web site. Then, copy and paste the code into the Arduino IDE.

Okay, so after you've typed in the sketch, you've probably got some questions. Maybe a lot of questions! Believe it or not, Listing 4-1 is actually a very short and simple sketch. Many sketches can run pages in length, and some complex sketches can be thousands and thousands of lines long! The sketch here consists of less than 20 lines, so let's walk through a couple important areas. It won't take long, and then you'll be ready to run the challenge!

ANDREW 5.0

My apologies for interrupting, but I'd like to point out that you can find many examples of sketches by visiting `http://arduino.cc/en/Tutorial/HomePage`.

On this page, you'll see sketches that do a variety of things. You don't necessarily need to understand what they're doing right now, but you might find it useful to take a look at the examples to see the variations in length and complexity.

You may even find a sketch or two that is of interest to you and, if you like, you can follow the instructions in the tutorials to run those sketches.

Beginning the Sketch

First, let's start with how a sketch is created. Take a look at that first line in Listing 4-1:

```
void setup {
```

You don't need to understand right now why the sketch uses the word void or what that strange symbol { (often called a curly brace) is for. What you do need to know is that all of the sketches you'll use in this book start this way. If you forget that first line, your sketch won't work. You're probably familiar with parentheses (like the ones at the beginning and end of this phrase). They're used to contain a bit of text, and the beginning parenthesis is always matched with an ending parenthesis. Well, the { symbol works the same way. Anything found between { and } in a sketch is related and works together as part of the sketch. Got it? If not, don't worry. It will start to make sense over time.

The word "setup" probably does make some sense to you, however. When the sketch is executed (run) by your Arduino, anything that's inserted between the opening { symbol and the closing } symbol is part of the setup process of the sketch. The setup section simply tells the Arduino how to prepare itself. In the case of Challenge #1, the text (also called code) you see between the { and } symbols of the setup section tell the Arduino to listen to the variable resistor in the circuit (refer back to Chapter 3) and to communicate with the Serial Monitor.

But how is the Arduino actually doing that listening? Good question! Let's keep examining the sketch.

Configuring the Serial Port

We already looked at the first line, so let's move to the second, third and fourth lines:

```
// setup serial port
  Serial.begin(9600);
}
```

That second line is a comment line. Have you ever read an instruction manual? Well, comments provide the instructions for deciphering a sketch. Good programmers (or coders) know that as they write a sketch, it's always a good idea to explain what a line of code or a section of code is doing. And with the Arduino IDE, you specify that a bit of text is a comment by putting // marks at the front. Your explanation goes after these marks.

So, the second line of code is //setup serial port—a comment line that says what follows will help the Arduino communicate with the serial monitor (using what's called a serial port—or the USB connection).

The third line of code may look cryptic, but it's simply telling the Arduino the speed at which it should communicate. In this case, the serial monitor will communicate with the Arduino at a speed of 9600 bits per second. That means 9600 ones and zeros per second.

And notice that the fourth line is the closing } symbol. That tells us we're done with the setup section of the sketch.

> **Note**   Again, it may seem strange and confusing right now, but you'll begin to pick up on bits and pieces of programming as you work through the book, so don't sweat it right now if none of this makes sense. Just put on your "Guru in Training" hat and keep moving forward!

Listening on the Serial Port

Now that you've configured the serial port, the next step is to "listen" to what it's telling you. Take a look at the next part of the code:

```
void loop() {
```

What's that `void loop()` stuff? Good question. Don't worry too much about the `void` part right now, but pay attention to the `loop()` part. What does a loop do? It keeps going around and around and around... forever, right? What this part of the sketch is doing is setting up a process that will keep going and going until you choose to end it, maybe by disconnecting the Arduino from the computer, for example.

The (and) symbols are for more advanced programming. All you really need to know now is that some text can be tucked between the parentheses, though most often it's simply left blank. But the (`...`)sequence is required! So, the `void loop() {` part of the sketch is setting up another section that will run continually. And anything between the opening { and the closing } will run and run and run....

But what's going to run and run and run?

That's what makes up the next bit of the code:

```
// set sensorValue to the reading on analog input 0
int sensorValue = analogRead(A0);
```

Once again we see a comment: `// set sensorValue to the reading on analog input 0.`

ANDREW 5.0

That comment about setting the sensor value is definitely confusing, so let me try to explain. What it's saying is that the next bit of code will tell the Arduino to take a reading of whatever is connected to one of its ports, specifically, the analog port with the number 0. You learn about the difference between analog and digital ports later in the book, but right now what you need to know is that the Arduino can have electronic components connected to it using both analog and digital ports, and each of those ports has a number assigned to it. If you look closely at your Arduino, you may even notice some of the headers (refer back to Chapter 2) are labeled A0, A1, A2... all the way up to A5. The same goes for the digital ports, although these don't have a D in front of their number and they range in values from 0 to 13.

Okay, so what Andrew is telling you is that the variable resistor will be providing a value to the Arduino. What that value will be is not known at the moment, and it can change with a simple turn of the knob on the component. Remember that the variable resistor (also called a potentiometer) will resist the flow of electrons, either with a high or low resistance depending on where the potentiometer is set. And that resistance value will be provided by the Arduino to the serial monitor using analog port 0.

And how does the Arduino do this? Easy! The Arduino stores the value from the variable resistor in a special holding area called a variable. Variables are just that—variable. They can change. Think of a variable as a pocket in the Arduino where it can place text or numbers and store them until it needs them later. The Arduino can hold a large number of variables, and the fun thing is that you get to name them! In this instance, we've created a variable called `sensorValue` and set it to equal whatever value is being read for analog port 0.

You're probably wondering about that int part, right? That stands for integer—a whole number—and simply means that the value provided to the Arduino must be an integer value, like 1 or 5 or 1000. No decimals! And negative numbers are okay, too. So the variable resistor will report a setting of 5 or 50 but not 5.532 or 50.89. The number will be stored as an integer, which will be easier for you to interpret.

Translating the Input into Digits

Now, the next few lines of code also need some explanation:

```
// set the mappedSensorValue to the value of the map() function
int mappedSensorValue = map(sensorValue, 0, 1023, 0, 9);
```

In a nutshell, the comment says that the variable resistor is going to give us a value (that we know will be large) and that we must convert it using a special tool called a function. A function performs one specific action. You use a function by typing it into the program along with some parameters. In this case, you'll be using the map function, which takes a large number and divides it up in such a way that it can be represented by a smaller set of numbers.

A variable resistor doesn't report settings from 0 to 9. It reports values from 0 to 1023. If you could turn the variable resistor a teeny-tiny amount, you'd increase the value from, say, 1001 to 1002 or from 348 to 349. But this level of control is very difficult with our human fingers. Instead, we can make it easier on ourselves by dividing up that 1024 range into 10 parts of approximate equal length – we'll squeeze in the leftover bits into the last part. (We have 1024 parts because we include zero, so 0 to 1023 equals 1024 parts). When the dial is positioned from 0 to 102, we'll say that's equal to 0. And from 103 to 205, we'll say that's a 1. Table 4-1 shows the ranges 0 through 9 based upon the pattern we've just described.

Table 4-1. Potentiometer Settings Mapped into Ten Buckets

Low	High	Bucket #
0	To 102	0
103	To 205	1
206	To 308	2
309	To 411	3
412	To 514	4
515	To 617	5
618	To 720	6
721	To 823	7
824	To 926	8
927	To 1023	9

So the `int mappedSensorValue = map(sensorValue, 0, 1023, 0, 9);` part of the program simply takes the value from the variable resistor stored in the `sensorValue` variable (between 0 and 1023) and converts it to fit a range of 10 numbers, 0 to 9. This new value is stored in a new integer variable called `mappedSensorValue`. This number will always be in the range of 0 to 9.

Remember that Elle and Cade have to provide a code to the locked door's keypad. This four-digit number will consist of four numbers from 0 to 9. The code could be 1234 or 8207 or 4488 or even 9999. But these nine values are what we, as humans, are used to using.

Displaying the Result

Simply turning the variable resistor to a location won't tell us what the resulting value from 0 to 9 is, however. We need to be able to see it! And that's where the serial monitor comes in. We'll include some code in the sketch that sends the mapped potentiometer value to be displayed on the screen. And to do that, we use this last bit of code:

```
// send mappedSensorValue to the serial port.
Serial.println(mappedSensorValue, DEC);
}
```

Hopefully you can now decipher these last two lines of code. The first is a comment, simply telling anyone viewing the sketch that the next line of code will take whatever value is stored in the `mappedSensorValue` variable and send it to the serial port.

The final bit of code sends the `mappedSensorValue` variable value to the serial monitor in decimal (DEC) format. This simply means you'll see numbers scrolling down the screen like those in Figure 4-2.

But what do these numbers mean and how do they help you with the challenge?

Let's finish up Challenge #1 now by seeing how the gizmo and sketch work together.

Figure 4-2. Scrolling values give you a real-time display of the setting on the potentiometer

Solving Challenge #1

Here's the big secret… are you ready?

The password is 8294. Got it? 8. 2. 9. 4. You need to calibrate the variable resistor by using a small screwdriver to turn the dial on the poteniometer so you see different values on the serial monitor. You'll want to make note of the position for each number (from 0 to 9) by somehow making a mark on a piece of paper. Think of a volume control dial for music, or the numbers going around an oven dial that represent the oven's temperature setting.

First, download and print the Challenge #1 Challenge Card from http://arduinoadventurer.com. Print it out on card stock that's a bit heavier than standard printer paper and grab a pen or pencil. Now, follow these steps to run Challenge #1.

1. Connect your Arduino gizmo to your computer with the USB cable.

2. Open the Arduino IDE and enter the sketch from Listing 4-1.

3. Press the Upload button on the Arduino IDE to upload the sketch to your Arduino.

4. Open the serial monitor by pressing the serial monitor button at the top right corner of the Arduino IDE. (It is the button that has an image that looks like a magnifying glass).

5. Observe the values scrolling up the screen.

6. Turn the variable resistor dial counterclockwise all the way until it stops. Make a small dot on the potentiometer's moving dial with a permanent marker or a tiny dab of paint.

7. Calibrate the variable resistor by marking on the Challenge Card where each number from 0 to 9 is located. For example, after turning the variable resistor a small amount and seeing the number 1 scrolling on the screen consistenly, write the number 1 on the Challenge Card where the small dot or mark on the potentiometer is located. Do this for all values from 0 to 9, creating your own dial with numbers.

8. After you've identified all nine-digit locations on the Challenge Card, enter in the password of 8294 by dialing in 8 first. Then dial in 2, then 9. And, finally, dial in the last password value of 4.

Congratulations! You've successfully configured a variable resistor to supply values from 0 to 9, to enable Cade and Elle to fool the keypad into accepting the passcode from the Arduino instead of the damaged keypad.

And another congratulations for making it all the way to the end of the first challenge!

Chapter 5

Damage Assessment

Elle dialed in the last digit of the door's entry code provided by Andrew. The Arduino and the variable resistor were dangling by jumper wires, and Elle was careful not to bump the assembly Andrew had instructed them to build.

"Okay, Andrew," said Elle. "That should do it." There was no buzzer or click to acknowledge that the code had been properly submitted. Elle crossed her fingers and looked at Cade.

Cade nodded at Elle and smiled. "Nice work."

"Okay, wave a hand in front of the door," replied Andrew, his voice muffled slightly by the closed door.

Cade held his hand up and waved it back and forth. The look on his face told Elle that he didn't believe the small circuit they'd spent the last fifteen minutes assembling had worked.

But the door opened with a loud grinding noise.

"It worked!" yelled Cade and Elle together.

Cade turned and gave Elle a hug.

Elle's face reddened, but she gave Cade a pat on the back and then pushed him through the door and into the Andrew 5.0 exhibition room.

The Face of Andrew

Cade and Elle both looked around at the white walls enclosing the large room. Four rows of ten chairs were crowded slightly in the center of the room, but that was the only furniture present. All four walls had colorful light presentations that moved and shifted randomly. It was a beautiful pattern and almost made the students forget about their current situation.

"Andrew… is that you?" asked Cade.

The colors on three of the walls shifted and then slowly morphed into a computer-generated male face on the wall that Cade and Elle were facing. It was a face that both students recognized, having seen it in history books, and it was smiling back at them.

"Hello, Cade. Hello, Elle. Nice to meet you both."

Elle brushed a wisp of blond hair away from her eye, and smiled. "Nice to meet you, too, Andrew. Thanks for your help."

"You're welcome. But there is little time to waste. Both you and Cade need to exit the station as quickly as possible. I do not know what the emergency is, but a mandatory evacuation has been ordered by the station's AI," replied Andrew.

Cade nodded toward another doorway, directly opposite the damaged door they had used to enter the room. "That door looks okay. Where does it go?"

Andrew's eyes moved to the other door and then back to Cade. "I can give you directions to the nearest escape pods, which are on the first level. But first I need to make certain I'm not sending you toward any danger. There are other escape pods on Level 6 and Level 10, but I'll need to communicate with the station's AI and find out what has happened and determine where to send you so you can exit the station."

"I thought you couldn't communicate with the station's AI," said Elle.

"I can't. I will need your assistance to unlock the communication node that prevents me from accessing the station," said Andrew.

"Okay," said Cade. "How do we do that?"

A loud popping sound made the students jump. Cade and Elle turned and watched as a large white floor panel at the back of the room slowly lifted until it was perpendicular to the floor.

"One of you will need to locate my primary control unit that's stored in the access area below the room. There's a safety release down there that will release controls up here and allow you access to my communication node."

Elle's eyes widened as she stared at the exposed hole in the floor. "You know I hate tight spaces, Cade," she said.

"And I hate spiders," Cade replied. "No problem, Elle. I'll do it."

Elle sighed and returned the grin. "Thanks."

Cade walked to the rear of the room and stood looking down into the access area. "It's a bit dark down there, Andrew."

"Yes, now that emergency lighting has been activated, all secondary light sources have been disabled to conserve power. Do you or Elle have a flashlight?"

Cade looked at Elle and shook his head.

"No, Andrew, we don't," responded Elle. "Sorry."

"There are a number of turns down there that Cade must make to get to my communication node. Cade will also need to be able to see and read some identifying text on various components down there."

Elle looked around the room. "Nothing in here. What about the room we were just in? You said you have an inventory of all the stuff stored in there—any flashlights?"

"Checking…," replied Andrew. "No flashlights found in the inventory. But there are 2,735 light-emitting diodes in stock, 587 of which are white."

"Light-emitting diodes?" asked Elle. "You mean LEDs?"

"Yes. LEDs. These would be suitable for making a lighting device with an Arduino microcontroller."

Cade smiled at Elle and then stared at the wall displaying Andrew's digital face. "Sounds like a plan. Let's do it."

An Embarrassed Cade

Ten minutes later Cade was frowning.

"Stop it," said Elle. "No one else is going to see you."

"If any photos of this show up at school, you will pay," said Cade.

Elle giggled. "You should let me take one just so we'll always remember this moment."

"Elle…"

"Kidding."

"Are you ready, Cade?" asked Andrew.

Cade turned to stare directly at Andrew. "No, Andrew… I think Elle needs to add more lights."

"The room's light sensors are detecting sufficient lumens for you to be able to navigate the access area," said Andrew.

"He's being sarcastic, Andrew. He's just a bit embarrassed at my improvised lighting solution," said Elle.

Cade looked down at his shirt and pants and then back to Elle. "I'll remember this."

Elle nodded with a laugh. "So will I."

After Andrew told them how to connect together an Arduino, some LEDs, and a battery harness, he gave them instructions for programming the hand-made flashlight. While Cade typed in the program on the ancient laptop they had used earlier for the Arduino door-code gizmo, Elle had grabbed a few more Arduinos, LEDs, and batteries to make more flashlights. She had then used a roll of duct tape from one of the toolboxes to attach each of the new flashlights to Cade's clothing. He had one strapped to his chest, one on top of each wrist, and one on top of each shoulder.

Cade shook his head. "You're going in the next tight space. No arguments."

Elle tried to remove the smile from her face. "I'm sorry. Come on, Cade… in you go."

Cade stepped down through the opening in the floor. The space between the floor and the bottom of the access area was less than three feet deep, so Cade was going to have to crawl on his hands and knees to find the communication node.

"I'll provide directions to you, Elle," said Andrew. "You may have to yell for Cade to hear you. Cade, you'll need to move down approximately fifteen feet in the direction of my screen."

"Got it," said Cade, and he began crawling down the tight space.

"When he gets to the T-junction, tell him to turn left and go forward ten feet."

Elle stuck her head down into the opening and repeated the instructions in Cade's direction in a loud voice.

"No need to yell!" replied Cade. "Everything echoes down here."

"Sorry!" exclaimed Elle.

"Elle! No yelling!"

"Sorry," she whispered.

"Okay, Elle… tell Cade to pull the red handle to his right that's labeled Node Access. Another panel should open and he should proceed down that tunnel ten feet."

"Cade, you need to pull the red handle…"

The Unlocking

Cade followed the instructions relayed by Elle and found the safety release switch. Pulling on the switch released a hidden panel on the wall near Andrew's projected face—and it startled Elle when it popped open. She was looking over at the small panel when Cade gave her another scare as he stood up from inside the access area and said "I'm back!"

"I think it's safe to turn off the lights, Flashlight-Man," said Elle, walking over and holding out her hand to help Cade exit the access space.

Cade began pulling the tape and electronic devices off his clothes. "Ha ha. You're funny. Okay, so I pulled the switch you told me to… anything happen?"

Elle pointed over her shoulder. "Yep. That panel opened."

"We're just all about secret panels today, aren't we, Andrew?" asked Cade. "What is it? Looks like a keyboard and screen to me."

"When I was moved here, this interface panel was installed to limit my access to the station. It's basically a lock and key that prevents me from joining the station's network," replied Andrew.

"Why would anyone want to limit your access to the station?" asked Elle.

Cade frowned. "Yeah, that doesn't sound so good. You're basically trapped in this room?"

"I can receive datafeeds that allow me to stay informed about whatever is happening around the system, but my assigned duties are to inform and educate visitors on my development," said Andrew. "But to answer your question, Elle, the station's staff wishes to have only one AI monitoring all systems. Two or more AIs monitoring the station is a waste of resources."

"And locking you in a room is a perfectly good use of an AI?" asked Cade.

"It is my assigned duty," responded Andrew.

"Well, I don't like it," said Elle. "When we're off this station, I'm going to complain about it. It's like a prison cell."

"I appreciate your concern, Elle, but let's focus on the problem at hand. You both need to get off this station as soon as possible. If you'll help me restore my connection with the station's AI, I'll try and assess the situation and get you both to safety."

Elle frowned. "Okay, just tell us what you need us to do."

"I simply need you to provide a password to the communication node. You can use the keyboard to type it in."

"Okay, what's the password?" asked Elle.

"Please don't tell me it's *password*," said Cade with a smirk. "Or 1-2-3-4."

Andrew's on-screen face smiled widely. "No, Cade. It's actually quite complicated, and you'll only get three chances to enter it correctly. So please type carefully, Elle."

"Ready," Elle replied.

"5 – A – 7 – 9 – 4 – B – Q – 2 – T – 7 – 9….," Andrew began reciting, with a two-second pause between each number or letter.

Elle continued to enter the password. Thirty characters later, she was done.

"Would you like me to repeat it so you can verify your entry?" asked Andrew.

"Please," said Elle.

"5 – A – 7 – 9 – 4 – B…." Andrew repeated the entire password once more.

"Not bad, Elle," said Cade.

"Thanks. That's it, Andrew. Press Enter?"

Yes, Elle."

Elle tapped the Enter key on the keyboard, expecting some loud noise or some sudden change on the display walls that Andrew was using. But nothing happened.

"Andrew?" asked Elle.

Andrew's face froze on the screen. Elle gasped, thinking that something had gone wrong, but then Andrew's eyes shifted to look directly into Elle's own. And he smiled.

"I have access to the entire station. Give me a moment to assess the situation, please."

Cade looked at Elle, a worried look on his face. "How about you and I start collecting toolboxes and Arduinos? I have a feeling we're not done building gadgets, Elle."

Elle nodded. "Yeah, grab whatever you can carry."

Andrew's voice made both of them jump. "Station assessment complete. Cade… Elle… it's not good. Please hurry and grab the following boxes. Box 12. Box 52. Box 31…"

Challenge 2: Fun Stuff to Know

We thought about naming this Chapter 6: Non-Boring Stuff (We Promise!), but our editors thought readers might just skip it and go on to Chapter 7. Our next try was calling it Chapter 6: More Details About Arduino, but this made our editors fall asleep. So we decided to stick with what works and keep it fun.

So now you've got your first Arduino gizmo built and tested. Some of you might be wanting to build really advanced Arduino gizmos—but would you attempt to build an automobile without a solid understanding of the engine, the doors, the wheels, the brakes, and all the hundreds of other parts and systems that make up a running car? Okay, we might try it, too, but that's not the point. The point is that you've got to start small and understand the basics before you can accomplish bigger projects. All of the projects we include in this book teach you bits and pieces that will get you familiar and confident with the basics of Arduino. Then you can move on to more advanced books that will show you, for example, how to take an Arduino and make a remote-controlled lawnmower.

As you know by now, the purpose of the chapter immediately following each piece of Cade and Elle's story is to give you a little bit of technical knowledge. Sometimes it will be specific to the current challenge and sometimes it will be information you need for what you'll be doing in the rest of the book. So don't skip these chapters, okay? We know you want to jump right to the building and programming, so we'll keep these "theory" chapters short… promise!

Once again, Andrew 5.0 will be jumping in when he wishes to provide more assistance—he's got some great suggestions for books and web sites for you to check out.

And now it's time to learn a little more about our favorite microcontroller. The information here will help you in the next challenge, where you'll be building your very own Arduino-Light. Okay, maybe a little less glamorous—you'll be building a flashlight. And an expensive flashlight at that! But the point of building a flashlight with the Arduino is to give you more hands-on practice with wiring things up, as well as more programming knowledge.

> **Note**   When you're done, you can break the flashlight down for the next challenge or take a look at the arduinoadventurer.com web site and find a Bonus Challenge where you modify your flashlight to add another feature.

Now… let's get started. It's pretty dark in the tunnels beneath Andrew's room, and Cade is going to need a strong light to find his way around. Let's talk about some of the things you'll need to know to make this flashlight work.

Let's Look at a Battery

Your flashlight is going to be powered by a 9V battery. No doubt you're familiar with batteries—you've probably had toys all your life that relied on batteries for movement and sound. We're not going to go into the technical aspects of batteries here (we'll let your chemistry teacher take that one), but we do want to go over some important details for dealing with not just batteries but power in general. Your Arduino is capable of providing power to connected components and it gets this power from batteries or from an AC adapter (sometimes called a wall wart because it's usually a big black block that plugs into the wall).

For many of the challenges in this book, you'll use a standard 9V battery. For others, you'll use an AC adapter. In either case, the Arduino is going to take the power and share it with any components you've connected. What kinds of components? Light emitting diodes (LEDs) are one example. You'll use one in Challenge 2, actually. You can provide power to small speakers for sound, to sensors for light or temperature detection, and even to small motors.

In just about every situation you encounter with components connecting to the Arduino, you're going to want to know a little bit about polarity. Take a look at Figure 6-1, which shows a 9V battery and a 1.5 AA (double-A) battery. You may never have noticed this before, but batteries are almost always labeled with a positive (+) end (or terminal) and a negative (–) end. A 9V battery's terminals are on the same end of the battery, but a 1.5V battery has the terminals on opposite ends.

Figure 6-1. Batteries have positive and negative terminals for supplying power

We don't want to get too deep into the technical aspects of batteries, but the one thing to take from this discussion is that when it comes to batteries, current flows from the negative terminal to the positive. When you connect the two terminals of a battery with a wire (but do NOT do this—it can be very dangerous), electrons speed down the wire, leaving the negative terminal and going into the positive terminal. The process continues until you disconnect the wire or until, eventually, all the electrons get used up. When that happens, we say the battery is *drained*, or *dead*.

Alert   Please do not ever short-circuit a battery. That's what happens when you connect the two terminals of a battery with a wire or piece of metal. The wire gets extremely hot and the battery can even explode! When you create a closed loop using a battery, you've created a circuit. But if there are no other components in the circuit (such as an LED or a resistor or potentiometer), you've created a *short circuit*, and that's a big no-no.

And Now a Circuit

Believe it or not—and please believe it—a simple wire connecting the two terminals of a battery is considered a circuit. But it's called a short-circuit and we've told you to always avoid these. Instead, what you'll be doing is placing electronics components into the circuit that will limit some of the current through the circuit. But how many components must you insert? That's an important question and we'll cover it in a bit more detail in Chapter 7 when you learn about the two key electronics components used in Challenge #2—the LED and the resistor.

ANDREW 5.0

I'd like to add that the Arduino itself can be treated as a component and inserted without risk into a circuit. There is no harm in connecting a 9V battery to the Arduino. In fact, the Arduino is designed for that purpose.

Take a look at Figure 6-2 for a moment. Don't worry if it doesn't make sense to you. You're looking at the circuit you'll be creating for Challenge #2. What we want to point out is how the 9V battery is connected to the power port on the end of the Arduino.

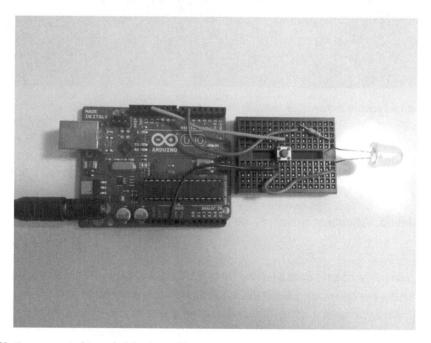

Figure 6-2. A 9V battery connected to an Arduino to provide power

Now note the small square to the left of the Arduino. That's a mini-breadboard into which you'll be inserting various electronics components to create a simple flashlight circuit.

Again, you don't need to understand (yet) what you're looking at; just focus on the fact that the Arduino will be getting power from the 9V battery and distributing it via the small wires that connect the Arduino to the mini-breadboard.

Also notice the following:

- The LED on the far left. It's a white LED that will give off a strong, white light.

- A small odd-shaped component nearby that has colored bands running around its body—it's called a resistor.

- A small push-button in the direct center of the mini-breadboard

You'll learn how these components work together to let you create a very simple flashlight. And you'll learn what the Arduino brings to the party when you add a bit of programming to the mix!

ANDREW 5.0

I'd like to suggest a book your readers might like to investigate once they finish your book. Anyone interested in learning more about the basics of batteries and other electronics components should check out *Make: Electronics* by Charles Platt. It's a must-read for everyone who wants to learn about electronics.

Let's return to the idea of the battery's positive and negative terminals. Why is this important to know? As you'll learn in Chapter 7, certain electronics components will work in a circuit only if they are inserted so they are oriented properly with respect to the positive and negative terminals. If they're not added to the circuit properly, they just won't work. And some components can even become damaged should you not insert them properly! But don't worry—we'll look further at this and explain how you can make sure you don't ever damage a component by inserting it incorrectly.

Current Flow

Here's one final fact to know about a circuit: any break in the circuit will keep the electricity from flowing. Cut the wire or place something in the circuit that breaks the loop and the current stops flowing. (Remember, electrons flow out the negative terminal and want to return to the positive terminal, making a loop.) The switch on a real flashlight performs just this function. Turn it to on and electricity flows out the negative terminal of the batteries inside, through the lightbulb, and then back into the positive terminal of the batteries. Turn the switch to off and you break the loop or circuit and the light turns off. Keep this in mind as you move into Chapter 7 and see if you can guess which component in Figure 6-2 will be used to control the current flowing through the circuit. We'll give you the answer in Chapter 7.

| ANDREW 5.0 |

Readers might like to know that current can be measured. We use the term *amperage* to describe how strong a current is, or how much force it has. We measure a current's amperage, its strength, in units called *amperes*, commonly called amps.

- On a hot day, you might ask the temperature and get an answer back in degrees.

- With a cool Arduino project, you can ask what the amperage is and get an answer back in amperes.

An ampere is a whole lot of electricity for such a tiny device as an Arduino. An ampere of current would melt your device. The projects you build will use milliamps of current. A milliamp is 1/1000th of an amp. That's right! It doesn't take much current to do some very fun and useful things.

Ready to Build Something?

We hope the little bit of technical discussion didn't overwhelm you. Even if some of this stuff is still confusing, just keep pushing forward—we promise things will start to clear up once you get your hands involved and start building the circuit.

Before you start building, be sure to take a look at Appendix A, which contains the parts list you'll need to complete Challenge #2. It's not a long list of parts, but each piece is required. Once you've got the components in your hands along with the Arduino and a 9V battery, turn to Chapter 7. You're going to have some fun wiring up a simple flashlight circuit and you'll learn more about various components that will come in handy for later challenges.

Time to build!

Challenge 2: Examining the Hardware

Ok! We're ready to put together a few key circuits to make a flashlight to help Cade find his way to Andrew's primary controls. But first we need to learn about the new hardware before we start putting the flashlight together.

As with every project in this book, we encourage you to visit Appendix A first and make certain you have all the components you need, purchased and ready to go. If you're like us, you're probably wondering about the choice to use the Arduino to make a flashlight, and we don't blame you! A flashlight is one of those objects we all tend to take for granted—flip a switch and the light comes on. But what do you do if you don't have a flashlight? What if you only have a handful of LEDs and a battery or two?

Well, one answer is to just connect an LED to the terminals of the battery. But that isn't a good idea. First, the battery might supply too much current and damage the LED, so the LED won't shine brightly. And one LED might not be enough, but ten LEDs might be perfect. How would you connect ten LEDs to a single battery? And how might you ensure you don't damage all ten LEDs?

We're going to answer those questions by showing you exactly how to connect an LED to an Arduino. Safely. And once you know how to connect one LED to an Arduino, you can connect as many more as you like, making a much brighter flashlight.

Let's go see how this is done. The next few sections discuss the new pieces of hardware you'll be using for this challenge.

The Push Button

The push button is a very common electrical component that allows you to turn an LED (or any other electrical device) on or off when you please, without physically connecting and disconnecting the battery. There are many types of push buttons out there, but we'll be focusing on the normally open push button. That means the push button does not make a connection until the button is pressed. Figure 7-1 illustrates various push buttons.

Figure 7-1. Push buttons

ANDREW 5.0

The term *open* comes from *open circuit,* describing a circuit in which no current is flowing. Thus, a *normally open* switch is one that does *not* allow current to flow unless you actively press the button. Normally open switches are commonly used on devices that you operate only briefly. A car horn is an example. Car horn switches are normally open, and only pass current when you press the horn button.

Imagine how funny it would be for car horn switches to be normally closed! A normally closed switch allows current to flow all the time, *except* when you're pressing the button. Think of how awkward it would feel to drive all the time with one hand on the horn to keep it quiet. Normally closed switches do have their place, though. They are often used in burglar-alarm circuits.

The Light Emitting Diode

You can't have a flashlight without light, and that's precisely what a light emitting diode (LED) provides. LEDs are special because they have a long life—providing they are properly protected. An LED has two leads: a negative cathode (–) and a positive anode (+). The anode lead is the longer of the two.

> **Tip**   "You can be positive the anode lead is longer." This is a convention followed in the industry to help engineers avoid errors. Positive = Anode = Longer.

We will be connecting the anode of the LED to one of the digital pins on the Arduino, and the cathode will be connected to ground. We will also be protecting the LED with a resistor because the LED will draw too much current and if that occurs you could burn out the LED or worse you could damage the Arduino. For the 5V that the Arduino supplies a 330ohm resistor works well to protect the LED and Arduino. Figure 7-2 illustrates various LEDs.

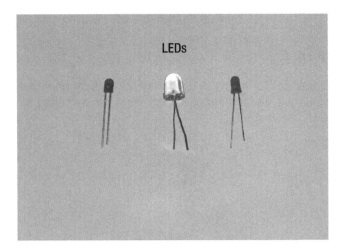

Figure 7-2. LEDs

The Resistor

Remember the potentiometer from the last gadget (Chapter 3)? Well, as we noted, a potentiometer is a variable resistor. A resistor looks like a very small peanut that has a few rings of colors on it to help identify its resistance.

What does a resistor do, you ask? A resistor impedes (blocks) the progress of current; LEDs are sensitive to current, so if too much current passes through an LED, that LED will burn out. You need to put a resistor in series with the LED to impede some of the current the LED will draw. (Oh, and just in case you're wondering, resistance is measured in units called *ohms*.) Figure 7-3 illustrates various resistors.

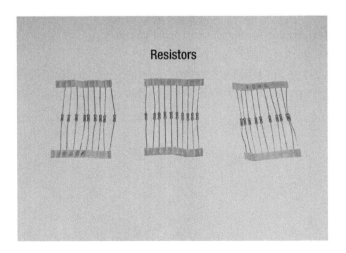

Figure 7-3. Resistors

Now you have the particulars of the electrical components we'll use for this challenge. It all may seem a bit overwhelming, but just keep moving forward. With each challenge, we'll give you a bit more information and things will start to fall into place. And, remember, the idea is to have fun with these challenges!

Let's Build Gizmo #2

Now it's time to build the flashlight to help Cade get to Andrew's primary controller. So, without further ado, let's build the circuit. Remember that all of the parts you need for this challenge can be found in Appendix A under Challenge 2.

Here are the steps to follow:

1. Connect the 9V battery connector to the Arduino, as illustrated in Figure 7-4.

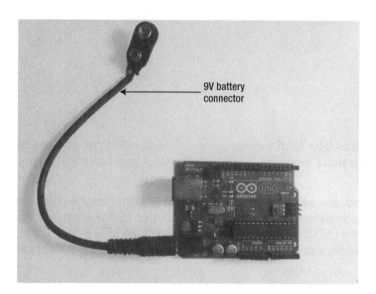

Figure 7-4. Connecting the 9V battery connector to the Arduino

2. Connect the LED to the small solderless breadboard, as shown in Figure 7-5. Place the longer, positive leg into E-1. Place the shorter, negative leg into F-1.

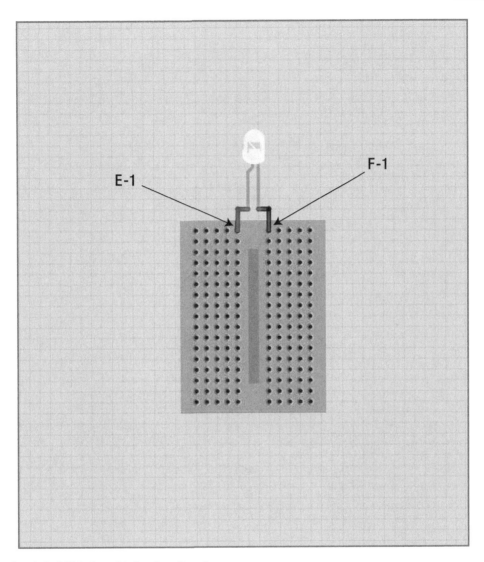

Figure 7-5. Attach the LED to the solderless breadboard

As you can see, the LED is inserted with one of its metal legs on one side of the mini-breadboard near the top. The other leg is inserted into the opposite side of the mini-breadboard on the same row.

The mini-breadboard doesn't have its columns and rows labeled (with letters and numbers, respectively), but if it did, the LED would have its longer leg inserted into E-1 and its shorter leg inserted into F-1. Label the columns A through J (10 columns in all) and number the rows 1 to 18 (running from top to bottom). You'll probably need to do this lettering and numbering in your head as there's very little room on the mini-breadboard to write the letters and numbers.

3. Add a 330 ohm resistor by inserting one of its legs into D-1 and the other leg into A-7. Figure 7-6 illustrates this process. Remember that all the pins in Row 1 are connected inside the breadboard. The resistor leg in D-1 thus connects to the LED leg in E-1.

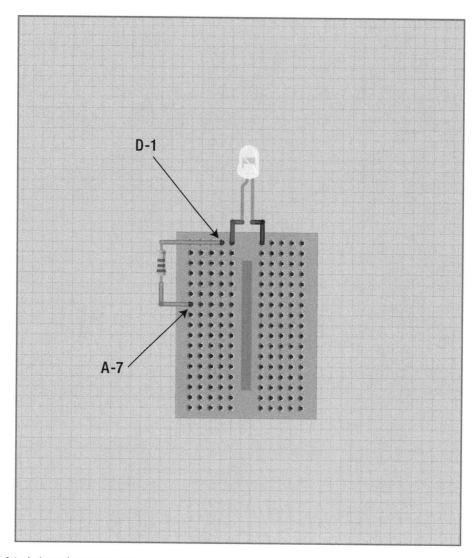

Figure 7-6. Attach the resistor to the solderless breadboard

4. Attach the push button to the solderless breadboard. One set of pins will be inserted into E-9 and E-11. The other set of pins will be inserted into F-9 and F-11. Figure 7-7 illustrates this process.

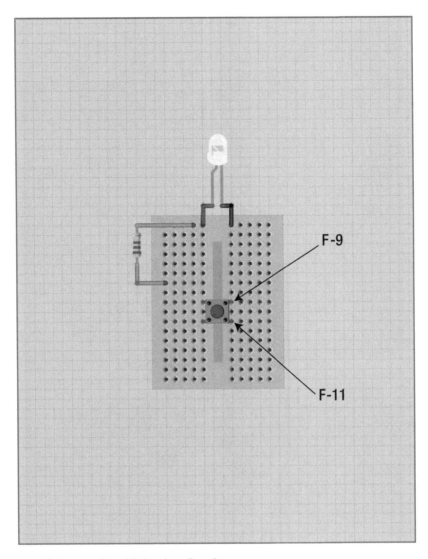

Figure 7-7. Attach the push button to the solderless breadboard

The push button is inserted so that it straddles the center break of the breadboard. Remember that the center of the breadboard breaks one row into two rows of five holes. Each of the five-hole rows has a small metal plate inside the mini-breadboard that physically connects those five holes and any components inserted into them. The push button doesn't allow current to flow through it until the button is pressed—this means no current flows across Row 9 or Row 11 until the button is pressed.

5. Attach a black wire from ground (GND) on the Arduino to G-11; this will connect ground to one side of the push button, as shown in Figure 7-8.

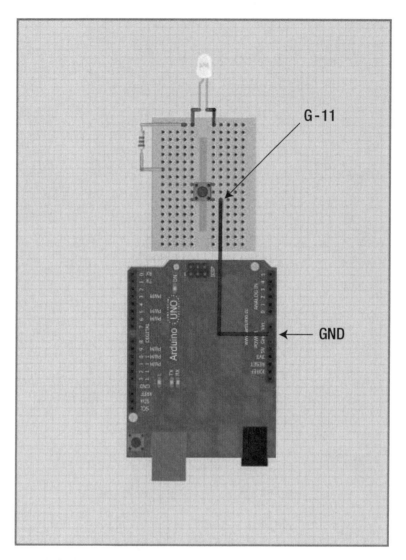

Figure 7-8. *Attach the ground wire from the Arduino to the push button*

When you add that wire to G-11, it's actually sharing a connection with the pin on the push button that's pressed into F-11. Putting that wire into G-11 performs the same duty as if you had touched the end of the wire to the push button's pin. The metal plate inside the mini-breadboard allows the wire (G-11) and the pin on the push button (F-11) to behave as if they are touching one another because the metal plate treats F-11, G-11, H-11, I-11, and J-11 as a single connecting point.

6.   Insert another jumper wire (we used green) from H-11 to H-1, the LED's shorter (Cathode) leg. Figure 7-9 illustrates this process.

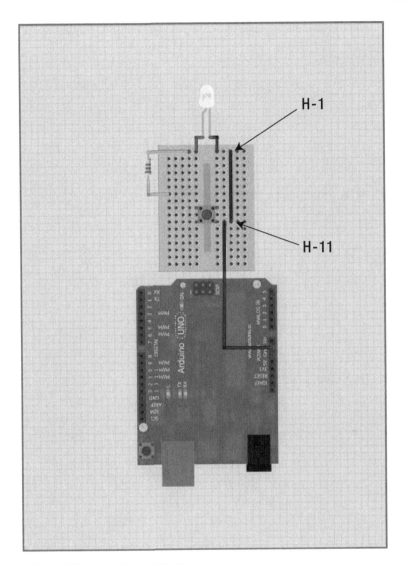

Figure 7-9. Attach ground from LED to ground on push button

7. Insert one end of another jumper wire (we used red) into digital pin 12 (D12) on the Arduino and the other end of the jumper wire into D-9 on the mini-breadboard. Figure 7-10 illustrates this process.

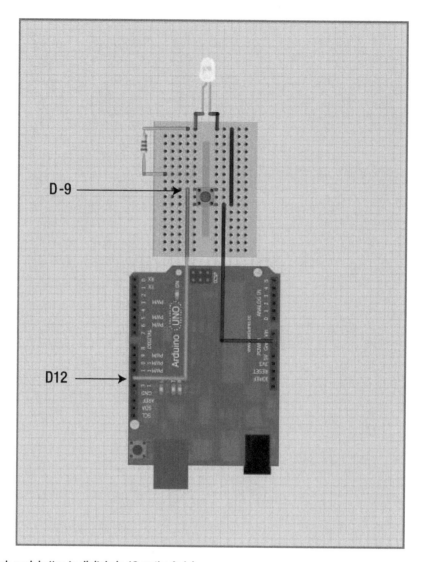

Figure 7-10. Attach push button to digital pin 12 on the Arduino

8. Insert one end of another jumper wire (we used green again) into D6 on the
    Arduino and the other end of the jumper wire into B-7 on the
    mini-breadboard. Figure 7-11 illustrates this process.

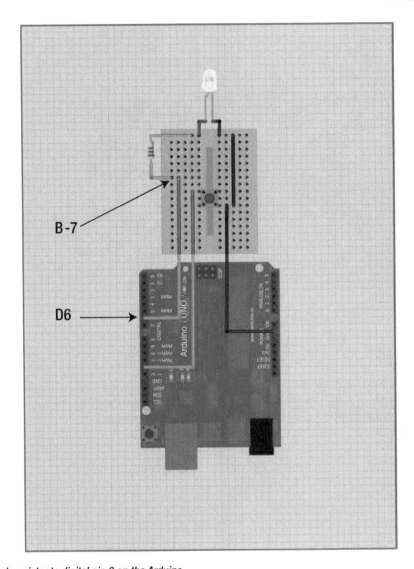

Figure 7-11. Attach resistor to digital pin 6 on the Arduino

By running this jumper wire to B-7, you're actually adding the resistor to the circuit because one of the resistor's ends is inserted into A-7. Remember, A7 through E7 are a shared connection point.

9. This last step is optional, but you might find it fun. Make sure your wires are lying down like those shown in Figure 7-11. Then visit our web site at http://arduinoadventurer.com and download a PDF file to print on card stock to create an enclosure for your gizmo.

Figure 7-12 shows a photo of the completed gizmo. Your device may look slightly different from ours, depending upon how you routed the wires.

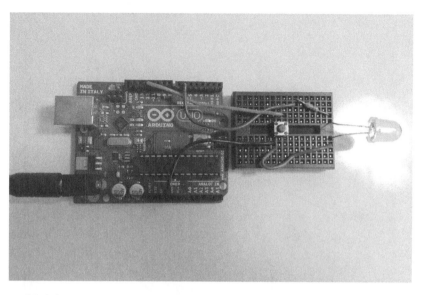

Figure 7-12. The completed gizmo

What's Next?

Now that we've built the gadget, we can move on to the next chapter and examine the sketch that will be uploaded to the Arduino. Remember, you can't do anything with the Arduino yet. Don't plug a 9V battery into the 9V battery connector until Chapter 8 is completed!

Challenge 2: Examining the Software

Now that you have your Arduino flashlight built, it's time to create the sketch that will be uploaded to the Arduino so you can actually use it. A flashlight is a fairly simple device, and the sketch is fairly simple, too—we'll go over the entire sketch in this chapter. And guess what? Even though your Challenge #2 gizmo has only one LED, you can easily add more. That's the benefit of using an Arduino to power the LEDs. If you find that your flashlight isn't bright enough, just add another LED!

As you saw in Chapter 7, each LED has a resistor that helps protect it from receiving too much current (it also protects the Arduino as it can only source 24 milliamperes). Also, each LED can be connected to its own digital pin on the Arduino so you can use the sketch to determine how many LEDs light up. We won't be doing it with this sketch, but it would be a simple matter to program the Arduino to turn on one LED with one press of the button, two LEDs with another press, three LEDs with a third press, and then turn off all LEDs with a fourth press of the button. In this manner, you could easily choose just the amount of lighting you need and nothing more—which means longer battery life!

Before we get to the sketch, we want to get you ready to use digital inputs and digital outputs. The next section will explain a few new functions we'll use for this challenge.

Functions Explained

The new functions for this chapter are digitalWrite, and digitalRead. You use them only with the digital pins on the Arduino (D0 to D13), so this means for the Challenge #2 gizmo you could have a flashlight with up to 12 individually controlled LEDs. (You can have more LEDs, but you'll only have control over

13 digital pins). Why 13 and not 14? Because one of the digital pins we'll be using is connected to a pushbutton. Here are the functions you'll be using to control the LEDs in your new gizmo:

- digitalWrite(pin number, state): This special function writes a HIGH or LOW to a digital I/O pin on the Arduino. A HIGH signal means that power (5V) will be applied to a pin; a LOW signal means no power (0V) will be applied to a pin. The pin number value is represented by the digital I/O pin you use, and the state value is represented by a HIGH or LOW value, so if you wanted to turn digital pin 5 ON, you'd use this statement: digitalWrite(5, HIGH). To turn an LED off that is currently connected to pin 5 that is set to HIGH, you'd use digitalWrite(5, LOW) and the LED will turn off.

- digitalRead(pin number): This function reads the state of a digital device—for example the input of a button. All you need to do is supply the digital pin you're using. So if you want to read the state of digital pin 3, all you'd have to write is: digitalRead(3). If the button is being pressed, the digitalRead(3) will detect a flow of voltage and read that as HIGH.

These two function will come in handy in many of the later challenges in this book, so be sure you understand how they work in the sketch.

The Challenge 2 Sketch

And now it's time to create the sketch we'll upload to the Arduino. Cade will be using an Arduino flashlight in the tunnel, and this sketch will give him the ability to turn the LED on and off with the push of a button. Take a look at Listing 8-1, which shows the sketch for this challenge. A breakdown of the sketch follows.

Listing 8-1. Software for the Second Challenge

```
int buttonPin = 12;  // Arduino pin the button is connected to.
int LEDPin = 6; // Arduino pin the LED is connected to.

int buttonState = 0; // Keeps track of button

void setup()
{
  // Set button as an input
  pinMode(buttonPin, INPUT);
  // Set LED as an output
  pinMode(LEDPin, OUTPUT);
  // Use Arduinos internal pull-up resistor
  digitalWrite(buttonPin, HIGH);
}
void loop()
{
  // Read button value on Arduino
  buttonState = digitalRead(buttonPin);
```

```
// Conditional If Statement
if(buttonState == LOW)
{
 // Turn ON LED when button is pressed
 digitalWrite(LEDPin, HIGH);
}
else
  // Turn OFF LED when button is not pressed
  digitalWrite(LEDPin, LOW);
}
```

Now let's take a look at some sections in more detail. The first bit of the sketch contains variables that let the Arduino know which digital pins are connected to various components:

```
int buttonPin = 12;  // Arduino pin the button is connected to.
int LEDPin = 6; // Arduino pin the LED is connected to.

int buttonState = 0; // Keeps track of button
```

Here, we've created an integer variable called buttonPin that contains the value 12. This means that the push button connects to the Arduino using digital pin 12 (D12). Look at your Challenge #2 gizmo and trace the wire from the push button on the breadboard to the Arduino; it should lead to D12. If it doesn't, go back to Chapter 7 and check your wiring.

Likewise, the LED we added in Chapter 7 connects to digital pin 6 (D6). We specify this in the sketch by defining an integer variable called LEDPin and setting its value to 6. Again, look for the LED on the breadboard and trace a connection back to D6 on the Arduino to verify this configuration.

Finally, we set the initial state of the button to 0; this means it's not being pressed. When the button is pressed, the variable buttonState will have its value changed to 1.

Next, we need to look at the setup portion of the sketch:

```
void setup()
{
  // Set button as an input
  pinMode(buttonPin, INPUT);
  // Set LED as an output
  pinMode(LEDPin, OUTPUT);
  // Use Arduinos internal pull-up resistor
  digitalWrite(buttonPin, HIGH);
}
```

Remember, anything between the first { bracket after void setup() and the last } closing bracket after digitalWrite(buttonPin, HIGH); is part of the setup section. We start with a simple comment // Set button as an input, and then use pinMode(buttonPin, INPU T) to define the push button as an input on the Arduino. Keep in mind that buttonPin has a value of 12, so the Arduino will be monitoring digital pin 12 (D12) to see whether it's value is 0 or 1, pressed or not pressed. The INPUT part of the sketch means that a value will be sent to digital pin 12.

Likewise, the next bit of the sketch defines the LED as an output device: pinMode(LEDPin, OUTPUT). Earlier, we set LEDPin to a value of 6, meaning the LED is connected to digital pin 6. The OUTPUT part means that voltage will be applied to pin 6 by the Arduino, which will cause the LED to light up.

The setup section closes with digitalWrite(buttonPin, HIGH).This digital write function is special because it is using the Arduino's internal resistor as a *pull-up resistor*. Yep, the Arduino has its own built-in resistor that's different from the resistor you insert into a breadboard. A pull-up resistor is used to make sure that a component such as our push button settles at its correct state. Push buttons can act a little funny at times—as if they were pressed when in fact they are not. To prevent this behavior, we'll use the pull-up resistor to set the push button to a known state that is HIGH so when the button is off the Arduino is reading 5V on digital pin 12 and when the push button is pressed D12 is reading a LOW state (0V).

Next we have the loop section of the code. It starts out with this little snippet:

```
void loop()
{
  // Read button value on Arduino
  buttonState = digitalRead(buttonPin);
```

After the opening { bracket in the void loop() section, the Arduino takes a reading of the state of the button—is it pressed or not pressed? It checks by setting the buttonState variable to either 1 or 0. The digitalRead(buttonPin) simply looks at digital pin 12 (D12) and then sets buttonState to 0 if the button is pressed and 1 if it is not pressed.

Once the button state has been read, the next bit of the sketch either turns on the LED or turns it off depending on whether the buttonState is LOW (0) or HIGH (1). Here's that bit of the sketch:

```
  // Conditional If Statement
  if(buttonState == LOW)
  {
   // Turn ON LED when button is pressed
   digitalWrite(LEDPin, HIGH);
  }
  else
    // Turn OFF LED when button is not pressed
    digitalWrite(LEDPin, LOW);
```

As you can see, this part of the sketch simply loops over and over and over, constantly checking the buttonState. Press the button, and the buttonState changes to LOW and the LED is turned on. Release the button, and the buttonState goes back to HIGH and the LED turns off.

Solve Challenge #2

If you'd like to wrap your Challenge #2 gizmo with the challenge card, you can download the card from http://arduinoadventurer.com and print it out. This challenge card wraps around the Arduino and breadboard to create an enclosure for your project. Then you simply attach the battery to the Arduino and press the push button to turn on the LED. Boom! You are now lighting the way with your Arduino.

If you want to have some fun with your Arduino flashlight, see if you can modify the sketch a bit to allow for lighting up two or more LEDs. All you need to do is insert additional LEDs on the breadboard, give each a resistor just as you did with the first LED, and then wire these to their own digital pins on the Arduino. Create variables that hold the pin numbers for these new LEDs (remember, the variables must have different names, so you could create LEDPin2 or LEDPin3 and so on). When the button is pressed, you simply need to change the state of each LED to HIGH and when the button is released, turn off all LEDs.

Now that the flashlight is built, Cade can get to Andrew's primary control so he can be released and help Elle and Cade get out of the space station.

Chapter 9

Feeling The Heat

Elle and Cade shuffled down the long hallway on Level 2, with Elle carrying a laptop bag over one shoulder and both carrying a toolbox full of electronics in each hand. After they had rounded up all of the parts and components on the shopping list Andrew had given them, they had to consolidate everything into fewer boxes so they could carry it all.

"Do we really need all this stuff?" asked Cade.

Andrew's voice responded over the station's communication system, allowing Elle and Cade to hear his instructions as he navigated them through the level. "Much of the station's internal systems are damaged beyond my ability to repair. I do have limited access to some of the station's auto-repair droids and the maintenance bots, but station-wide electrical damage has occurred. You may find yourselves blocked again by damaged doors. And there are reports of fires in a few locations as well as some compartments venting atmosphere. Turn left at the next junction, please."

"Are you sure it was a satellite impact?" asked Elle, turning left and following Cade down another dark hallway. "If it was a meteor shower, there might be more impacts coming."

"I now have access to the planet's communication network," said Andrew. "There are a number of reports that a communication satellite experienced a rupture in a thruster fuel tank. The trajectories of the satellite fragments were not calculated in time to warn the station and begin evacuations. Emergency vehicles are on their way, but they are still hours away. I think it is best to get both of you off the station now rather than wait for rescue. Stop a few feet before the Holographic Exhibit door for a moment, please."

Cade and Elle set their cases on the floor and waited for Andrew to assess the status of the room they were about to enter. Andrew's directions had gotten them safely down a ladder to Level 2, but the access panel to open the emergency exit to enter Level 1 was in ruins.

"The room is safe to enter," said Andrew. "Please proceed through it to the next area."

Cade sighed and picked up his two cases. "Has our school reported us missing yet?"

Elle frowned as she grabbed a case handle in each hand. "I hadn't even thought about that," she said. "Mrs. Hondulora is going to be furious."

"Checking," said Andrew.

A few seconds of silence passed.

"Records indicate thirty-five students and two instructors checked into the station. Eight escape pods have been launched with thirty-five seat restraints engaged. I believe it is safe to say your absence has been noticed."

"We're in so much trouble," said Elle.

On a Pedestal

Cade walked to the door, which opened automatically, and looked over his shoulder. "Look at it this way…maybe we'll get extra credit for all the new things we're learning." His smile was not convincing.

Elle and Cade moved toward the center of the new room. Numerous pedestals were visible against the walls of the round-shaped room. Cade looked closer and could see a small gold plate on each pedestal engraved with a name.

Elle pointed at a door on the opposite side of the room. She consulted the map of the station from memory, trying to recall what exhibit was in the next room.

"What is this room?" asked Cade. "It's kinda creepy."

Andrew responded immediately. "The Holographic Exhibit allows visitors to interact with various celebrities, scientists, and politicians from the last two hundred years. The holograms are currently disabled."

"Oh, no," said Elle.

Cade stopped and turned to face his friend. "Elle, I really don't think we have time to chat with…," he squinted at one of the small name plates. "Bre Pettis? Who is that?"

"Bre Pettis," said Andrew. "A key individual from the early twenty-first century, responsible for the widespread acceptance of three-dimensional printing as a valid form of fast prototyping for small businesses. A major breakthrough by his team in 2015 led to…"

"Yeah, yeah, smart guy," said Cade. "Elle, we gotta move."

Elle continued to stare at the door as she shook her head. "Andrew, you need to find us a different route."

"What?" asked Cade. "Elle, are you alright?"

"We can't go this way," she said. "There has to be a different route."

"I'm sorry, Elle," replied Andrew. "This is not only the fastest way to Level 1, it's also the only one available. There are no other routes to Level 1."

Elle stared hard at Cade. "This way leads to the maintenance tunnels."

Cade shook his head, not understanding. "Yeah? So? What's wrong with that?"

"I wasn't kidding back in Andrew's room, Cade. I really can't handle tight spaces."

Cade put his hand on Elle's shoulder. "We're in some serious danger here, Elle... could you just close your eyes and let me lead you?"

Elle shook her head. "I'm serious. I can't do this. I just…"

"Okay," said Cade. "Let's, uh…see what our options are. Andrew, how long of a crawl is it through the maintenance tunnels?"

"Seventy-eight meters from entrance to exit," said Andrew. "I estimate it will take you ninety-two seconds to complete the transit."

"Not gonna happen," said Elle. "Find us another way, Andrew. I'm not kidding." Ell's voice was tense, and Cade could tell just from her facial expression that her mind was made up.

"Elle, I understand your reluctance, but…"

"Find us another way, Andrew!"

Cade took a step back, shocked at Elle's outburst. His friend was not going to be crawling through any tunnels, that much seemed certain.

Chutes and Ladders

"Andrew, there's got to be another way to the escape pods on Level 1," said Cade.

"There is not, Cade," said Andrew. "The only other option I can provide is to guide you to Level 6. But I am unable to access the station's video surveillance functions and most of the station's environmental sensors are damaged. The ones I can access I'm not certain I'm willing to trust due to the damage to the station."

"Is Level 6 accessible with the emergency ladder tube we used to climb down from Level 3 to 2?" asked Cade.

"No. That tube's access controls for moving up are damaged and I am unable to override. There is another emergency access tube that moves from Level 2 to Level 5 that I can access, but I can't verify the environmental status of Levels 3 and 4. If you had emergency suits, I wouldn't be concerned. All breaches have been sealed, so oxygen isn't a problem. But the station's AI is informing me that there is a fire on Level 4. Damage control droids haven't yet been able to confirm that it has been extinguished."

"But what if there's no fire?" asked Elle. "Then we could get to Level 5 and then to the escape pods on Level 6, right?"

"The risk is too high," replied Andrew. "Elle, it would be safer and faster for the two of you to attempt to cross the access tunnels that lead to Level 1."

Elle ignored Andrew's request, and stared down at the heavy boxes in her hands. Something Andrew had said about the emergency tunnels triggered a thought. "Wait, you said you could open the hatches between levels, right?"

"That's correct, Elle," said Andrew.

"Well, couldn't we put a piece of cloth or paper on Level 3 to detect a fire? We come back down to Level 2, close the hatch, and you open up the hatch that leads to Level 4. If there's no fire, the paper or cloth will let us know it's safe to proceed."

"That won't take into account a high temperature that would be unsafe for humans," said Andrew. "If there's a fire on Level 4, the temperature in the access tunnel could still be too high for you to cross."

"I can't believe this," said Elle. "We can't proceed because we lack a simple thermometer?" She shook her head in frustration.

"Wait," said Andrew.

Cade looked at Elle. "If he tells us we left a digital thermometer back in the room, I'm going to scream."

"I'm sorry about this," said Elle. "I really am. But there's no way I'd make it through the maintenance tunnel."

Cade smiled. "It's okay, Elle. I trust you. If you can't do it, we'll find another way."

"Please open Box 12," said Andrew.

Cade looked at the numbers on his and Elle's boxes. "One of mine," he said, sitting his boxes down and opening up Box 12. "Okay…what next?"

"Please verify you have part number Q91-XB-4."

Cade dug through the boxes various trays, not finding the specified part. He lifted up the top tray and began pulling out the bags and boxes in the bottom of the toolbox.

"Wait," said Elle, reaching forward. "Here it is."

Cade smiled. "Good eyes. Okay, Andrew. We've got it. What is it?"

"Please pack up your boxes and proceed out the Holographic Exhibit's entry door. Turn right, go twenty feet, and turn left. Please hurry."

Cade and Elle began to repack Box 12.

"Keep that part safe, "said Cade. "I have a feeling it's that part that's gonna keep me from dragging you kicking and screaming down the maintenance tunnels."

Elle stood up, grabbed her stuff, and smiled at Cade. "Let's go."

Green-eyed Hatches

Ten minutes later, Cade and Elle stood inside a small room with a metal ladder in the center. Two round, green-painted hatches could be seen, one on the ceiling and one on the floor, with the vertical bars of the ladder extending up and through the hatches. The seal was tight, but Cade and Elle could see that when a hatch opened, a person would be able to continue climbing up or down the ladder.

"I'm going to open the hatch between Levels 2 and 3," said Andrew.

The green hatch split into two halves, each half disappearing into the ceiling. Cade and Elle looked up into the next section of the emergency access tunnel.

"You're okay with the size of this room?" asked Cade.

"Don't ask me to explain," said Elle. "This is plenty of room to move around. Those maintenance tunnels are only two feet wide."

"Okay," said Cade with a nod. "Andrew, what do you need us to do now?"

"I'm going to have you create a small circuit that will test the temperature in Level 4. Part number Q91-XB-4 is critical, but you're also going to need some other components. Please open your boxes and I'll tell you which pieces you'll need."

Cade and Elle sat down on the smooth floor. Elle opened up the laptop bag she'd been carrying and pulled out the antique computer.

"First, you'll need one Arduino Uno..."

Chapter 10

Challenge 3: Fun Stuff to Know

Are you starting to get more comfortable inserting wires into a breadboard and connecting the Arduino Uno to your computer to upload a sketch? We hope so. The folks who design the Arduino microcontrollers had many goals when they were developing the device, and one of those was to make it as simple as possible for non-technical people to build things. You don't necessarily need to know how a resistor works or how its chemical makeup makes it do what it does. You don't need to understand why an LED only works when inserted in the breadboard one way and won't work when inserted the other way. These are things you can find out about later, with some extra research and reading, should you decide you want a deeper understanding of electronics.

But right now . . . what you want is more hands-on activities, right? Well, that's what you're going to get with Challenge 3. This is the last challenge in the book that will have you focusing on a single component. Challenges 4 through 8 will be more involved, and will take advantage of electronic components you've already used (such as resistors, potentiometers, and LEDs), as well as some new ones you haven't yet examined.

So let's get moving. Andrew now has access to all parts of Gemini Station, and he needs to get Elle and Cade to the escape pods. But as you read in Chapter 9, the team needs to move up to Level 5 through a series of hatches, and there's a possibility that Level 4 might be too hot for humans. The only way they can check is to take a temperature reading, and for that they're going to use a new component—a temperature sensor.

Looking at the Temperature Sensor

You're probably quite familiar with the kind of thermometer used to take your temperature—a long glass tube filled with mercury that you stick under your tongue. The mercury moves up the tube and indicates your body's temperature using a bunch of small, numbered lines on the tube. Depending on the country you live in, temperatures are given in either Celsius (C) or Fahrenheit (F).

Using a glass-tube thermometer isn't ideal when dealing with electronics, however. Sure, you could go crazy and build a super-complicated gizmo that uses a visual sensor of some sort to actually read the gauge on the tube, just as a human would read it. But that would probably require both expensive hardware and advanced programming skills. Fortunately, when you need to take a temperature with an Arduino microcontroller, there's a much simpler way.

Take a look at Figure 10-1. It doesn't look anything like a glass-tube thermometer but, believe it or not, it's a temperature sensor. It is fully capable of taking a temperature reading of its current environment and providing that reading back. The sensor in Figure 10-1 happens to return values in Celsius, but you can easily convert to Fahrenheit if you prefer.

Figure 10-1. A temperature sensor is a tiny device; this is close to its actual size

If you've already got your temperature sensor in hand, go ahead and take a closer look at it. If you don't have one yet, check the parts list in Appendix A to find what you need.

The first thing to notice is how easy the three prongs are to bend. You don't want to bend them back and forth, over and over again, but the flexibility of the three prongs will allow you to easily insert them into a breadboard. You can trim them down if you find the temperature sensor is too tall, and you can bend the temperature sensor down or away from other components. And that little black barrel? Inside is an amazingly sensitive and accurate bit of electronics that allows the sensor to detect the temperature of its immediate surroundings. If you're surprised about the small size of this sensor, you'll be even more amazed to know that there are even smaller versions!

While you're examining your temperature sensor, let's talk about how it provides a numeric value that represents temperature. We mentioned that the sensor reports in Celsius, but here in the United States, temperature is typically given in Fahrenheit. However, you've probably learned in school that there's a simple equation for converting a Celsius value to a Fahrenheit value, so this is no big deal. But guess what? You don't even need to worry about converting to Fahrenheit with a pen or pencil, you can just add this requirement to the sketch and make the Arduino do the Celsius-to-Fahrenheit conversion for you! How cool is that?

Many temperature sensors look just like the one in Figure 10-1, but they may not measure temperature in exactly the same manner. Some temperature sensors have a wider range than others, meaning one temperature sensor might be able to take a reading between 0 and 120 degrees Celsius, for example, while another might only be able to read between 40 and 150 degrees Celsius. For the purposes of Challenge 3, we'll be looking for a safe temperature for humans, so the recommended temperature sensor found in Appendix A should work fine.

ANDREW 5.0

It's probably a bit more technical than your readers might care for, but the datasheet for the specific temperature sensor used in Challenge 3 can be found at www.sparkfun.com/products/10988. Even I got drowsy reading over it, so just beware that it's full of charts and equations and other sleep-inducing content.

As long as your readers use a similar temperature sensor, they should get reasonably trustworthy readings and they won't be required to wire up the sensor any differently than is shown in Chapter 11.

And please warn your readers that the gizmo they'll be building for Challenge 3 is for testing and educational purposes only. No one should rely on this Arduino gizmo and temperature sensor for real-world use—checking your own temperature, for example. Testing for a fever is much better performed with a thermometer designed for that purpose. The goal here is for your readers to understand how a temperature sensor can connect to an Arduino microcontroller and provide temperature data.

As Andrew said, it's probably not a good idea to use this gizmo to test anything other than the temperature of the room you're working in. So please don't go putting it into the oven or the microwave or the freezer. First, your parents probably won't like the mess this makes (melted electronics everywhere); and second, your Arduino might not survive. There are methods for creating real-world gizmos that can withstand high and low temperatures, but the gizmo you'll be building in Chapter 11 won't be capable of dealing with temperature extremes.

We're jumping ahead a bit, but take a look at Figure 10-2 to see what the final wired-up gizmo for Challenge 3 looks like. (You'll find the instructions for actually assembling it in Chapter 11.)

Figure 10-2. An Arduino gizmo, complete with temperature sensor

There are a few things you might notice in Figure 10-2 in addition to the temperature sensor. First, you'll see a resistor and an LED. As you learned in Challenge 2, it's always good to pair an LED with a resistor to protect the LED from burnout should it receive too much power. We'll talk about the function of the LED is in Chapter 11, but try and make some guesses about how an LED might be used with a gizmo that's designed to determine the temperature in a room. Any ideas?

Notice that we're once again using jumper wires to make some connections. In Chapter 11, we'll be telling you how to connect everything together. For now, Figure 10-2 should give you an idea of the simplicity of this gizmo. Imagine it—an Arduino and a tiny temperature sensor, when connected to a computer, can give you real-time feedback on the temperature. Can you think of any possible uses for this combination of components?

ANDREW 5.0

Your readers might like to know some of the uses I can think of for a temperature sensor. Here are a couple suggestions that might spark some ideas for future gizmos.

1. *Fan controller:* Use the temperature sensor to start and stop a battery-operated fan. Use the fan to keep cool at your desk or workbench.

2. *Automatic plant watering device:* Use a temperature sensor to determine when it's time to tip a motor-controlled watering can to give a plant a drink of water. Even better, you could investigate a humidity sensor and how best to integrate it into your automatic plant watering device! (You'll start learning about motors with Challenge 4.)

3. *Flowerbed protection device:* Tape a temperature sensor to the inside of a window to determine when the temperature outside drops below a certain point. Program the gizmo to alert you to cover up your plants so they'll survive the cold night.

Andrew's got some great ideas and we're sure you have some of your own. As we stated earlier, your imagination is your best source of future gizmo designs. When you finish Challenge 3, you'll have been introduced to the potentiometer, LED, temperature sensor, resistor, jumper wires, battery harness, and push button. But we're not done... not even close. In upcoming challenges, you'll be combining many different components you've experimented with individually and making some more-complex gizmos that'll give you an even better idea of just how far you can push your Arduino microcontroller with some extra parts, a little bit of reading, and a fun bit of tinkering.

Ready to Build Something?

Are you starting to see some of the possibilities Arduino microcontrollers offer? Just think about this—if you can imagine a gizmo that can perform a certain function, you can probably figure out how to actually build it. You may have to do some more research, post some questions on a few Web forums, and possibly burn out a few components as you try different solutions, but that's also part of the fun of experimenting with an Arduino—trying new things, testing them out, learning what works and what doesn't work, and then finally having that big breakthrough where you wow the world (okay, maybe just your friends and family) with your new invention.

Remember to check out Appendix A for the hardware you'll need to build the Challenge 3 gizmo. Again, it's not a long list, so it shouldn't take you long to gather the parts and it shouldn't cost you a fortune, either. Turn to Chapter 11 when you're ready to begin assembling the temperature sensing gizmo.

Time to build!

Challenge 3: Examining the Hardware

Ready for the next hardware challenge? This time we'll create the temperature gizmo Cade and Elle need for checking the temperature between levels. This gizmo is extremely simple, but that doesn't mean it's not important! Think about it—some of the most important things you do in life require only one or two components—brushing your teeth, writing an essay, even riding a bike. But it's often the simplest things that require the most preparation.

Take riding a bike: there's basically just one component—the bike—but you've got to have a good sense of balance, two feet for the pedals, two hands to steer, and the bike needs to be assembled properly or you risk injury. The same goes for any gizmo you build with the Arduino! You need to understand each simple component used in the gizmo, plus how to properly program it and wire it up on a breadboard.

So, before building the Challenge 3 gizmo, let's learn a little bit about the temperature sensor we're going to use. Once that's out of the way, we'll start creating the circuit.

Let's get moving!

What Is a Sensor?

As we mentioned, we'll be using a temperature sensor for the Challenge 3 gizmo. But what is a sensor? Well, a sensor is a component that allows you to convert values of natural phenomenon to a readable unit, such as voltage. Think about it this way: the temperature sensor will take a reading of the room's temperature—that's the natural phenomenon. Other readings could be the light level in a room, the sound level in an auditorium, or even the water level in a flooded basement.

Sensors you use with an Arduino Uno, however, often don't report values the way we humans read them. For example, the temperature outside right now is 80 degrees Fahrenheit, but the temperature value provided by a working temperature sensor won't show up as 80.

The sensor translates temperature into voltage. The Arduino Uno senses the voltage level and reports that to you as a number. For example, 80 degrees might trigger the sensor to return 4.503 volts and that's the value the Arduino Uno gives you. It's up to you to do the math to translate 4.503 into 80 to represent degrees Fahrenheit. That math is done in software. You'll see it in the next chapter.

For the Challenge 3 gizmo, we'll be using the TMP36 temperature sensor. Sounds technical, doesn't it? Well, if you take a look at Figure 11-1, you'll see that there's really nothing complicated about it at all.

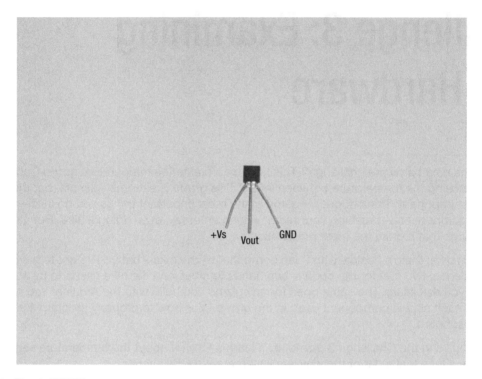

Figure 11-1. Pinout of TMP36

Figure 11-1 doesn't just show what the TMP36 looks like. See how the flat side is facing up? That's a good reference point for you. When you use this sensor, you need to make sure to connect it correctly or you can damage it.

Now take a look at the sensor's pinout in Figure 11-1. The pinout simply shows the function of each of the three metal legs (pins) and how they should be inserted into a breadboard circuit. As you can see, the sensor has one pin for the input voltage (5v or 3.3v), one for ground, and one for output voltage. The output voltage lead is going to be connected to the Arduino's analog input, and it's the voltage provided by this pin that will be converted into a temperature we can all understand.

ANDREW 5.0

There's a lot going on inside the TMP36 temperature sensor, and I know you'd like to understand how that little device works. First, the actual temperature the TMP36 detects is converted to a voltage value. As the temperature climbs, the voltage climbs, and if the temperature drops, the voltage value is reduced. This voltage value is what's reported using the middle wire—the voltage-out pin.

In addition to the temperature sensor, we'll also be using some components you already know—an LED and a resistor. For the Challenge 3 gizmo, you'll use the LED to indicate when the detected temperature falls above or below a certain value. You'll use the program to define whether you want it light up when the temperature drops below a value (say, below 90 degrees Fahrenheit) or when the temperature exceeds a value (above 100 degrees Fahrenheit, for example).

You'll also need your mini breadboard, your Arduino Uno, and five jumper wires. We're using three black wires and two red wires, but the color isn't all that important so use what you have.

Let's Build Gizmo 3!

Now let's build the circuit. Remember, you can find a list of all the hardware for this challenge, and all of the projects, in Appendix A.

1. The first step is to attach the LED to the solderless bread board, as shown in Figure 11-2. Insert the longer, positive LED lead into Row 26, Column E (E-26). Insert the shorter, negative lead into Row 30, Column E (E-30).

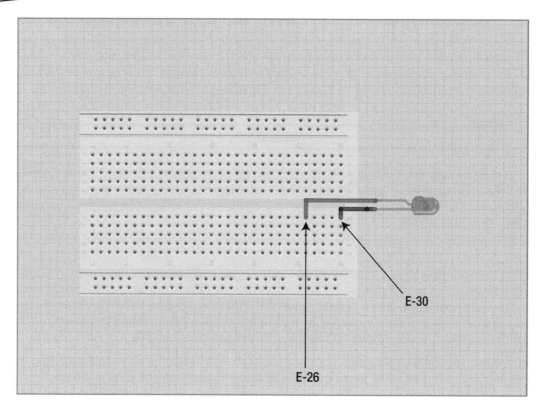

E-30

E-26

Figure 11-2. LED attached to the solderless breadboard

2. Next, attach the 150-ohm resistor to the positive lead of the LED, as
    illustrated in Figure 11-3. The 150-ohm resistor has a series of colored bands
    with the pattern brown-green-red. (You may also have either a gold or a silver
    band following the red one). Insert one of the resistor leads into Row 26,
    Column D (D-26) and the other into Row 24, Column B (B-24).

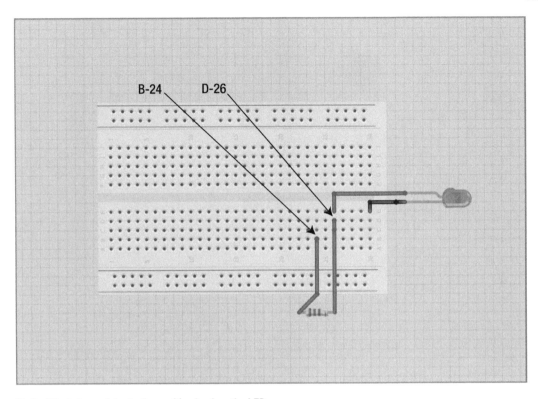

Figure 11-3. *Attach the resistor to the positive lead on the LED*

3. Attach ground from the Arduino to the bottom ground strip of the solderless bread board. Then attach the ground strip of the solderless bread board to A-30 of the solderless bread board. Figure 11-4 illustrates this process.

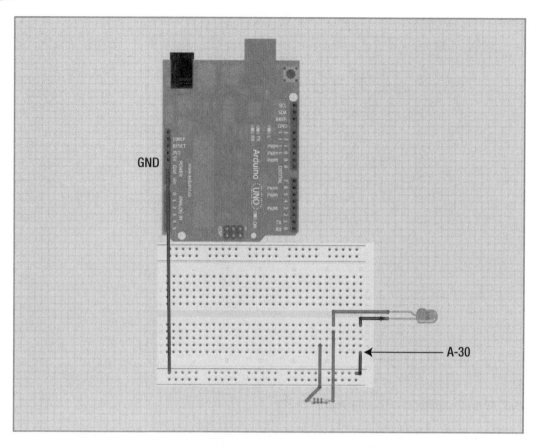

Figure 11-4. Attach ground from the Arduino to the solderless bread board and to the LED

4. Attach digital pin 13 of the Arduino to the other side of the resistor (E-24 of the solderless bread board), as shown in Figure 11-5.

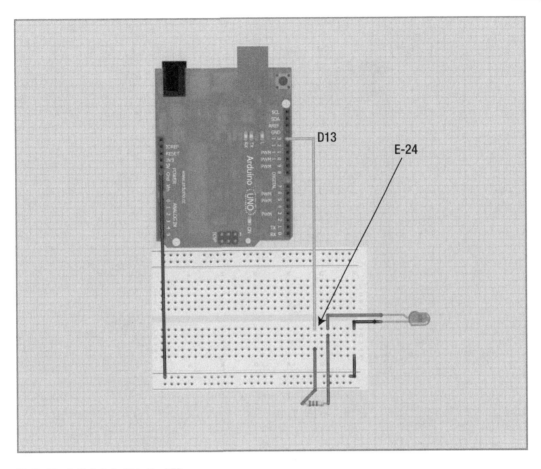

Figure 11-5. Attach digital pin 13 to the LED

5. Now you're ready for the temperature sensor. Insert the TMP36 sensor into the solderless bread board as shown in Figure 11-6, making sure the flat side is facing away from the Arduino—assuming you have the two boards oriented as we do in the figure.

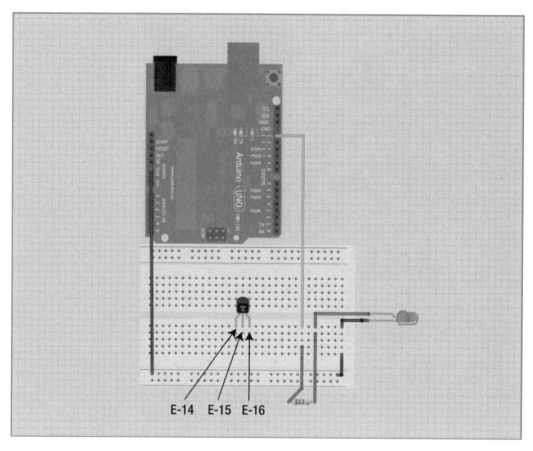

Figure 11-6. Attach the TMP36 to the solderless breadboard

> **Caution**   Use care when adding the temperature sensor to the breadboard. There is some risk of damage if you mix up the pins. Pay close attention to the next paragraph.

You want the Vs pin (on the left when looking at the TMP36 with flat side facing you) inserted into Row 14, Column E (E-14), the middle pin (Vout) inserted into Row 15, Column E (E-15), and the GND pin inserted into Row 16, Column E (E-16).

6.   Now you'll connect the temperature sensor to the other components. First, connect the 5V pin on the Arduino to the +Vs pin on the TMP36 using a jumper wire. Insert one end of the jumper wire into Row 14, Column D (D-14) and the other end into the +5V header on the Arduino. (We used a red wire, but any color will work.) Next, connect ground from the ground strip of the solderless breadboard to the ground pin on the TMP36. Use another Jumper

wire with one end inserted into Row 16, Column A (A-16) and the other end going into the ground strip of the solderless bread board. (We used a black wire but any color will work fine.) Figure 11-7 illustrates this process.

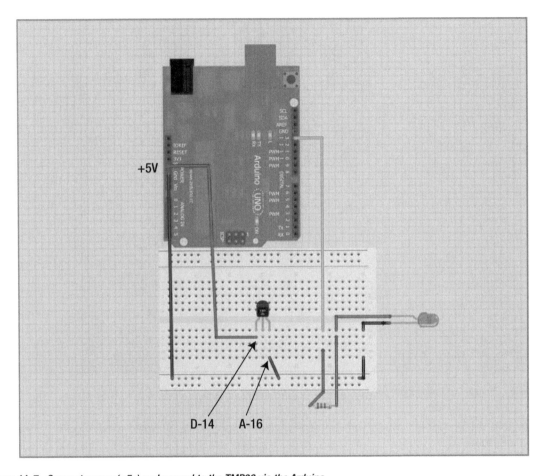

+5V

D-14   A-16

Figure 11-7. Connect power (+5v) and ground to the TMP36 via the Arduino

7. Finally, you'll use your last jumper wire to connect the Vout pin on the TMP36 to the analog 0 header on the Arduino, as shown in Figure 11-8. Insert one end of the jumper wire into Row 15, Column D (D-15) and the other end into the A0 header on the Arduino. (We used a green wire but any color will work.)

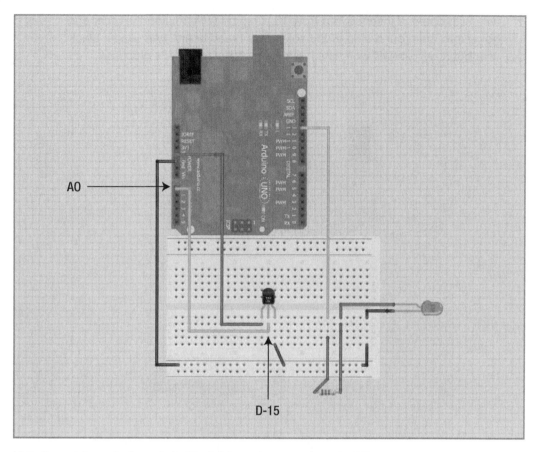

Figure 11-8. Connect the analog input pin 0 of the Arduino to the center pin on the TMP36

And that's it! You've got a temperature-detecting gizmo ready to be programmed! Figure 11-9 shows the one we built.

Figure 11-9. The authors' version

Be sure to check that the LED is connected correctly with the negative pin (the anode) inserted into E-30 and the positive pin (the cathode) inserted into E-26. Also, make sure you're sending 5v to the TMP36 and not 3.3v; this wouldn't cause damage, but it would result in incorrect readings or possibly a gizmo that just won't work. If your wiring is correct you are ready to program!

Chapter 12 will provide the simple sketch that must be uploaded to your Challenge 3 gizmo to make the detector work. So turn the page and get moving—Cade and Elle are counting on you!

Chapter 12

Challenge 3: Examining the Software

If you ask a dozen students about their favorite part of designing gizmos with an Arduino, you're likely to get a dozen unique answers. One might like experimenting with new sensors, another might like building motorized devices, and a third might prefer the programming portion of a design. Even your authors have their own favorite parts of designing a gizmo. Harold, for example, enjoys the programming part of a project, and he's quite good at it. But James Floyd, on the other hand, prefers laying out circuits on a breadboard instead of typing up bits of code to make a sketch.

But an Arduino gizmo requires some skill in all areas. Harold is also quite good at building circuits, and James Floyd is getting better at programming. You're probably already starting to identify your strengths and weaknesses when it comes to building the gizmos in the book, right? Maybe you really enjoy building the circuits, or maybe you've discovered you've got a special knack for programming. Whatever you enjoy doing, keep doing it! But don't forget that a properly working gizmo requires a good understanding of both aspects of its design—hardware and software.

Well, we're here in the Challenge 3 programming chapter, and that means learning a bit more about how sketches work and control an Arduino and its various components. In the case of the Challenge 3 gizmo, the temperature sensor is the newest element. Thankfully, it's not a complicated component!

Before we get into showing you the complete sketch for the Challenge 3 gizmo, we want to introduce you to another fundamental concept of programming. Once again, don't sweat it if the programming doesn't seem to come naturally to you—it doesn't to James Floyd, either. Programming is something you learn a little at a time, piece by piece. Over time, your brain will start to organize all the techniques and methods you pick up as you program various gizmos and, the next thing you know, you're an Arduino programming guru!

But let's just take it a step at a time. For the Challenge 3 gizmo, you're going to want to continually monitor the feedback from the temperature sensor. And in order to do this, you need to revisit a concept from Chapter 4 called a loop. What does a loop do? Pick any point on a loop and start moving—and you'll return to your starting position eventually. It's the same with a programming loop. At some point, the sketch starts doing something and, after a period of time, it starts over. It's not complicated, and the actual programming code required to do this is pretty short, so let's take a look at how we can tell the Arduino to repeat an action over and over again.

The Conditional If-Else Statement

Imagine sitting in a race car on a race track. It doesn't matter if the track is circular or oval or some other pattern. If you start driving, eventually you'll come back to your starting point, which we'll call the Starting Line.

Now, you've got a few things you want to monitor. The first is your fuel level and there's a gauge you're watching. A needle points to either Full or Empty. Another gauge tells you whether your tires are Good or Need Replacing.

Punch the gas and let's race! You finish your first lap and as you cross the Starting Line, you look at your gauges. Gas is still Full and Tires are Good. Keep going! You go lap after lap after lap… eventually the gas gauge says Empty. Do you head in for a pit stop and refuel? Of course! Without fuel, you're out of the race. After refueling, you'll continue to monitor your gauges and make decisions based on the conditions of your car.

Let's think of how we might do a bit of decision making. We could make a list of conditions like this:

- If Gas >= 4 gallons and Tire tread >= 40%, keep racing.
- Else make a pit stop.

Notice that the Gas and Tire tread variables have the >= and then a number after them. Those numbers are called limits, and limits are extremely important in all aspects of programming. For example, the two limits used in this example are 4 and 40, but they could have been 2 and 65. It just depends on the limits you need for your specific application.

Imagine if we replaced you (the driver) with an Arduino that could somehow drive the race car. We'd need to create a sketch to steer, obviously, and another to press the gas pedal or hit the brakes. If we assume that the steering and driving parts of the sketch have already been written, then what's left is the part of the sketch that determines when to make a pit stop and when to keep racing. To do that, we'd need to periodically check the conditions of the gas tank and the tires.

When it comes to Arduino programming, these kinds of tests are most often performed using an extremely easy bit of code called an If-Else statement. An If-Else statement is a kind of Conditional Statement and it works like this:

If Gas is >= 4 gallons and Tires are >= 40% tread left—RACE!

Else MAKE A PIT STOP!

Pretty simple test, isn't it? Based on a condition, we do one or the other! If the gas tank has 4 or more gallons and the tires have 40% or more tread left, keep racing. But if the gas is less than 4 gallons or the tire tread is less than 40%, or both conditions exist (gas < 4gallons, tire tread < 40%), then we make a pit stop.

And what does an If-Else statement look like when implemented in a sketch? Take a look:

```
if (test condition or test conditions)
{
    // Code here
}
else
{
    // Code to run when no previous condition is a match
}
```

Look closely at the code. The first thing that happens is that one or more conditions—whatever's inside the parentheses—are tested. Suppose we want to test just for an empty gas tank. We could use if (gastank >= 4), which basically says, "If the gastank variable is greater than or equal to 4 gallons, then perform whatever instructions we provide next between the { and } brackets.

But we've also got the tires to check, so we could modify our if statement as follows: if (gastank >= 4 && tires >= 40), which essentially says "If the gastank variable is greater than or equal to 4 gallons AND the tires variable is greater than or equal to 40%, then perform the instructions between the { and } brackets.

Only if both conditions (gas tank > 4 gallons and tire treads > 40%) are true will whatever code we put in between the first set of brackets be executed. Otherwise, the sketch jumps to the else clause and executes whatever *fall-through statement* is between the { and } brackets that follow the else keyword. Here's a modified version of the If-Else statement:

```
if (gastank  >= 4 && tires >= 40)
{
    RACE
}
else
{
    MAKE PITSTOP
}
```

The key to really learning to use an If-Else statement is figuring out how to create the conditions that are tested. We created two fake variables, gastank and tires, that would monitor the conditions of your race car, but there is really no limit to the conditions you could place within the parentheses—if (motiondetector <>0) or if (temperature>90), for example.

This example illustrates how to set up a loop when you want an action to repeat over and over again, but be able to break out of it when certain conditions are met. Hopefully you are beginning to understand the basics of the If-Else statement. We're now going to show you how we implement an If-Else statement in the Challenge 3 gizmo's sketch. Things should begin to crystalize for you as you read the next section.

The Challenge #3 Sketch

Now that you understand the If-Else statement you can use it in this next listing to control an LED whenever the temperature reaches a certain limit. The limit for this sketch can change from household to household. For example, your house may be warmer than 75 degrees, so you might have to adjust that limit when you are running the program.

Listing 12-1 is the sketch you should upload for Challenge 3 to your Arduino with a USB cable.

Listing 12-1. The Sketch for Reading Temperature

```
int tempPin = 0;
int LEDPin = 13;

void setup()
{
   pinMode(LEDPin, OUTPUT);
   Serial.begin(9600);
}

void loop()
{
 //get voltage reading from the temperature sensor
 int reading = analogRead(tempPin);

 float voltage = reading * 5.0;
 voltage /= 1024.0;   // short way of stating voltage = voltage / 1024.0

 // Convert voltage to Celsius
 float tempC = (voltage - 0.5) * 100 ;

 // convert Celsius to Fahrenheit
 float tempF = (tempC * 9.0 / 5.0) + 32.0;

 // if Temperature is greater-than or equal to 75 turn LED on else leave
 // LED off
 if(tempF >= 75)
 {
   digitalWrite(LEDPin, HIGH);
 }
 else
 {
   digitalWrite(LEDPin, LOW);
 }

 // for debugging purposes shpow tempF data on Serial monitor
 Serial.println(tempF); //Send tempF data to serial port.

 delay(500);    //waiting a half second
}
```

Go ahead and read through the entire sketch—it isn't long at all. You'll probably recognize some parts of the sketch because of the previous gizmo sketches. But you'll also see some new stuff. So let's break it down and examine some of the key parts and learn how they work.

Here's the first part of the sketch:

```
int tempPin = 0;
int LEDPin = 13;

void setup()
{
   pinMode(LEDPin, OUTPUT);
   Serial.begin(9600);
}
```

Pretty straightforward—we create two variables, tempPin and LEDPin, that define where these two components are inserted into the Arduino. The temperature sensor has one of its pins inserted into A0 and the LED has one of its pins connected to D13. (Refer back to Chapter 11 for details on how the components connect to the Arduino microcontroller.)

After the variables are defined, we add a bit of code that specifies how the LEDPin will be used. OUTPUT means voltage will be applied to pin 13 to light up the LED. We'll also be using the serial monitor again so we can see actual temperature feedback from the sensor.

Here's the next piece of the sketch:

```
void loop()
{
 //get voltage reading from the temperature sensor
 int reading = analogRead(tempPin);

 float voltage = reading * 5.0; // convert analog reading to a voltage level
 voltage /= 1024.0;   // voltage = voltage / 1024.0

 // Convert voltage to Celsius
 float tempC = (voltage - 0.5) * 100 ;

 // convert Celsius to Fahrenheit
 float tempF = (tempC * 9.0 / 5.0) + 32.0;
```

You'll recognize the void loop() part as the main area of the sketch. The sketch will take a reading from the temperature sensor by reading the data received on A0 (tempPin=0, remember?) and storing it in a temporary integer variable called reading. The reading variable stores an analog value that we also need to convert.

We create a temporary variable called voltage that will be calculated by taking the value stored in the reading variable and multiplying it by 5 (because the Arduino is supplying 5V of power). The value of the voltage variable needs to be converted to something a human can understand, so we divide the current value by 1024 (1024 bits) to get a voltage value (from 0 to 5v).

The voltage value can then be converted into both Celsius and Fahrenheit. To calculate the Celsius temperature, we take the voltage value and subtract .5 before multiplying by 100. If you live in a country that uses Celsius for displaying temperature, you could stop here. But in the USA, we use Fahrenheit, so there's one more calculation that needs to be done. We take the Celsius value (stored in variable tempC) and multiply it by 9 and then divide that by 5. Add 32 as the final step, and tempF will hold the Fahrenheit value provided by the temperature sensor.

And now let's finish up by examining the last bit of the sketch:

```
// if Temperature is greater-than or equal to 75 turn LED on else leave
// LED off
if(tempF >= 75)
  {
    digitalWrite(LEDPin, HIGH);
  }
  else
  {
    digitalWrite(LEDPin, LOW);
  }

  // for debugging purposes shpow tempF data on Serial monitor
  Serial.println(tempF); //Send tempF data to serial port.

  delay(500);    //waiting a half second
}
```

Here's that If-Else statement you just read about. Look at the first line: if(tempF >=75). This is a simple test to determine if the temperature being detected by the sensor is greater than or equal to 75. If the test is found to be true, the LED lights up because the code between the { and } brackets below the if statement, digitalWrite(LEDPIn, HIGH), is executed.

If the test is false (maybe the temperature is 74 degrees F), then the code found between the { and } brackets below the else statement is executed. If the temperature is 40 degrees F, for example, the sketch executes digitalWrite(LEDpin, LOW), which simply turns off the LED.

The remaining bit of the sketch puts the current value of tempF on the screen so you can use the serial monitor to actually read the value that the temperature sensor is detecting. You can have some fun with this by cupping the sensor in your hands or holding a candle near (but without touching) the sensor. You should see immediate changes in the temperature reading.

The delay(500) simply pauses for half a second between readings.

You can tweak the sketch a number of ways:

- ■ Changing to if(tempF < 75) tests whether the temperature value is less than 75.
- ■ Changing to if(tempC >23) tests using Celsius values.
- ■ You could test if(tempF < 75) and set the LED to LOW to test the same condition, but this time turning on the LED (LED to HIGH) in the else statement. If the temperature is less than 75, the if statement is false and the else statement will execute, turning on the LED.

You'll find the If-Else statement to be very common in Arduino sketches. There's no better method for testing conditions and using the true or false nature of those conditions to control the actions of a gizmo.

```
╔═══════════════════════════════════════════════════════════════╗
║                         ANDREW 5.0                            ║
╚═══════════════════════════════════════════════════════════════╝
```

You should also note that if-else statements can be combined to test a much larger set of conditions. This practice is called nesting and looks like this:

```
if (test condition 1)
{
        if (test condition 2)
                { //Code here
                }
        else
                { //Code here
                }

}

else if (testcondition 3)
{
  // Code here
}
```

You can even nest another if-else statement in the original else portion of the code. This nesting can get tricky, but it's completely allowable and is a great way to test multiple conditions.

Solve Challenge #3

After uploading the sketch to the Arduino microcontroller, open up the serial monitor and start watching the temperature value being returned. Carefully grab the temperature sensor between your finger and thumb. (We like to put a finger or thumb right up against the flat portion). Your body heat will warm the sensor. You should see the values in the serial monitor climb when you hold the sensor, and fall back down once you let go of it.

You will notice that the LED will turn on only if the temperature is 75 degrees Fahrenheit or greater. You can modify the code to check, for example, that the temperature is greater than 75 and less than 95 (or whatever upper limit you want to set). We'll leave it up to you to modify the code to test for a lower and upper value.

Keep in mind that Cade and Elle don't want the temperature in the emergency tube to be too low or too high. A good challenge for you is to figure out how to modify your sketch so it will light up the LED if the temperature is over 75 but blink the LED if it's above a higher value (85 degrees, for example).

Congratulations on getting your temperature sensor up and running! Now Elle and Cade can make certain it's safe to move between levels and that the temperature isn't so high it'll hurt them.

Chapter 13

Uninvited Guest

"Temperature in the compartment is reading 74 degrees Fahrenheit," said Cade.

Elle verified the sensor reading on the laptop screen, scooping up the Arduino gizmo she and Cade had assembled and left sitting on the floor of Level 3. Above her head, the hatch seal between Level 3 and Level 4 was closed.

Cade climbed up from Level 2 to join his friend, staring up at the closed hatch seal.

Andrew's voice echoed from the small wall-mounted speaker in the compartment. "No vacuum and no fire in the Level 4 emergency escape tube. Proceed immediately to Level 5."

Upward

The hatch seal above the students opened quickly, allowing them to see all the way up to the Level 5 compartment.

"You go first, Cade," said Elle. "I'll hand you the laptop and cases when you're ready."

Cade climbed the ladder and pulled himself into the Level 4 compartment. He spun around, dropping his left arm down. "Okay, gimme…"

Elle closed the laptop, carefully placed it in its bag, and climbed up a few steps until Cade was able to grab the strap. She repeated the process with the four toolboxes full of electronic components, and then joined Cade on Level 4.

"Great… now we get to do that again," complained Cade with a grin.

"Let me take a turn pulling up the stuff," replied Elle, already climbing the ladder to Level 5. "I know that's got to be tiring."

Cade didn't argue.

Spooky?

A few minutes later, Cade and Elle peered out of the open door into the hallways of Level 5.

"Tell me again why the emergency access tube doesn't go straight to the Level 6 escape pods," said Cade. "That seems like really poor design."

"There are multiple emergency access tubes throughout the station. No one tube runs completely through the station," said Andrew. "The design was intentional to provide multiple locations to exit the station using escape pods."

Cade shook his head. "Yeah, yeah… okay. Still, would've been nice to have a straight shot to the pods."

Elle was catching her breath from the climb and pulling up the toolboxes and was too tired to voice her complaint, but she felt the same as Cade.

"The Level 6 escape pods are still functional," said Andrew. "The estimated time to reach them is approximately four minutes. The emergency response team from the planet's surface isn't scheduled to arrive for another three hours."

Elle frowned. "Is the station safe, Andrew? Has it been knocked out of orbit? Are we running out of oxygen?"

"Is there any food," asked Cade. "I'm really hungry."

Elle nudged Cade with her shoulder. "Bigger problems here, Cade," she said.

"Doesn't change the fact that I'm starving."

"I'm running another station-wide scan," said Andrew. "Thirty-two percent of the station's damage-control reporting capabilities are offline, however. And the station's AI is still only responding to a few of my queries, not all. One moment…"

Cade and Elle both looked down the dark hallway, lit only with emergency lighting.

"A bit spooky, isn't it?" said Elle. She then whistled an eerie little tune from a popular horror movie.

"Stop it," said Cade.

Elle grinned, aware that her friend did not like scary movies. "Reminds me of that Experi-Vid we saw last year. What was the name of it? 'What Lurks on Station Five?' Yeah, remember that scene in the dark hallway…?"

"Elle, I will drag you down that tunnel,," said Cade.

"Level 5 has very little damage," interrupted Andrew. "I will guide you quickly to the other emergency access tube that will take you to Level 6. I'll continue to try to gather information about Level 6. Please proceed down the hallway for fifty feet and then turn right…"

Urgency!

"Stop!" said Andrew, surprising Elle and Cade who were now standing in front of the closed door that would let them enter the emergency access tube for Levels 5 to 10.

"A fire?" asked Elle.

"Vacuum?" asked Cade.

"One moment…," said Andrew.

Cade and Elle stood in silence, staring at the closed door. Only an occasional pop or creak echoing throughout the station could be heard, and both students wondered what was giving Andrew reservations about opening the door.

"Andrew?" asked Cade. "Is everything okay?"

Elle swallowed nervously, aware that if they were unable to gain access to Level 6 using the emergency escape tube, their only option would be to return to the maintenance tunnels.

"A ship has docked on Level 11," replied Andrew. "I am trying to determine the origin of the ship and verify the identity of its passenger."

"One passenger?" asked Elle.

"The station's AI is providing me with only minimum details at the moment. A ship has docked, but its configuration is not consistent with emergency vehicles from M-392. And its identification beacon is not broadcasting. This is a violation of vehicle protocols."

"Maybe a private ship offering help?" suggested Cade.

"I am trying to access any of the ten video feeds from the shuttle bay on Level 11. One moment…." said Andrew.

Cade nodded and smiled at Elle. "One moment," he mimicked.

Elle smiled. "Let Andrew check it out… be patient."

"Bigger problems, remember," replied Cade. "Patience isn't on my mind right now."

The door to the emergency access tube opened with a whoosh, making Cade and Elle jump.

"Please hurry," said Andrew. "You need to make your way up to Level 6 right now."

The emotion in Andrew's voice surprised Elle. There was a sense of urgency she had never heard before from the AI.

"Andrew? What's going on?" Cade asked. He, too, had picked up on the change in Andrew's conversational tone.

"I will explain as you climb. Please, Cade… Elle… climb."

Elle shrugged off the laptop bag and set the boxes down on the floor as the hatch above her head opened to reveal Level 6. "Alright. One more climb," she said.

"Let's do this," replied Cade. "I'm heading up."

Danger!

"The single passenger is currently trying to access Command and Control on Level 12," said Andrew. "He tried to hack the control panel, but failed. The station's AI performed an identification check and has verified his identity. His name is Gunther Canvin. He is an ore hauler from Taurus Station. He has a criminal record."

Elle moved down the hallway behind Cade, carrying her toolboxes and laptop bag. "What's he doing here? Is he responsible for the damage to the station?"

"Intersection, Andrew," interrupted Cade. "Left, right, or forward?"

"Left and forty feet forward to the station's cargo hold," replied Andrew. "Elle, I do not know what his intentions are, but I do not believe he was responsible for the satellite's destruction. The most likely scenario is that he was traveling to Taurus Station and became aware of the damage to Gemini Station."

"Maybe he's here to help?" asked Elle.

"Unlikely," said Andrew. "He's not responding to the station's AI to identify himself or his intentions. You need to hurry."

Elle and Cade both increased their walking speed, but the heavy cases weren't helping.

"Is there something you're not telling us, Andrew?" asked Cade, giving Elle a quick glance over his shoulder.

"Gunther is now attempting to access Command and Control using an emergency override protocol."

Elle shook her head. "What does that mean?"

"He can't get in using security credentials, so he's attempting to sabotage the life support controls."

"What?" both students yelled.

"Why would he do that?" asked Cade, stopping suddenly and causing Elle to bump into him from behind. "Oh, man... watch your step."

Elle stepped aside and looked in front of Cade. A fifteen-foot-wide gap ran completely from left to right of the station's sides, blocking Cade and Elle from the door on the far side that was labeled Emergency Access.

"If Gunther can sabotage the life support controls, all security overrides will be lifted. The station will unlock all secure rooms. This is to allow emergency personnel full access to the station, but it will give him access to the station's master control room."

Elle took a cautious step forward and looked down. The gap was at least thirty feet deep, and she could see cargo boxes and other items stacked or knocked over in the station's cargo bay. On the opposite side of the bay were two large metal grates in a raised position.

"Shouldn't those grates be down so we can cross?" asked Cade.

"I am trying to access the controls to lower them, but the system appears to be damaged."

"We can't jump across that gap, Andrew," said Elle. "It's too wide."

Cade looked around. "Maybe there's something we can use to throw at one and hook it? Pull it down?"

"The motors controlling the lowering of the grates will be locked. There is no way to pull the grates down without damaging them and possibly pulling them off their hinges," replied Andrew.

"Whose idea was it to put both grates on the same side?" asked Cade. "Really? I'm not believing this!"

Bucket

"There is another option for crossing the gap, but you're going to have to listen to me carefully and work fast," said Andrew. "Look to your left and you'll see a tool transfer bucket mounted to the wall."

Elle and Cade turned and looked. Mounted on a track running along the wall was a small rectangular box.

"You've got to be kidding!" said Cade.

"You want us to ride in that?" asked Elle. "It's not big enough."

"It's large enough to hold one person at a time, but that's not the problem," replied Andrew. "The controls for the bucket appear to be damaged. I was unable to visually verify that before directing you to this level. I apologize."

"So we need to head back to the maintenance tunnels," said Cade. "Sorry, Elle. It's our only option."

"There's no time," said Andrew. "If Gunther succeeds in disabling life support, all escape pods will automatically eject after a five-minute countdown."

"No way!" yelled Cade. "That's crazy!"

"There's no time to waste. I'll guide you through fixing the tool bucket controls so you can cross the bay. The bucket still has power, and the motor does not appear to be damaged. You will need to simply create your own override to instruct the motor to spin in both directions."

Cade grinned. "Sure! All we need to do is create an override," he said, looking at Elle while shaking his head.

"Easy!" said Elle with a matching grin. She followed Cade as he walked over to the tool transfer bucket.

"Good," said Andrew. "Unpack your boxes and laptop, and let me explain what you need to do."

"He's not so good with sarcasm, is he?" asked Cade, dropping his boxes and sitting down on the floor with Elle.

Challenge 4: Fun Stuff to Know

Your brain is definitely going to get a workout with Challenge 4. Elle and Cade need to cross the room in the tool-transfer bucket, and they're going to need to create a controller that will allow them to move the bucket across the gap with one of them in it. They'll also need to reverse the bucket and bring it back to pick up their supplies… and to carry the remaining person across. (We know Cade will let Elle go first—he's polite that way.)

For Challenge 3, you built a simple gizmo that could take a temperature reading. Think about it for a moment—you took an Arduino Uno, a few wires, a sensor, and an LED and wired it all up so it would alert you when a certain temperature value was reached. We're betting that before you started reading this book, you probably knew of no other way to take a temperature reading than a thermometer, right? Could you have imagined such a tiny, little temperature sensor could make it so easy for you to determine the temperature indoors or outdoors? And looking back at Challenge 2, we're guessing you've never actually built a flashlight before, have you?

That's the great thing about tinkering with an Arduino Uno—there are thousands of electronic components out there that can do all sorts of amazing things. Some of them can even do fairly normal things, or even do boring things. But that's the point. With your Arduino Uno, you can put together some fairly cool gizmos of your own if you're willing to spend some time reading, tinkering, and testing.

And that's what you're going to do right now. With Challenge 4, you're going to use a larger selection of components that will need to work together to do something interesting. We're going to show you how to build the gizmo and program it, and when you're done, you'll see a much more complicated gizmo than in previous challenges.

Are you nervous? Don't be. Excited? You should be! Completely overwhelmed? If so, take a deep breath and just know that everyone who has ever started tinkering with electronics has been in your position. This stuff will start to make sense over time, and much of what will end up sticking (as opposed to being forgotten) will be the stuff you do with your own hands. That's why hands-on experiences are so important—they engage multiple senses (touch, sound, and sight, for example. Don't go tasting your electronics, okay?) and this helps your brain start making sense of what you're doing and learning.

The Challenge 4 gizmo is about controlling the forward and backward movement of the motor that drives the bucket across the gap... and back. Did we just say a motor? Yes, we did. Challenge 4 will involve a motor—a bucket-mover motor—and you're going to have some fun with it.

Looking at the Bucket Mover

Go ahead and take a look at Appendix A if you haven't already assembled all the parts you'll need for Challenge 4. It's not a long list, but there are a couple of new items you may need to order online if you don't have a locally accessible parts provider.

Before we start handling these items and examining them, take a look at Figure 14-1. This is the final circuit you'll be building (minus the motor). If you look carefully, you should notice a few items you've already experimented with, as well as some new ones.

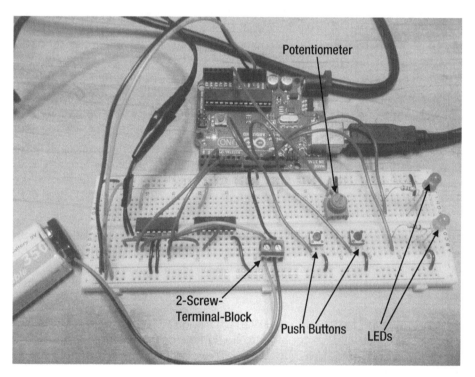

Figure 14-1. *The Challenge 4 gizmo wired up and ready to be connected to a motor*

Let's start with the familiar. You should see two LEDs, one red and one green. The green LED will light up when the motor is spinning clockwise, and the red LED will light up when the motor is spinning counter-clockwise . Just below the potentiometer (it has a dial on the top of it) are two push buttons. Press one of the buttons and the motor will turn clockwise; press the other button and the motor will spin in the opposite direction (counter-clockwise).

Finally, you should see a 9V battery connected to a battery harness. Because the wires of the battery harness are thin and stranded (versus solid), they are brittle and difficult to push into the breadboard. For that reason, you can use a two-screw terminal post, like the one in Figure 14-1, that can be tightened down on the two wires from the battery harness. When that's done, you simply insert the screw terminal into the breadboard (it has its own tiny little posts that will fit into the breadboard) and make the power from the battery available to the rest of the breadboard with some wiring that we'll cover in Chapter 15. Finally, there are a couple of resistors added to protect the LEDs.

But what about those other two items? Those two small black rectangular bits? They are called ICs, short for integrated circuits. ICs are electronic components that will allow you to do some powerful things and we'll talk more about them shortly, but for now we'll focus on the two used in the Challenge 4 gizmo. One of them is called a hex inverter and the other is called an H-bridge. Feel free to take a closer look if you have them on hand, but be careful! Those tiny little posts (legs) are extremely delicate and can be easily bent.

ANDREW 5.0

Please remind your readers that integrated circuits are also very sensitive to static electricity. You know that little zap you get when you walk across carpet and touch a doorknob? Well, that little bit of static electricity is more than enough to damage an IC, so take precautions when handling ICs by discharging any static charge that might be built up on your person. Sit down and touch a piece of metal on your desk or chair, and then you should be okay to handle the IC.

Even better, consider purchasing and wearing an anti-static wrist strap. You can read more about them at http://en.wikipedia.org/wiki/Antistatic_wrist_strap. They usually cost less than $10.00—a good investment if you plan on diving deeper into electronics!

Understanding the ICs

Here's the thing about ICs… they're powerful but somewhat complicated to explain. Think of each IC (also commonly referred to as a chip) as a small circuit in itself. They're not powerful enough to do everything, so they're often designed to do one thing—and do it well. When you insert a chip into the breadboard, each leg is typically wired up in such a way that the chip is either receiving voltage on a pin or sending voltage out. When no voltage is being received or sent, the voltage on a pin is said to be low or zero. If a signal is being sent or received on a pin, we say the voltage on that pin is high or that voltage is being provided to the circuit (such as 5 volts or 3.3 volts).

An IC uses a series of high and low voltage signals to perform calculations that are then provided to other components—motors, LEDs, and even other ICs! ICs can be either digital or analog circuits, but this explanation is meant to be about digital ICs as that's what we will be using in this challenge. As an example, one of the ICs you'll be using in the Challenge 4 gizmo is the hex inverter. Just as the name states, it inverts something. What does it invert? Easy—if it receives a value of 1 (5V in this case) on a particular pin, it sends out a value of 0 (0V in this case) on a different pin. Not all that complicated-sounding, sure… but the stuff going on inside the chip is hidden from you, so it looks uncomplicated. In reality, this IC and every other IC out there is doing some amazing things internally so that you, the user, can worry about other parts of your circuit.

Note that ICs are way beyond what we have time to cover in this book, but we're going to point you to another resource later in this book that can turn you into an IC expert in no time. Our goal with the Challenge 4 gizmo is to simply introduce you to the concepts of ICs and let you use a few simple ones so you'll see how powerful they can be in your own gizmos.

We'll come back to the other IC in your collection in a moment, but before we do that, take a look at Figure 14-2. These are examples of DC motors, one of which you'll be using for Challenge 4. In real life, of course, motors can be much larger, but they all work basically the same.

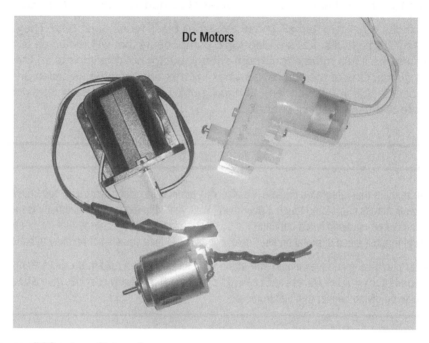

DC Motors

Figure 14-2. *A few small DC motors with two wires*

Take a close look at your own motor. Do you see two wires coming out of it? One wire will always be connected to ground and one will be wired up to receive positive voltage. The wire that gets the positive voltage determines which direction the motor spins. You can test this out right now by taking your 9V battery and touching one wire from the motor to one terminal on the battery and the other wire to the other terminal. Don't hold the wires to the terminals for more than a few seconds — holding them too long might damage the motor (as this motor is a 6V motor). But a few seconds of holding should show you which direction the motor will spin.

Now, reverse the wires and touch them to the battery terminals. Can you see the motor spinning in the opposite direction?

> **Tip**   You can take a tiny piece of clear tape and wrap it around the motor's axle to make a little flag on the end. This little flag will make it easier for you to see which direction the motor is spinning.

In Challenge 4, Cade and Elle need to cross a large span in the cargo bay, but only one of them can cross at a time. That means the bucket one of them will ride over in will need to reverse direction and go back to pick up the other person. This is done by simply reversing the direction the motor spins.

But creating a circuit with a breadboard that can easily reverse a motor's spin by changing which wire provides voltage is tricky. Very tricky, and it's also unnecessary.

That's what the other IC is for—to provide an easier method for reversing the direction of the motor's spin! It's called an H-bridge and if you want to get into robot-building and more advanced gizmos that use motors, an H-bridge is going to be a very good IC to have in your possession.

ANDREW 5.0

An H-bridge can be tricky to explain, so just remember that it's used to allow for a change of direction a DC motor will spin. If you really want more details, be sure to visit http://en.wikipedia.org/wiki/H-bridge. You'll also learn how the H-bridge gets its name and what's going on inside the IC.

And you're right about needing to become familiar with its function for building robots and other motorized gadgets. An H-bridge removes the complexity of trying to wire up a motor to spin in both directions and makes building a circuit with a motor that can spin in either direction extremely easy. But as with all ICs, be careful when handling it and avoid static electricity and any damage to its pins.

As Andrew stated, an H-bridge is not the easiest thing to explain, and our goal with this book isn't to overwhelm you with all the technical details. (A great book for learning about ICs is *Make: Electronics* by Charles Platt. It's an outstanding book for learning even more electronics skills.) For now, what you need to know about the H-bridge IC is that you'll be using it to easily allow the changing of the motor's spin direction. We'll go into more detail on how to wire it up properly and how it actually helps you in Chapter 15 when we show you how to build the gizmo.

Ready to Build Something?

We chose Challenge 4 as the point in the book to start ramping up the projects. We didn't want to overwhelm you with something like the Challenge 4 gizmo too early. Hopefully by this point, you're pretty comfortable using a breadboard and inserting wires and other components. As long as you work slowly and follow our instructions in Chapters 15 and 16, you'll do fine.

If you haven't collected the parts for Challenge 4 yet, go ahead and make your shopping list. Again, Appendix A contains a complete list for you, including some variations in places to purchase.

Chapter 15 is waiting for you, so grab your components, your breadboard, the battery, and your Arduino Uno, and let's go help Cade and Elle get across the room safely.

Time to build!

Challenge 4: Examining the Hardware

So far, you haven't been working with complex systems of circuitry, but you've been building a foundation for using circuitry with the Arduino. But things are about to change, and some of the gizmos you're going to create will be a bit more involved in terms of building and programming. But that's a good thing! You're learning more and more about the Arduino and how other electronic components work with it, plus you're delving deeper into the programming aspect of gadget design. At this point, you've definitely moved beyond Arduino novice, and you should congratulate yourself on that. We also hope you're beginning to look around and ask questions about how exactly things work in your world—the lights, the computers, and even the vehicles and machines that these days all have electronics inside them. Your Arduino and electronics skills will continue to improve if you always ask questions and look for answers, and your status as an Arduino guru will become a certainty.

Now, you're going to take what you learned in previous challenges and apply it to this challenge, but first we want to go over the new pieces of hardware you need to help Cade and Elle override the controls on the tool bucket—two new components called an H-bridge and a hex inverter.

New Hardware

An H-bridge is shown in Figure 15-1. It gets its name from how it often appears in circuit diagrams known as schematics. In a schematic, an H-bridge is represented by a shape resembling the letter "H."

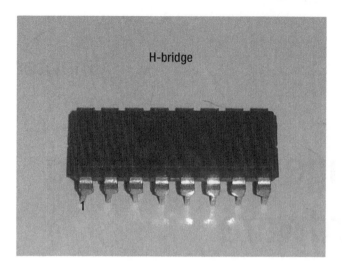

Figure 15-1. An H-bridge

H-bridges are small and not much to look at, but they're key components that you'll want to get familiar with if you want to advance your Arduino skills. They're especially useful in building anything involving motors. H-bridges allow you to control a DC motor (in our case) in both forward and reverse directions, as well as to control the speed of a motor via a pulse-width modulation (PWM) pin on the Arduino.

Pulse-width modulation uses increases and decreases in voltage to control the speed of a motor. The pulses happen so fast that you don't perceive them yourself. Instead, they control just how fast a motor spins by applying bursts of power at a frequency needed to hold a given spin rate.

We mentioned that an H-bridge lets you determine the direction of spin of a motor, and it does this by changing the wire on a motor to which it applies voltage. If a particular wire gets the voltage, the motor spins in one direction; when another wire gets the voltage, the motor spins in the other direction.

This isn't the most detailed explanation, but it should give you an idea of how an H-bridge can help you build a gizmo to control the direction of the tool bucket. Also, we don't want Cade or Elle jolted in the bucket too much by a sudden increase in speed, so some sort of control is necessary to slowly build up the speed of the motor. The H-bridge solves both problems.

We also need to use an H-bridge because we can't use the Arduino itself to control the DC motor—the motor draws more amperage than the Arduino can handle. The solution is to have the Arduino control the H-bridge, and then the H-bridge controls the motor.

Caution   Never try to plug a DC motor into the Arduino—it will burn up your Arduino!

ANDREW 5.0

If your readers really want to know more about pulse-width modulation, have them visit this great online video tutorial:

`http://blog.makezine.com/2011/06/01/circuit-skills-pwm-pulse-width-modulation-sponsored-by-jameco-electronics/`

Collin Cunningham is one of the 21st century's best video educators on electronic components, so be sure to search for his other videos at `makezine.com`. He has videos on resistors, capacitors, and many more, and they're easy to follow and fun to watch.

The other new piece of hardware you'll be using is the hex inverter, shown in Figure 15-2. This little integrated circuit (IC chip) allows us to control the direction of the DC motor with just one pin on the Arduino. And how does it accomplish that? Well, the hex inverter is just what its name implies: it's an inverter that changes a digital 1 into a digital 0, and a digital 0 into a digital 1.

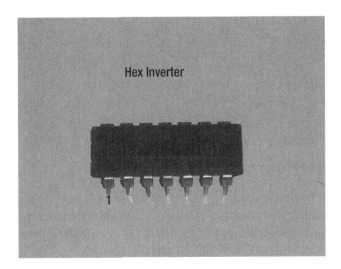

Figure 15-2. A Hex Inverter

For example, say we have a digital signal of 1 (HIGH); we put that signal through the hex inverter and then read the signal that comes out. The digital signal is now 0 (LOW). (We'll explain the software side of hex inverters in the next chapter).

How can you tell the H-bridge and the hex inverter apart? Hex inverters have only 14 pins while H-bridges have 16 pins.

Now that you know a bit about the new hardware being used in the challenge, you can create the gadget that will help Elle and Cade cross the gap safely using the tool bucket. Let's get building!

Let's Build Gadget #4

To build the gizmo that will help Cade and Elle cross the room in the tool bucket, you'll need some of the electronic components you used in the previous challenges. Remember that all of the parts for this project are listed in Appendix A. Now, let's get started.

1.   First, be sure your breadboard is in the correct orientation, with the blue line at the top. Now insert the H-bridge in the breadboard, making sure the notch on the H-bridge (it will be either a small dot or a U-shaped notch) is facing to the left, as shown in Figure 15-3. Notice that the left side of the chip starts at E-9 and continues to E-16. Likewise, the other side of the chip has its pins inserted into F-9 through F-16.

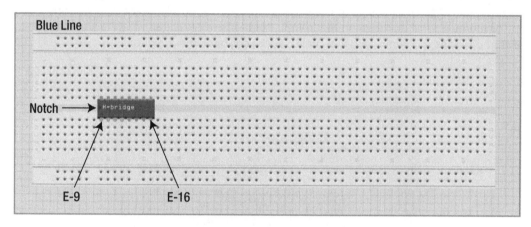

Figure 15-3. Attach the H-bridge to the breadboard

2.   Insert the hex inverter in the breadboard as shown in Figure 15-4, making sure the dot on the chip's surface is facing to the left. The seven pins on one side of the chip are inserted into E-20 through E-26, while the seven pins on the other side are inserted into F-20 through F-26.

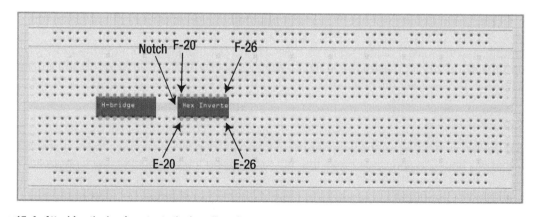

Figure 15-4. Attaching the hex inverter to the breadboard

3. Next, attach the 9V connector to the blue two-position terminal block; tighten down on the screws to make certain the wires are held in good and tight. If possible, insert the red wire to the left of the black wire, as shown in Figure 15-5, before plugging the terminal block into the solderless breadboard so that its pins are inserted into A-32 and A-34.

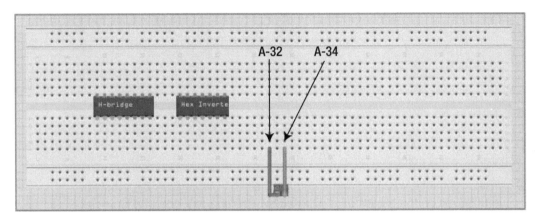

Figure 15-5. Attach the 2-position terminal block to the solderless breadboard

Now we need to attach the 5V and 9V power to the various pins on the IC's and terminal block. We'll do this with a number of red jumper wires, but you can use any color wire you like.

Pins on the H-bridge and hex inverter begin at pin 1 located in the lower left corner of each chip. So, on the H-bridge, pin 1 is inserted at E-9 and pin 8 is inserted into E-16. Numbering wraps to the opposite side so that pin 9 is inserted into F-16, and numbering continues up the side of the chip and ends with pin 16 inserted into F-9.

4. Now insert a jumper wire that connects pin 16 to the 5V power rail of the solderless breadboard. Insert the wire into H-9 and plug the other end of the jumper wire into any available hole next to the red line on the breadboard (indicating +5V power that will come from the Arduino, not the 9V battery).

5. Connect pin 14 of the hex inverter to the 5V rail of the breadboard as well by inserting one end of a jumper wire into H-20 and the other end of the jumper wire into any available hole near the red line on the breadboard.

6. Attach the positive side of the two-position terminal block to pin 8 of the H-bridge (this is the only place where 9V power is needed) by inserting a jumper wire into D-32 and its other end into D-16.

7. Finally, connect the power rail on one side of the breadboard to the other power rail on the opposite side of the breadboard by inserting a longer jumper wire into two available holes, one near each of the red lines. Figure 15-6 illustrates this process.

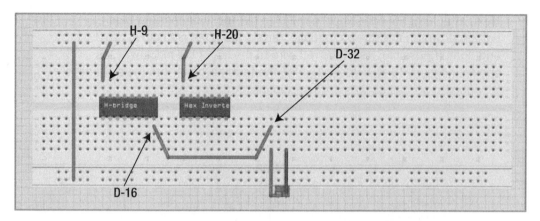

Figure 15-6. Supply power: +5V to the circuit and 9V to the H-bridge

Now it's time to add the connections to ground for this project. We've used black jumper wires but, again, you can use any color you have available.

8. First, connect a wire from pin 4 and pin 5 on the H-bridge to the closest ground rail on the breadboard. Do this by inserting one end of a jumper wire into D-12 and the other end into a free hole near the blue line on the breadboard (that will be wired to GND). Insert another jumper wire into D-13 and its other end into a free hole near the blue line as well.

9. Now connect a jumper wire from a free hole near one blue line of the breadboard to a free hole on the other side of the breadboard nearest the blue line.

10. Connect pin 7 of the hex inverter to ground by inserting a jumper wire into D-26 and its other end into a hole nearest the blue line on the breadboard.

11. Connect the black wire of the two-position terminal block to the ground rail on the breadboard by inserting a jumper wire into D-34 and its other end into a free hole nearest a blue line on the breadboard. Figure 15-7 illustrates this process.

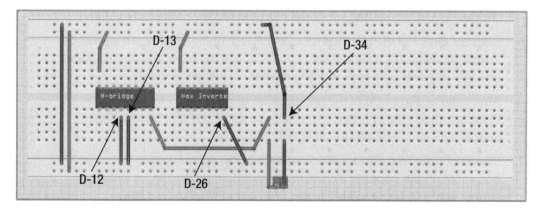

Figure 15-7. Attach ground to the circuit

12. Connect pin 3 of the H-bridge to an empty space on the solderless breadboard. We used a green wire (but you can use any color you have available), with one end plugged into C-11 and the other into C-7.

13. Connect pin 6 of the H-bridge to an empty space on the breadboard. We used a green jumper wire inserted into D-14 with the other end inserted into D-8, as shown in Figure 15-8.

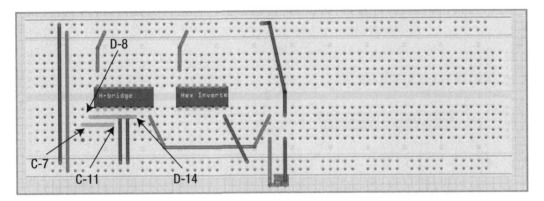

Figure 15-8. Attach wires from pins 3 and 6 to an open area on the solderless breadboard

14. Once again, we'll use green jumper wires, but use whatever color you have available. Attach pin 7 of the H-bridge to pin 1 of the hex inverter by inserting a jumper wire into C-15 and its other end into C-20.

15. Attach pin 2 of the H-bridge to pin 2 of the hex inverter by inserting one end of a jumper wire into B-10 and the other end into B-21. Figure 15-9 illustrates this process.

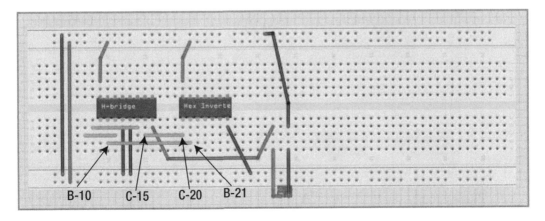

Figure 15-9. Set up the hex inverter

16. Now connect the wire from pins 3 and 6 of the H-bridge to the DC motor. Insert one of the DC motor's wires into E-7 and the other into E-8—it doesn't matter which wire you choose to insert into E-7 or E-8. Figure 15-10 illustrates this process.

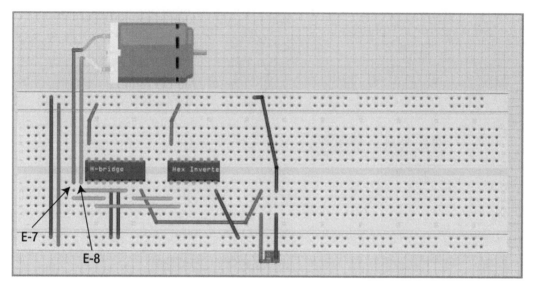

Figure 15-10. Attach the motor to the H-bridge via pins 3 and 6

17. Add the 3-pin potentiometer to the solderless breadboard and attach the leftmost pin of the potentiometer to 5V power. Do this by inserting the potentiometer so its pins are plugged into G-44 through G-46. Figure 15-11 illustrates this process.

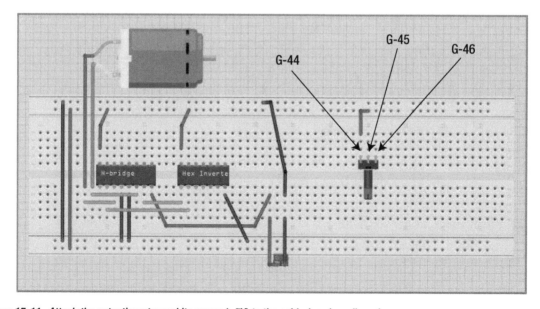

Figure 15-11. Attach the potentiometer and its power (+5V) to the solderless breadboard

18. Now add the two push buttons to the breadboard. Insert the first one so its pins plug into B-40 and B-42 and E-40 and E-42. Insert the pins of the other push button into B-47 and B-49 and E-47 and E-49. Figure 15-12 illustrates this process.

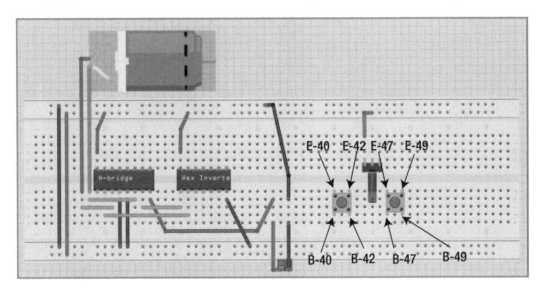

Figure 15-12. Attach the push buttons to the solderless breadboard

19. Attach the red and green LEDs to the breadboard, making sure you have enough room to attach other components. Insert the longer leg (the anode) of the red LED into F-58 and the shorter leg (the cathode) into H-60. Insert the longer leg of the green LED into E-58 and the shorter leg into C-60. Figure 15-13 illustrates this process.

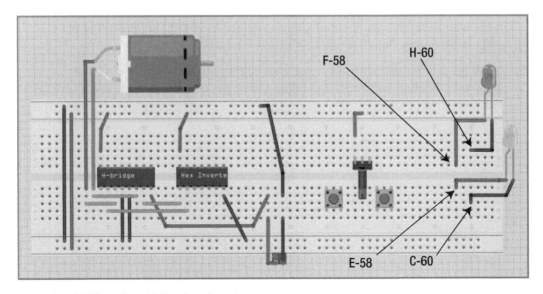

Figure 15-13. Attach LEDs to the solderless breadboard

20.   Next, add a 330-ohm resistor to the anode (longer lead) of the red LED by inserting one leg at H-58 and the other at H-54, and then attach another 330-ohm resistor to the anode of the green LED at C-58 and C-54, as shown in Figure 15-14.

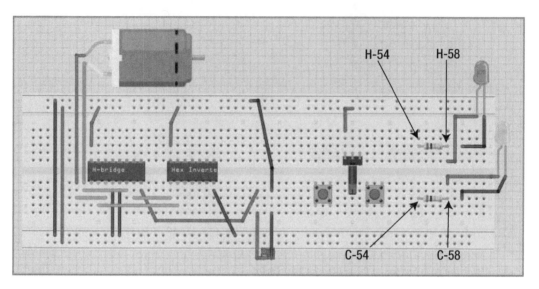

Figure 15-14. Attach resistors to the anode (long lead) side of the LEDs

21.   Attach grounds to one side of each of the push buttons. We used two black jumper wires, one inserted at A-42 and the other inserted at A-49, each connecting to a free hole nearest the blue line on the breadboard.

22.   Insert another jumper from GND to the cathode (shorter leg) of both the red and green LEDs by inserting two jumper wires, one at A-60 and the other at J-60, each connecting to a free hole nearest the blue line.

23.   Insert another jumper wire at the rightmost pin of the potentiometer at J-46 and insert its other end into a free hole nearest the blue line. Figure 15-15 illustrates this process.

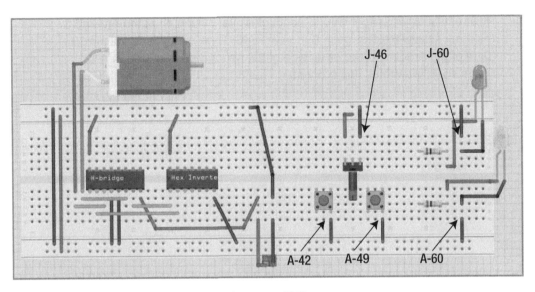

Figure 15-15. Attach ground to the push buttons, potentiometer, and LEDs

24. Now it's time to start connecting the circuit to the Arduino. First use a jumper wire to connect digital pin 3 (D3) of the Arduino to pin 1 of the H-bridge at B-9. Then attach digital pin 4 (D4) of the Arduino to pin 7 of the H-bridge at A-15. Figure 15-16 illustrates this process.

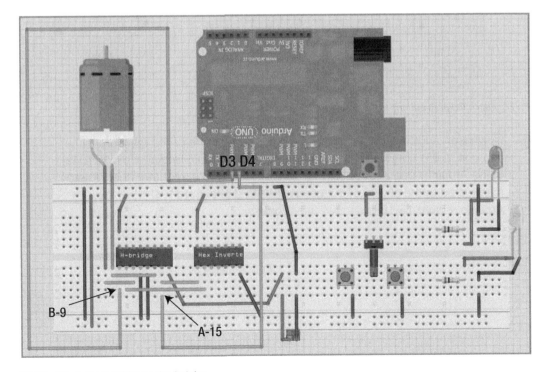

Figure 15-16. Attach the H-bridge to the Arduino

25. Next, use another jumper wire to connect digital pin 9 (D9) of the Arduino to the other side of the first push button at A-40. Then connect digital pin 10 (D10) of the Arduino to the other side of the second push button at A-47. Figure 15-17 illustrates this process.

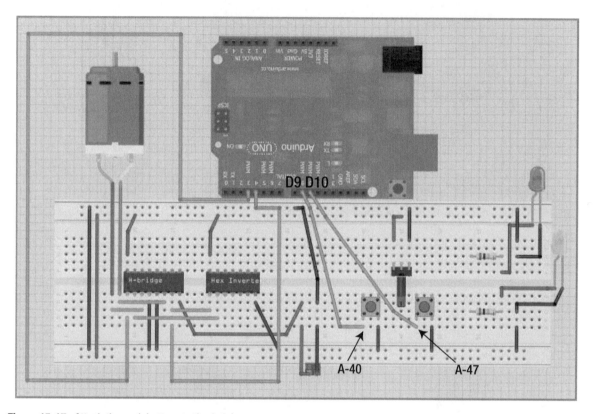

Figure 15-17. Attach the push buttons to the Arduino

26. Now insert another jumper wire at F-54 to connect one of the resistors (the one that is connected to the anode of the red LED) to digital pin 12 (D12) of the Arduino. Use another jumper wire at A-54 to connect the other resistor (connected to the anode of the green LED) to digital pin 11 (D11) of the Arduino. Figure 15-18 illustrates this process.

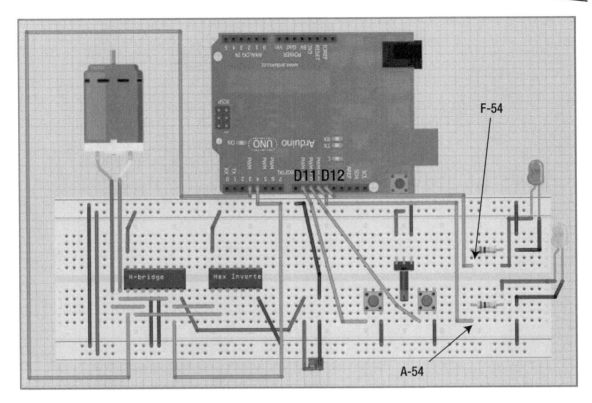

Figure 15-18. Attach the LEDs to the Arduino

27.   Now connect the middle pin of the potentiometer to analog pin 0 of the
      Arduino by inserting a jumper wire into J-45 and its other end into A0, as
      shown in Figure 15-19.

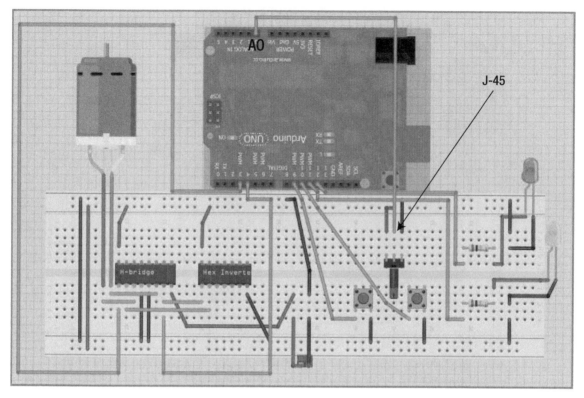

Figure 15-19. Attach the potentiometer to the Arduino

28. Connect power (+5V) to the red side of the power strip of the breadboard by inserting a jumper wire into a free hole nearest the red line and its other end to the +5V on the Arduino.

29. Connect GND to the blue side of the power strip of the breadboard by inserting a jumper wire into a free hole nearest the blue line and the other end into GND on the Arduino. Figure 15-20 illustrates this process.

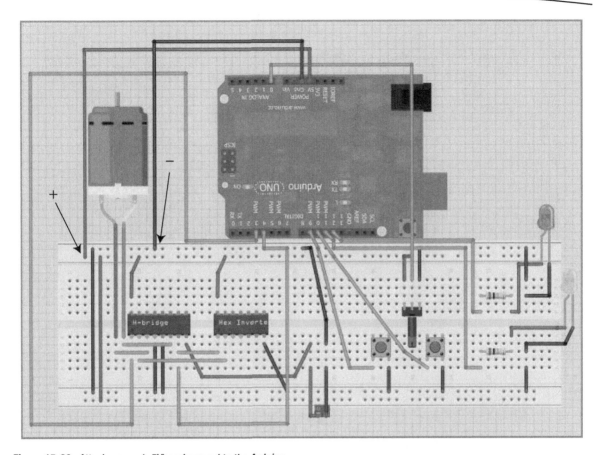

Figure 15-20. Attach power (+5V) and ground to the Arduino

That was a lot of wiring! (Figure 15-21 shows our own final version of the gizmo). It's always a good idea to go through the steps a second time and make sure you have everything connected correctly. (We sometimes go over our schematic ten times!) We suggest you review your wiring at least once. It's tedious, but the review will help you catch errors now and save you frustration later.

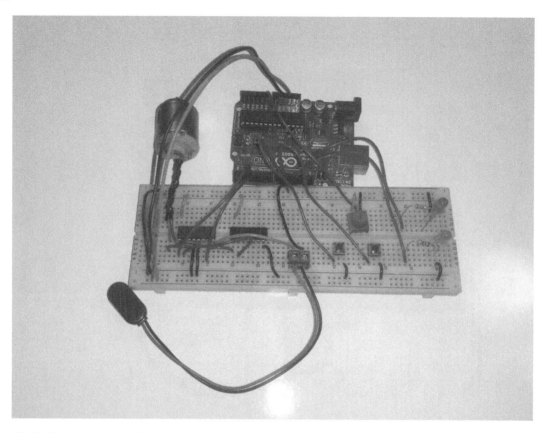

Figure 15-21. The motor-control gizmo as built by the authors

When you feel your wiring is correct, you are ready to move on to the final stage of this challenge, in which you'll be writing code to control a motor so that Elle and Cade can get across the gap that's in their way.

Chapter 16

Challenge 4: Examining the Software

It's possible you've already skimmed through this chapter and seen the sketch you'll be uploading to the Challenge 4 gizmo. If you haven't, go ahead... get it over with. Take a look at Listing 16-1 and then come back ... we'll wait.

Okay ... what did you think? Was it a bit longer than you expected? Does that make you nervous? Well, don't worry. Often the most scary-looking sketch is nothing more than a bunch of code repeated over and over. Back in Chapter 12, you learned about how you can insert an If-Else statement into the main program loop to check a condition again and again and again. But sometimes an If-Else statement isn't what's needed. Sometimes what you have to do is constantly check the status of a sensor or a motor or other component.

The sketch in Listing 16-1 is long, yes, but it's not complicated. The reason it's lengthy is that we're setting things up so our motor can spin in both directions, depending on which of two buttons are pressed. Rather than use If-Else statements, we simply copied the code that controls the spin of the motor counterclockwise if one button is pressed, and pasted it back in with some changes that will make it spin the motor in the opposite direction if another button is pressed. There's also some code to shut the motor down when no buttons are being pressed. Understand the code for one function, and you'll automatically get the others as well.

We've also got some LEDs and a potentiometer in the mix, but you're already quite familiar with those so they shouldn't trip you up when you're examining the sketch. In any case, we'll be going over the various sections of the sketch so you'll have a good understanding of how the Challenge 4 gizmo works.

You won't need to use new functions or structures as this challenge takes advantage of all of the things you learned in Challenge 1 through Challenge 3. We'll be using analog inputs on the Arduino microcontroller to read in the potentiometer values; digital outputs to turn the LEDs and motor on; and digital inputs to read values from the two push buttons. We've done all of this before in the previous challenges. The new challenge will teach you how to use these functions to create a system where everything works together. By the end of this chapter, you should have a working motor controller that uses LEDs to tell you which direction the motor is turning; the motor's direction will be controlled by the button you press, and the speed of the motor will be controlled by the potentiometer. Let's get to the details.

The Challenge 4 Sketch

Let's start with a breakdown of what we need to do in this sketch. By making a list we can be certain we don't miss anything, and it'll help when we begin to explore the different sections of the sketch. Here's what has to happen in the sketch:

1. We have to determine what variables are needed to communicate with all of the different IO (inputs and outputs).

2. We'll use the setup structure to initialize the outputs, and use a few of the Arduino's pull-up resistors.

3. In the loop structure, we'll read in the state of the push buttons.

4. We also need to read the state of the analog input (potentiometer).

5. We have to scale the potentiometer values to fall between 0 and 256. The potentiometer will give a value between 0 and 1023, but we'll divide by 4 to reduce that range to a more easily usable one. A smaller analog range means you will have the full range of the potentiometer rather than ¼ of the potentiometers range.

6. Next, we have to set up a conditional statement to compare the states of each of the push buttons to ON or OFF (0 or 1). Remember, because we chose to use the Arduino's internal pull-up resistors (we did this in Challenge 2) and because of the way we designed the circuit, the states for ON and OFF are backward; that is, 1 represents OFF and 0 represents ON. Sometimes design choices will cause you to code sketches in different ways.

7. Finally, we need a state that controls the condition when neither push buttons is pressed. We don't need to worry about both buttons being pressed as the motor will spin clockwise in this case due to the order of the If-Else statement.

Listing 16-1 is the final sketch for this challenge.

Listing 16-1. Final Sketch for Challenge 4

```
// Initialize all of the pins variables
int LEDPin1 = 12;
int LEDPin2 = 11;
int ButtonPin1 = 10;
int ButtonPin2 = 9;
```

```
int MotorPWMPin = 3;
int MotorDirPin = 4;
int PotPin = A0;

// Initialize value and state variables
int ButtonState1 = 0;
int ButtonState2 = 0;
int PotValue = 0;
int MappedPotValue = 0;

void setup()
{
  // Set pins to be outputs
  pinMode(LEDPin1, OUTPUT);
  pinMode(LEDPin2, OUTPUT);
  pinMode(MotorPWMPin, OUTPUT);
  pinMode(MotorDirPin, OUTPUT);

  // use the Arduino's internal pullup resistor for
  // the buttons so that the buttons do not float.
  digitalWrite(ButtonPin1, HIGH);
  digitalWrite(ButtonPin2, HIGH);
}

void loop()
{
  // Read in button values
  ButtonState1 = digitalRead(ButtonPin1);
  ButtonState2 = digitalRead(ButtonPin2);
  // Read in Potentiometer values
  PotValue = analogRead(PotPin);

  // Scale pot value from 0 to 256
  MappedPotValue = PotValue/4;

  if (ButtonState1 == 0)
  {
    // if button1 is pressed adjust speed to mapped
    // potentiometer value then turn motor on and turn
    // counterclockwise.
    analogWrite(MotorPWMPin, MappedPotValue);
    digitalWrite(MotorDirPin, HIGH);
    digitalWrite(LEDPin1, HIGH);
    digitalWrite(LEDPin2, LOW);
  }
  else if (ButtonState2 == 0)
  {
    // if button2 is pressed adjust speed to mapped
    // potentiometer value then turn motor on and turn
    // clockwise.
```

```
    analogWrite(MotorPWMPin, MappedPotValue);
    digitalWrite(MotorDirPin, LOW);
    digitalWrite(LEDPin2, HIGH);
    digitalWrite(LEDPin1, LOW);
  }
  else
  {
    // Turn motor off
    digitalWrite(MotorPWMPin, LOW);
    digitalWrite(MotorDirPin, LOW);
    digitalWrite(LEDPin2, LOW);
    digitalWrite(LEDPin1, LOW);
  }
}
```

Now, let's break down the sketch in Listing 16-1 into smaller sections so you can see exactly what's going on.

Breaking It Down

The first bit of code does nothing more than create some variables and set the initial values for them:

```
// Initialize all of the pins variables
int LEDPin1 = 12;
int LEDPin2 = 11;
int ButtonPin1 = 10;
int ButtonPin2 = 9;
int MotorPWMPin = 3;
int MotorDirPin = 4;
int PotPin = A0;

// Initialize value and state variables
int ButtonState1 = 0;
int ButtonState2 = 0;
int PotValue = 0;
int MappedPotValue = 0;
```

We've got two LEDs, so we assign them digital pins 11 and 12 on the Arduino. Analog pin (A0) connects to the potentiometer. Buttons 1 and 2 are assigned digital pins 9 and 10, while the motor gets two connections to the Arduino—D3 (digital pin 3 of the Arduino) and D4. The state variables are used to assign an initial value of 0 to the button states, meaning they are unpressed. The potentiometer's starting position is also set to 0. As noted, we'll use another variable to store a scaled value of the potentiometer. Remember, the potentiometer reports a value between 0 and 1023 but we want to reduce that range to values between 0 and 256, so we'll use the MappedPotValue to store the scaled-down value.

The next bit of the sketch is:

```
void setup()
{
  // Set pins to be Outputs
  pinMode(LEDPin1, OUTPUT);
  pinMode(LEDPin2, OUTPUT);
  pinMode(MotorPWMPin, OUTPUT);
  pinMode(MotorDirPin, OUTPUT);

  // use the Arduino's internal pullup resistor for
  // the buttons so that the buttons do not float.
  digitalWrite(ButtonPin1, HIGH);
  digitalWrite(ButtonPin2, HIGH);
}
```

Here we create the setup structure to set the LED's and motor pins to outputs. We're using the Arduino's built-in pull-up resistors so we don't have floating switches. With a floating switch you get intermittent on and off states. It's like noise in the circuit that you want to filter out, and it's really out of your control unless you use pull-up or pull-down resistors as we're doing here. Using the digitalWrite function, we set both buttons HIGH. This means each button is powered but pressing a button will cut its voltage and set its state to LOW (0).

And now we get into the last part of the sketch. This final bit involves a loop and an If statement. The following shows the loop without the If statement. The ellipsis shows where the If statement fits.

```
void loop()
{
  // Read in button values
  ButtonState1 = digitalRead(ButtonPin1);
  ButtonState2 = digitalRead(ButtonPin2);
  // Read in Potentiometer values
  PotValue = analogRead(PotPin);

  // Scale pot value from 0 to 256
  MappedPotValue = PotValue/4;

  ...

}
```

The main program loops forever, so it's constantly checking the states of both buttons (pressed or not pressed). The program stores the state of each button using the code bit ButtonState1 = digitalRead(ButtonPin1), for example.

The digitalRead command simply looks at the condition of a button (Button 1 in this example) to determine if it's pressed or not. Remember that we set the initial value of each button to HIGH, so it's got a value of 1. Pressing a button changes its state to LOW or 0, and this value (0) gets put into the ButtonState1 variable. The same happens for Button 2—its state is constantly being checked: pressed or not pressed?

Now, remember back in Challenge 3 where you learned about the If-Else statement. There's a variation of the If-Else statement that basically allows you to add an unlimited number of else clauses. It looks like this:

```
if (condition1)
{\\code here
}
else if (condition2)
{\\code here
}
else if (condition3)
{\\code here
}
else (condition4)
{\\code here
}
```

Notice that you can keep entering Else-If clauses. Commonly the last one is a simple Else. That's what's going to happen with this sketch. We'll enter a series of clauses to test for the following possible conditions:

1. Button 1 is pressed.

2. Button 2 is pressed.

3. Neither button is pressed.

4. Both buttons are pressed.

Here's the complete code, showing the loop and the If statement with all its clauses:

```
void loop()
{
  // Read in button values
  ButtonState1 = digitalRead(ButtonPin1);
  ButtonState2 = digitalRead(ButtonPin2);
  // Read in Potentiometer values
  PotValue = analogRead(PotPin);

  // Scale pot value from 0 to 256
  MappedPotValue = PotValue/4;

  if (ButtonState1 == 0)
  {
    // if button1 is pressed adjust speed to mapped
    // potentiometer value then turn motor on and turn
    // counterclockwise.
    analogWrite(MotorPWMPin, MappedPotValue);
    digitalWrite(MotorDirPin, HIGH);
    digitalWrite(LEDPin1, HIGH);
    digitalWrite(LEDPin2, LOW);
  }
```

```
  else if (ButtonState2 == 0)
  {
    // if button2 is pressed adjust speed to mapped
    // potentiometer value then turn motor on and turn
    // clockwise.
    analogWrite(MotorPWMPin, MappedPotValue);
    digitalWrite(MotorDirPin, LOW);
    digitalWrite(LEDPin2, HIGH);
    digitalWrite(LEDPin1, LOW);
  }
  else
  {
    // Turn motor off
    digitalWrite(MotorPWMPin, LOW);
    digitalWrite(MotorDirPin, LOW);
    digitalWrite(LEDPin2, LOW);
    digitalWrite(LEDPin1, LOW);
  }
}
```

The first clause, if(ButtonState1 == 0) is true, is triggered when Button 1 has been pressed. If that's the case, the code inside the curly braces immediately following the if clause is executed. This happens again with the else if (ButtonState2 ==0) clause that follows. If that condition is true, it means Button 2 has been pressed. Finally, the else clause comes last and is true if neither Button 1 nor Button 2 have been pressed.

Now, let's take a look inside the condition statements to see what happens when one button is pressed or when no buttons are pressed. Here's a snippet of code from inside that first If statement:

```
{
  // If button1 is pressed, adjust speed to mapped
  // potentiometer value, then turn motor on and spin
  // counterclockwise.
  analogWrite(MotorPWMPin, MappedPotValue);
  digitalWrite(MotorDirPin, HIGH);
  digitalWrite(LEDPin1, HIGH);
  digitalWrite(LEDPin2, LOW);
}
```

Don't let all this code stress you out! In a nutshell, here's how the If statement for the button works when Button 1 is pressed (the same steps apply for Button 2, but the motor spins clockwise):

1. The potentiometer's position is checked. When you press the button, you turn the potentiometer to increase the speed of the motor. So the value will constantly change as long as you hold down Button 1 and turn the potentiometer. Release the button and the motor stops. Stop turning the potentiometer (while holding Button 1) and the motor will stay at a constant speed.

2. The MotorDirPin value is either HIGH or LOW. When it's HIGH, the motor spins in one direction. When it's LOW, it spins in the other direction. (You can modify the sketch here and change which direction Button 1 controls

by changing HIGH to LOW. Just remember for Button 2 to change the MotorDirPin from LOW to HIGH.)

3. When you press Button 1, LED 1 lights up (its state goes to HIGH). Should LED 2 be lit up (from pressing Button 2) it will be turned off by setting its state to LOW.

The Else-If statement that follows the first If statement controls the motor if Button 2 is pressed. The only difference is which direction the motor spins and which LED lights up. Otherwise, the code inside is almost exactly the same as for a Button 1 push.

The last Else statement controls what happens when neither button is pressed. What do you think should happen? Yep—the motor should stop spinning! Here's the snippet of code that follows the Else condition statement:

```
else
{
  // Turn motor off
  digitalWrite(MotorPWMPin, LOW);
  digitalWrite(MotorDirPin, LOW);
  digitalWrite(LEDPin2, LOW);
  digitalWrite(LEDPin1, LOW);
  }
}
```

1. Power is cut to the motor.

2. The direction pin is set to LOW.

3. Both LEDs are turned off (their states are set to LOW).

Then the main program continues to loop, waiting for a button press to change the motor's condition (spinning or not spinning as well as its direction). The potentiometer's position is also constantly checked as the main program loops, but it has no effect on the motor unless a button is pressed.

And that's it! A bit of a longer sketch than you've seen so far, but definitely not all that complicated when you really examine how it works.

Solve Challenge 4

Now all that's left to do is to connect your Arduino to a computer and upload the code to your new gizmo. After you've done that, you can power the Arduino either from a computer's USB connection or by attaching a 9V battery to it, and then attach a 9V battery to the 2-postion-terminal-block, as shown in Figure 16-1.

Figure 16-1. Challenge 4 complete!

To operate the gizmo, simply press one of the push buttons. You'll notice that when you press one button the motor spins in one direction and one of the LEDs lights up. Release that button and press the other one. Now you should see the motor switch direction, the second LED light up, and the first LED turn off.

You've now got a simple device for controlling the direction and speed of a simple motor. Elle and Cade need a gadget like this to control the tool transfer bucket so they can take turns crossing the gap in the cargo area. Because they can control the direction, they can send the bucket across with one of them in it as well as return it to the original side for the other person to take a ride!

Chapter 17

Hide and Seek

"I have to tell you…I don't exactly feel safe in this bucket," said Cade as he crossed the halfway mark.

Cade had insisted on going first to test out the tool bucket and the override controls. Any other time, Elle would have laughed at her friend crammed tightly into the small metal box with his knees to his chest.

The Crossing

Elle examined the override device they had quickly assembled from Andrew's instructions. It appeared to be working properly and the motor was spinning in the proper direction to take Cade to the other side of the room.

"Five more feet," said Elle.

Cade couldn't turn in the bucket to see his destination, and the bucket was moving at a torturously slow speed.

"I should have just tried to run and jump. This is ridiculous," replied Cade with a frown. "What is this Gunther Canvin doing now, Andrew?"

"I'm having difficulty with the video surveillance system's position relative to his current location. He's already removed two panels from the wall, but I can't determine how far along he is with shutting down life support," replied Andrew.

The tool bucket bumped to a stop, and Cade looked down before stepping out. "Longest five-minute ride of my life," he said. "You'd think a tool transfer bucket would go much faster."

Elle shook her head and pressed a button on the override device. The bucket began moving toward her, but much faster this time. "I'm betting it's the weight," she said. "Look how fast it's moving now."

Cade stretched his back and then held his hands out wide. "Throw the boxes, Elle. We don't have time to send them over in the bucket."

Elle picked up one of the two component toolboxes and examined the distance between Cade and herself. "If you don't catch it and it falls down there, you're going after it."

"Just throw it."

Elle took two spins and slung the toolbox across the divide. She held her breath for half a second as she watched the toolbox arc across the open space before Cade reached up and caught it. The impact knocked the wind out of Cade, and he held up a finger to tell her to give him a moment.

One minute later the transfer bucket arrived back on Elle's side of the room just as Cade caught the second toolbox.

"Hurry, Elle," huffed Cade, setting the toolbox down to his left. "Grab the laptop and get in."

Elle stepped into the transfer bucket and slung the laptop bag's strap over her neck and shoulder. She leaned forward and pressed the button on the override device and sat down fast.

Cade smiled. "Longest ten-second delay you'll ever experience, Elle."

Elle counted to ten. The jolt as the bucket began to move forward startled her.

"Forgot to warn you about the bump," said Cade.

Elle couldn't turn to look at him. "Just tell me when I'm getting close, okay?"

The bucket was only a third of the way across when the station's alarm system began whooping. It was replaced by a female voice.

"Emergency protocols have been initiated. Please proceed immediately to the evacuation pods. Automatic launch of all pods will begin in five minutes."

"Oh, no," said Elle.

"Aw, come on! Really?" yelled Cade.

Five Minutes!

"Andrew, is there any chance you could turn off the alarm?" cried Elle.

The alarm sounded as if it had increased in volume and Elle worried that she and Cade wouldn't be able to hear Andrew. She was also worried that the bucket had only just now crossed half the distance.

Elle listened for a response, but just as she was about to yell out to Andrew again, the alarm's wail stopped.

"Is that better, Elle? I have limited control over the emergency system, but I was able to eliminate the alarm on this level only. I doubt Mr. Canvin will notice, given the other damage to the station."

"Four minutes until automatic launch of all evacuation pods. Please proceed immediately to the nearest evacuation compartment. Follow the lighted emergency signals on the walls to find your nearest evacuation compartment. Three minutes, forty seconds until automatic launch of all evacuation pods. Please proceed immediately..."

"Does that sound like Mrs. Kendrick to you," asked Cade. "She never liked me."

"Cade!" yelled Elle. "Focus! How close am I?"

"Almost here, Elle," replied Cade. "Sorry."

The emergency notice continued to repeat in the background. Elle focused on the most important part of the message. She and Cade had less than three minutes to get to the escape pods. "Andrew, how long will it take us to get to the pods on Level 6?" she asked.

"If you leave the electronics and laptop and run, you can reach the pods in approximately 70 seconds."

"Plenty of time," said Cade. "Another three feet, Elle, and you'll clear the drop."

Elle smiled, and then the tool bucket stopped moving. A loud grinding sound was followed by a couple of pops and a sizzle.

"Are you kidding me?" groaned Elle.

"The motor appears to have burned out," replied Andrew. "It was simply too much weight on the system."

Cade snickered. "Must be all those cheeseburgers, Elle."

"You'll pay for that," said Elle, unable to turn and give Cade the look he deserved. "Are you close enough to grab the laptop bag?" She pulled the strap over her head and held the bag behind her back.

"Swing it," said Cade.

Elle moved the bag forwards and backwards until she felt the swinging bag stop.

"Got it. Let go."

"Two minutes, thirty seconds until automatic launch of all evacuation pods. Please proceed immediately..."

"This isn't good," said Elle.

"You're gonna have to jump, Elle. I'll catch you," said Cade. "I promise. Just be careful standing up."

Elle shook her head. "This is nuts."

"Hold onto that rail mounted on the wall, Elle," said Andrew. "I've disabled the power to the bucket. You won't get shocked."

Elle squeezed her fingers into the small groove where the bucket's bearings were visible. When she was confident her grip was good, she slowly stood in the bucket and turned to face Cade.

"Hi," said Cade. He was only three feet from her, but the gulf between bucket and the edge of the floor felt like a mile. "You can do this. One foot up on the edge of the bucket and jump."

Elle looked down. Fifteen feet below her was a large metal container. "I don't think I'll bounce if I hit that," she said.

"Jump, Elle! Come on!"

Elle took a deep breath, put her right foot on the top edge of the bucket and pushed. Cade reached out, circling his arms around her shoulders, and leaned back. The two tumbled to the floor.

"Gotcha!"

Elle looked down at Cade. She thought he might actually be blushing.

"Another thing we never talk about, right?" she said.

Elle rolled to the left and she and Cade stood up. He had a smirk spreading across his face.

"Elle…Cade…run! Now!" said Andrew. "Follow the red arrows on the walls. Hurry."

Run!

"One minute, forty five seconds until automatic launch of all evacuation pods. Please proceed immediately…"

Cade raced down the hallways of Level 5, turning left, then right, then left again as he followed the glowing red arrows on the walls.

"There!" he yelled, as the emergency escape tube came into view. He could see the ladder that would take them to Level 6.

"Forty five seconds until automatic launch of all evacuation pods. Please proceed immediately…"

"Climb, climb," said Cade, stepping aside and letting Elle go up the ladder first.

"Never would have made it carrying the equipment," Elle huffed.

Cade nodded, out of breath, as he followed Elle up the ladder. Just as Cade reached the top of Level 5, his left hand slipped from the rung and he fell back, smacking his head against the circular hole between Levels 5 and 6. His vision flared and he lost his footing, falling to the floor.

"Cade!"

Cade rolled on the floor, holding his head.

Elle put her feet back on the ladder and began to climb down.

"No!" yelled Cade, staring up at Elle. "Get to the escape pods. Go, Elle!"

"Thirty seconds until automatic launch of all evacuation pods. Please proceed immediately…"

Elle reached the bottom of the ladder and kneeled down next to Cade. She reached out and looked at his head.

"No blood. Can you climb? Did you break anything?" she asked.

Cade shook his head. "Don't think so. Go, Elle. Hurry."

Elle helped Cade to stand and then put his hands on the ladder. "Climb."

"Too dizzy," he replied, but climbed anyway.

"Fifteen seconds until automatic launch of all evacuation pods."

"Andrew?" said Elle.

"I'm sorry, Elle," Andrew said.

"Ten seconds until automatic launch of all evacuation pods."

"Nine."

"Eight."

Cade jumped down from the ladder and stared at Elle. "Sorry, Elle. It's all my fault."

"Six."

"Five."

"Elle and Cade, I need you to return to the cargo area right now," said Andrew.

Cade looked at Elle, his eyebrows shooting up.

Elle looked at Cade and shook her head. "I will never sneak away on a field trip with you again."

"Three."

"Two."

"One."

"Evacuation pods launching."

A slight shudder could be felt under the students' feet as dozens of escape pods launched and sped away from the station.

"Let's go," said Cade. "I'm guessing you have a backup plan, Andrew?"

"I'll give you instructions on the way. Please return to the cargo bay. Hurry," said Andrew.

Walk

Cade wanted to run, but Elle could tell he was still hurting from the fall. She kept an eye on him, worried he might fall again or even lose consciousness.

"There's only one other way off the station," said Andrew. "Unfortunately, it's going to require you to climb up additional levels."

Elle frowned, trying to think about the layout of the station. All of the escape pods were gone, and as far as she could remember, the station had no backup shuttles. What other options did they have to leave the station?

Cade must have been wondering about the same thing, because they both stopped walking and looked at one another.

"Is he serious?" asked Cade.

Elle nodded. "I think so."

"It's the only way," interrupted Andrew. "You're going to have to get on board Mr. Canvin's shuttle to get away."

"Uh, Andrew," said Cade. "I don't think he's going let us do that. Criminal record, right?"

"He's definitely up to no good," added Elle. "I'm not sure we should even be moving in his direction."

"There are no other options, Elle. The station's life support is disabled, and there's less than ten hours of oxygen. Emergency vehicles will be here within three hours, but the temperature on the station is going to drop fast. You've got less than two hours to get to the shuttle and get away."

"What if we run into him?" asked Cade.

"The station's AI and security system controls are now offline, so I can't use the video security system."

"Great," interrupted Cade. "So we don't even know where he is right now."

"After you retrieve your equipment, I'm going to have you assemble a few devices that will help me monitor Mr. Canvin's activities and movement. He has to use the emergency escape tubes to move between levels, so I will track him there."

Elle pulled on Cade. "Come on. We've got to hurry. You alright now?"

Cade nodded. "Yeah. I'm feeling better. Let's go."

Andrew began to recite the list of components he wanted Elle and Cade to retrieve from their toolboxes. As he began to describe the components, Elle smiled.

"Kinda scary, but I think I'm actually beginning to understand this wiring and programming stuff," said Elle.

"Me, too. I wonder if we'll get extra credit for learning all this stuff," said Cade.

"Not unless you can build a gizmo to get us out of detention. We're going to be in so much trouble when this is over."

The students turned a corner and entered the cargo bay.

"There it is," said Elle, pointing at the laptop bag and toolboxes. "Time to start building."

"Motion detector, huh?" asked Cade. "These might come in handy on the next field trip."

"Cade!"

"Sorry."

Challenge 5: Fun Stuff to Know

So, how did you like Challenge 4? Pretty cool, huh? Motors are always fun, and we promise you're not done working with them yet. And if those ICs (integrated circuits) are still confusing you, don't worry—we still get confused by them, too. The thing about working with ICs is that they start to make sense the more you actually use them, so we'll go ahead and let you know you'll be working with ICs again later in the book.

But let's talk about the current challenge. Elle and Cade are going to have to be a bit sneaky if they want to get off Gemini Station. With the bad guy's current location unknown, they don't want to cross paths with him, so Andrew has a great idea to build some motion detectors to scatter around the station. (It's worth mentioning that the PIR sensor itself is not a motion detector, but it can be used as one.)

Let's think about this for a moment. There are a lot of ways to detect motion. You can visually see someone walking towards you, but if you're not around, how would you know if a little brother or sister entered your room without permission? In spy movies, you often see the spy sticking a small hair or a piece of rice on the top of a door as he leaves. When he returns to the room, if the rice or hair is no longer on top of the door or has shifted position, there was likely an intruder.

A dog makes a great motion detector, too, but a dog requires dog food, walking, bathing, and other care. Let's skip the dog and keep thinking more along the lines of a gizmo.

First, we'd like our gizmo to be small, right? If it's big, an intruder might see it and be able to quickly think of a way to get around it. So we want to keep the gizmo small so we can hide it. It also needs to be portable—connecting it to a laptop would work, but what if we quickly need to shift its position or move it to a completely different room in a hurry? Forget the laptop and let's make it battery-powered. And we want to make a bunch of them, so they need to be inexpensive, right? We can't really control the price of the official Arduino, but we can try and locate electronic components that are inexpensive. (You can buy Arduino-compatible boards, by the way, and they often can be as low as $10, but we prefer using the official Arduino product.)

And what should happen when the gizmo detects motion? Do we want it to let out a piercing alarm that will wake the neighborhood or would we like a silent alarm that doesn't alert the intruder but lets us know that someone is where he doesn't belong?

These are all great questions, and they also leave open a lot of opportunities for you to tinker and modify the gizmo we're going to have you build for Challenge 5. But before we build it, you know what we need to do first, right?

Yep, we need to go over a teeny-tiny bit of theory (did you just yawn???) and explain how the components you'll be using for Challenge 5 work.

But trust us… Challenge 5 is cool. Build it properly and you'll have a great little gizmo to scare that little brother or sister with a nice loud buzzer!

Let's Look at the Challenge 5 Gizmo

Once again, we want you to examine Appendix A and make sure you've gathered all the parts you'll need for Challenge 5. Don't let this short list of items fool you—it doesn't always take much to build a really cool gizmo.

Would you like to see just how simple your little motion-detecting gizmo really is? Take a look at Figure 18-1. That's the final circuit, and you should easily be able to pick out the two new items.

Figure 18-1. *The Challenge 5 gizmo wired up and ready for security duty!*

They're those two larger-than-usual items sticking out of the breadboard. And if you're wondering about them, well, let's clear up the mystery right now. In Figure 18-1, the square-shaped item in the upper left corner of the breadboard is the PIR sensor.

If you've already purchased the part and have it close by, pick it up and take a look. PIR stands for Passive Infrared. Yes, you'd think they could pick a better name for it. Well the passive part of the PIR sensor means that the PIR sensor does not send out any signals, it only reads in a signal. What signal does the PIR sensor read in? Simple—it reads in infrared light or heat, which is where the IR in PIR comes from. The PIR sensor then detects changes in infrared light (for example, when you wave your hand in front of it) and thus can detect motion of objects.

Look underneath the PIR sensor and you'll see three short pins. Just like the temperature sensor from Challenge 3, each of those pins will be wired into your final circuit. (You'll learn more about the function of each pin in Chapter 19, so stay tuned.) They're short, so you'll need to use what's called a 6-pin header to connect it to the breadboard. If you don't already have the 6-pin header, you'll need to get one so you can properly connect the PIR sensor to the breadboard.

ANDREW 5.0

One way to think of the PIR sensor is this: when the PIR sensor detects motion, what it's really detecting is changes in infrared light. All forms of matter give off infrared light because all forms of matter give off heat.

Andrew's right. There are a lot of different PIR sensors, but the one you'll be using is suitable for you to monitor a room or hallway. Just keep in mind that the dome on the PIR sensor must be able to "see" the room it's monitoring. You can't put it under a blanket or behind a book. Still, it's pretty small. Unless someone is actively looking for it, chances are it'll never be seen! Let's hope so—Elle and Cade aren't going to want the bad guy to know he's being monitored.

There's one additional new device you'll be using with Challenge 5. That's the item you'll see to the right of the PIR sensor in Figure 18-1—a buzzer. And just as you'd imagine, a buzzer does one thing and does it well… it buzzes.

The buzzer makes its noise when you supply current to the small disk inside the buzzer. The more current you supply, the higher the frequency of the noise. There is no plastic ball or metal ball bearing to rattle around. The volume of the buzzer is increased or decreased by changing a value in the sketch (program) that you'll learn about in Chapter 20.

Now it's time to collect the other things you need—your Arduino Uno, 8 jumper wires (we used two green, three red, and three black, but you can use any colors you like), a 9V battery harness and a 9V battery.

ANDREW 5.0

I'd like to make one last comment about the motion-detecting gizmo. While the authors are using a buzzer for their version of the Challenge 5 gizmo, I'm going to have Cade and Elle build their motion detectors with LEDs. I don't want Mr. Canvin hearing the loud buzzers and wondering who scattered these little gizmos around the space station. I've instructed Cade and Elle to modify the program to light up an LED that hopefully I'll be able to detect. Feel free to modify your gizmo to light up an LED if you like, but I think the buzzer option will be much more fun, especially if you want to scare an intruder.

Yes, we're going to have you use a buzzer instead of an LED. You already know how to use an LED with the Arduino and breadboard, so feel free to add one if you like. You may even feel confident enough to trigger a number of LEDs with a modified sketch, so go right ahead!

Other possibilities could include using the PIR sensor to trigger a spinning motor—maybe you want to design a small, rolling robot that runs away if it detects movement in the area. Or maybe you could use a sound sensor that picks up noise! Imagine designing a gizmo that detects movement or sound or both. You've got lots of possibilities when it comes to modifying the motion detector, so think about how you might want to expand the gizmo and give it more features.

Ready to Build Something?

Challenge 5 will have you building a gizmo that might offer a real-life function you'll use. You've tinkered with enough components in earlier challenges that you might be gaining some confidence to mix and match various components, such as resistors, LEDs, a temperature sensor, and even a motor. (Imagine the noise that little motor will make if it's set to turn on when a PIR or light or sound sensor is triggered!)

Well, it's time to actually go and build the Challenge 5 gizmo. If you haven't got the parts for Challenge 5 collected yet, turn to Appendix A for the complete parts list. Chapter 19 will give you the building instructions and Chapter 20 will provide the program (sketch). Time to help Cade and Elle create some motion-detecting gizmos they can scatter around the station to alert Andrew to Mr. Canvin's presence.

Time to build!

Challenge 5: Examining the Hardware

You've crossed the halfway point! Congratulations. You now have four gizmos under your belt and you're about ready to begin building the fifth. Hopefully at this point you're starting to gain some confidence in your hardware skills. Patience is always a good idea when building gizmos, and so is carefully observing where components are inserted and where the wires go that are used to connect everything.

One of the most common errors we experience when building circuits is simply connecting something improperly. Remember the LED and its short leg and long leg? We can't tell you how many times we've made the mistake of inserting an LED into the breadboard with the long leg (Anode) connected to the negative voltage side of the circuit and the short leg (Cathode) connected to the positive. While resistors don't care which way you insert them, most components do! You haven't used a transistor yet, but trust us—insert a transistor the wrong way and you could get a tiny little fizzle (the transistor could get really hot) when you apply power. So, always check your circuit before applying power, and double- and triple-check that you've got all the components inserted correctly and wired up properly.

Now let's start building the Challenge 5 gizmo. As you learned in Chapter 18, this little gizmo will use two new components (three if you count the 6-pin header)—a PIR sensor and a buzzer.

The PIR sensor is not a true motion detector, but it can be adapted to act as one. This challenge shows you how to use the sensor to detect changes in heat that you can interpret as being caused by the movement of a human into the sensor's field of view.

ANDREW 5.0

Let me interrupt to say that no motion detector detects motion directly. Passive infrared sensors detect body heat and interpret changing heat levels as indicating motion. Ultrasonic motion detectors interpret changing sound waves as representing motion. Microwave-based detectors function similarly to a police radar gun in detecting the time from sending a ping to its being received back. In all cases, it's not motion that's directly being detected, but something else that is interpreted as indicating motion.

Even humans can't directly detect motion! When you "see" motion, what your eyes really detect are changing patterns of light. Your brain interprets those patterns and you perceive that motion is occurring. When you touch something you perceive is moving, you are interpreting changing patterns of pressure and perhaps the reciprocal motion of your own body as an indication that what you are touching is moving.

No need to get too metaphysical. For our purposes, it is sufficient to treat changing patterns of heat as indicating that human motion is occurring.

Once again, Andrew is correct. We could apply all sorts of technology to the problem of detecting motion. It's often best, however, to choose the simplest approach that will solve the problem. Elle and Cade don't have time to spare. A passive infrared sensor is reliable in their situation, and can be built swiftly using the parts available. It is a good choice that will save the day.

A Closer Look at the PIR Sensor

One of the new pieces of hardware for Challenge 5 is the passive infrared (PIR) sensor shown in Figure 19-1. This PIR sensor detects changes in infrared (heat) radiation, which makes it very easy to adapt it to motion detecting as every object has some form of heat radiation. All forms of matter produce heat, especially people! The PIR sensor can detect the body heat given off by a person.

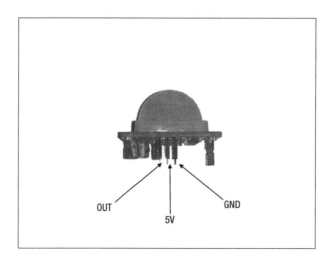

Figure 19-1. *A PIR sensor with its pinout*

Notice in Figure 19-1 that the PIR sensor has three pins (just like the temperature sensor you've already used). The 5V pin (in the center) is where you'll provide 5 volts; this will come from the Arduino.

ANDREW 5.0

You're probably already shaking your heads and saying "Wait—that's a 9-volt battery connected to the Arduino!" And you're correct. The Arduino Uno itself receives 9 volts from the battery, but it can provide either 5V or 3.3V to the electronics connected to it. For this circuit, you'll be connecting a wire from the Arduino header labeled 5V to the breadboard. That's how the PIR sensor will get its 5V!

We'll be connecting the GND pin on the PIR sensor to GND. You could run a wire from the GND header on the Arduino to this pin, but we're going to show you a different method. And, of course, the Out pin is how the PIR sensor will alert the Arduino (and the sketch that you'll upload to the Arduino in Chapter 20) that it has detected motion.

The other major component you'll be using with the Challenge 5 gizmo is the buzzer. A buzzer creates a noise by applying a current to a piezoelectric disk. This disk can increase or decrease its volume depending on a frequency you'll specify in the program. Figure 19-2 shows the buzzer you'll be adding to your circuit.

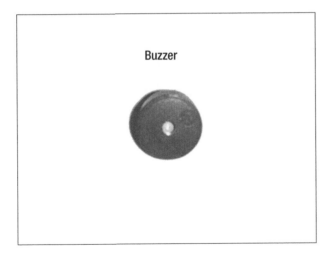

Buzzer

Figure 19-2. A buzzer

The only other new component you need is the 6-pin header. This functions as an extender because the pins on the PIR sensor are very short—too short to be inserted properly into a breadboard. You insert the header into the breadboard and then you'll insert the PIR into the header.

Now, let's build this thing!

Let's Build The Challenge 5 Gizmo

For this circuit, we need to connect all the digital pins on the PIR sensor and on the buzzer to the Arduino.

> **Note** We won't keep reminding you about the rows and columns on the breadboard. For the steps below, we'll just tell you in which row (a number) and column (a letter) to insert components. If your breadboard isn't numbered and/or lettered, you can use a Sharpie to add your own letters and numbers. Or you can simply keep track of where we insert wires and components and how they're connected.

1. Make sure that the jumper on the PIR sensor is set to the L setting. Figure 19-3 illustrates this process.

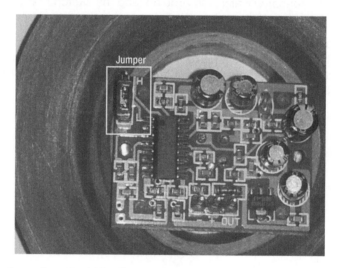

Figure 19-3. Make sure the jumper is on the right setting

2. Your first step is to attach the 6-pin-female-stackable-header to the solderless breadboard (J-5 through J-10), as illustrated in Figure 19-4.

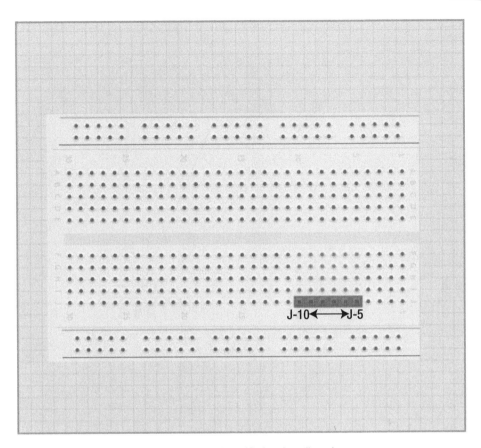

Figure 19-4. Attach the 6-pin-female-stackable-header to the solderless breadboard

3. Next, insert the PIR sensor into the far right pins of the 6-pin-female-stackable-header. This corresponds to J5, J6, and J7. Be sure the Out pin is inserted into J5, as shown in Figure 19-5. The PIR sensor you purchased may be difficult to fit on the 6-pin-female-stackable-header. What you can do is bend (gently) the capacitors that are in the way just enough to allow the PIR sensors header fit into the 6-pin-female-stackable-header.

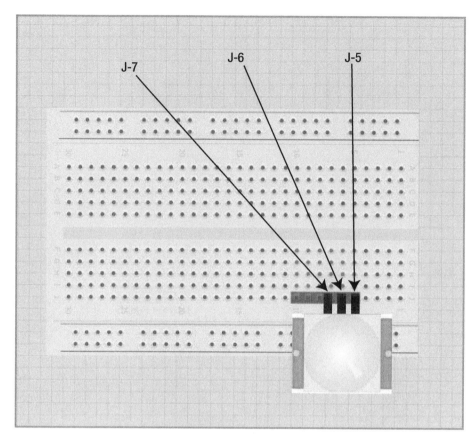

Figure 19-5. Attach the PIR sensor to the 6-pin-female-stackable-header

4. Now connect the 5V pin on the PIR sensor to what will become the 5V power source on the breadboard. In Figure 19-6, this corresponds to the column of holes that runs right next to the red line on the breadboard. We connected a red wire from I-6 to the power column at row 12. We connected a black wire from I-7 to the GND column at row 19.

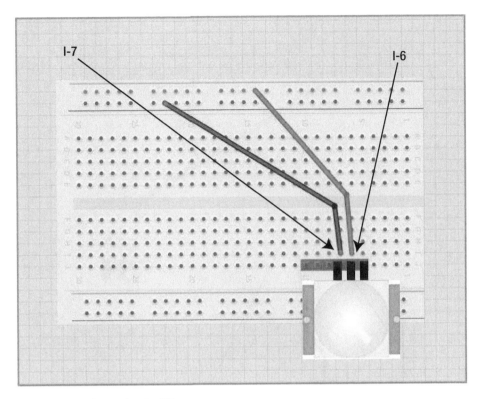

Figure 19-6. Attach power and ground to the PIR sensor

If your breadboard doesn't have the blue and red lines on it, you can add your own or just remember which column (column because it runs parallel to the lettered columns) you are going to use for power and which you'll use for GND (ground).

5. Remember, I-6 shares the same electrical connection as F-6, G-6, H-6, and J-6. So when you added the wire at I-6, it's just as if you wrapped the wire around the middle pin (5V) on the PIR sensor.

6. Now it's time to attach the buzzer. Insert the buzzer into the breadboard so that one of the buzzers pins goes into H-19 and the other pin into H-22. Figure 19-7 illustrates this process. If you're not sure which pin is which, take a close look because they are labeled.

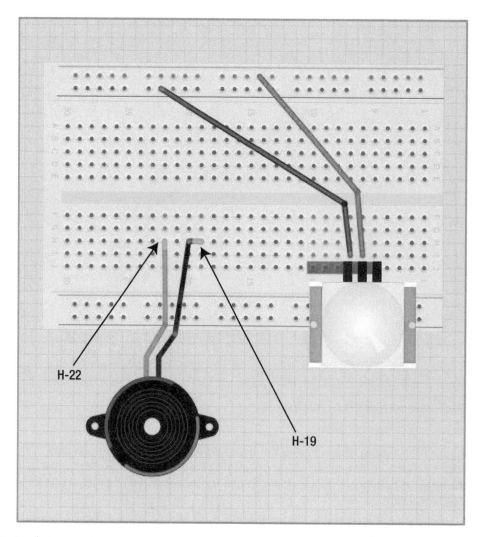

H-22

H-19

Figure 19-7. Attach the buzzer to the solderless breadboard

7. Now it's time to wire up the buzzer. Connect the buzzer (J-19) to the ground rail on the solderless bread board by adding a black wire from J-19 to the GND column row 19. Figure 19-8 illustrates this process.

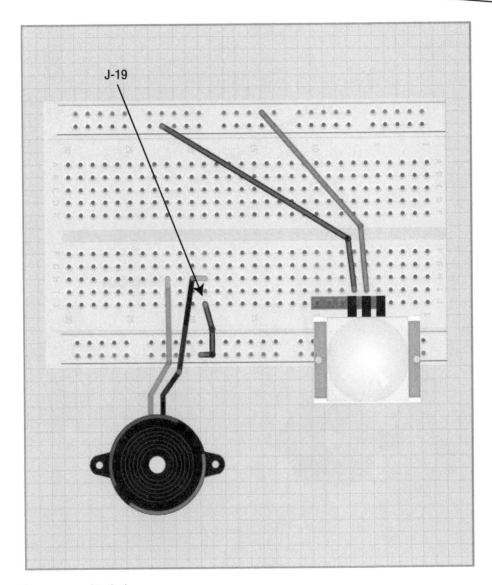

Figure 19-8. Connect ground to the buzzer

Note   As we have done in previous challenges we will be using both sides of the solderless bread board's power and ground rails this makes sure that the circuit is neat and easy to follow.

8. You don't want to connect a buzzer directly to 5V, so we're going to add a resistor in there to protect the component from receiving too much voltage. Insert one end of a 100-ohm resistor to the positive lead of the buzzer at F-22 and insert the other end of the resistor into H-25. Figure 19-9 illustrates this process.

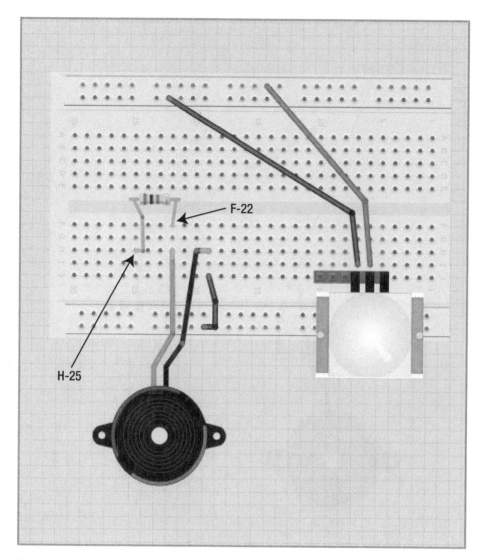

Figure 19-9. Attach the 100-ohm resistor to the positive side of the buzzer

9. Now, before we forget, let's make sure the power and GND columns on
    the breadboard are connected so that both sides can provide voltage and
    ground. Simply run a wire (we used red) from one of the power holes (the
    hole nearest to the top or bottom of the breadboard is always easiest) to a
    power hole on the other side of the breadboard. Do the same for the GND
    (we used a black wire). Insert one end of the wire into a hole on the GND
    column and the other end to a hole in the GND column on the other side of
    the breadboard, as shown in Figure 19-10.

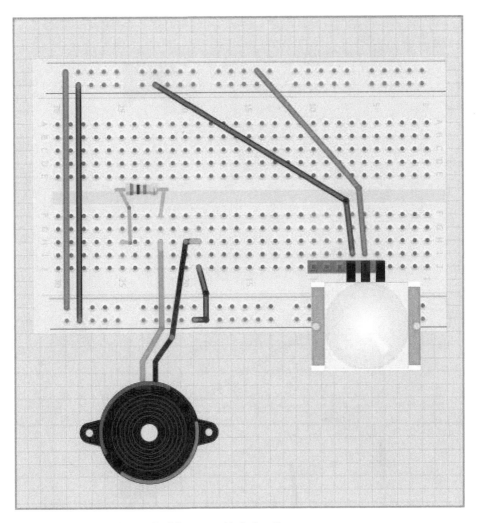

Figure 19-10. *Connect the power and ground rail from one side to the other*

10. Now let's bring the Arduino into the circuit. Connect the Out pin (refer to Figure 19-1) of the PIR sensor to the Arduino by running a wire (we used green) from I-5 to D6 (digital pin 6) on the Arduino. Figure 19-11 illustrates this process.

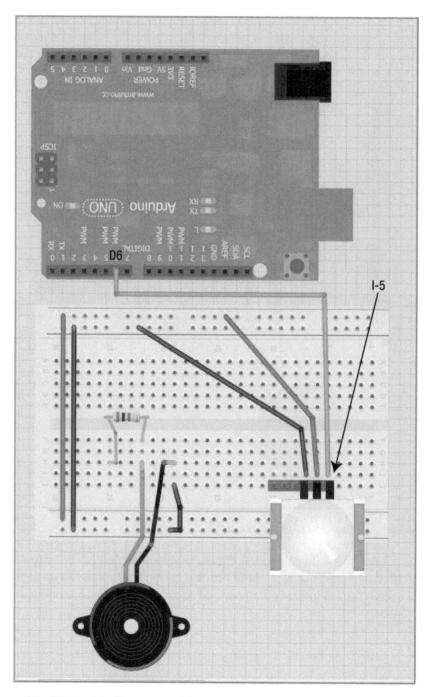

Figure 19-11. Connect the OUT pin of the PIR sensor to digital pin 6 of the Arduino

11. Next, connect digital pin 9 (D9) of the Arduino to F-25. This connects D9 to the 100-ohm resistor. Figure 19-12 illustrates this process.

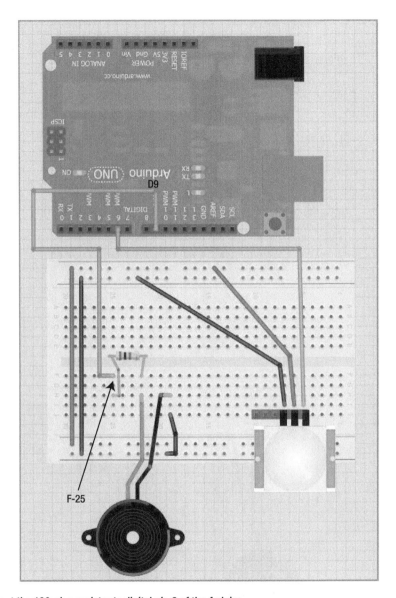

Figure 19-12. Connect the 100-ohm resistor to digital pin 9 of the Arduino

12. Now we need to connect both power and GND to the breadboard, which is done via the Arduino. The Arduino will get power from the 9V battery and then provide it to the breadboard using a wire (we used red) running from the +5V pin to the power column on the breadboard. Connect the wire to any free hole on the power column (power column row 13). Insert the end of another wire (we used black) into the GND header on the Arduino and the other end into the GND column (ground column row 12). Figure 19-13 illustrates this process.

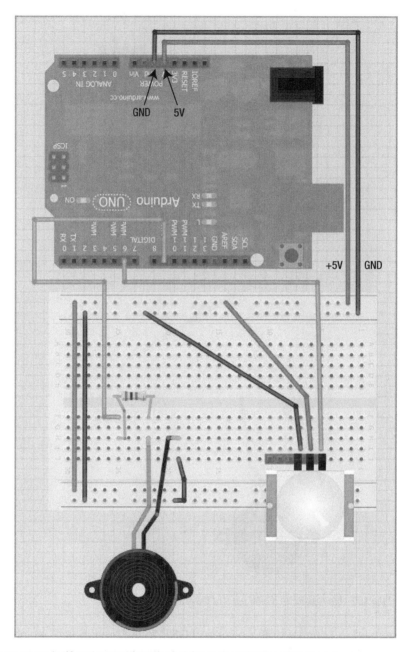

Figure 19-13. *Connect power (+5V) and ground from the Arduino to the solderless breadboard*

13. Finally, connect the 9V battery harness to the Arduino as shown in Figure 19-14.

Figure 19-14. Connect the power cord to the Arduino

That's it! Don't connect a battery just yet—you'll do that after you get the sketch uploaded to the Arduino. And Chapter 20 is all about programming the Challenge 5 gizmo, so keep reading and get that motion detector finished!

Challenge 5: Examining the Software

Well, you've crossed the halfway point in the book and now you're ready to tackle the sketch for the Challenge 5 gizmo. At this point you should have the Challenge 5 gizmo all wired up and ready to be placed in a secure location so it can detect intruders.

We have a specific device here with one specific duty—to detect motion by using the PIR sensor to detect changes in infrared radiation. What is infrared radiation? Well, to put it simply, it's heat. And all forms of matter give off heat. As matter (such as a person) moves in front of the sensor, the precise amount of heat reaching the sensor will vary.

We're going to give you the actual sketch to upload to your Arduino, but let's take just a moment and talk about how you might go about deciding how to structure this sketch if you were going to create it all on your own.

ANDREW 5.0

Don't let the idea of writing your own sketch scare you! On the book's website, the authors provide dozens of resources you can use to continue your education. Some of those resources will supply much more detail and explanation about programming an Arduino gizmo than you'll see in this book. There's a wealth of information out there, just waiting for you!

Thinking Through the Solution

Take a second and think about this little device (the PIR gadget), and what its sketch might look like in rough form. What does our device really need to do? Well, first, the sketch needs to have the PIR sensor and buzzer identified so the Arduino knows which pins to monitor, right? So we start off our sketch by initializing the pins that are connected most directly to the buzzer and the PIR sensor.

We also need to know which of these devices acts as an input and which acts as an output. That's pretty easy, isn't it? The buzzer makes noise, so it makes sense that it will be the output device. And the PIR sensor is always checking for infrared radiation—it waits for a change in radiation and then triggers the buzzer to sound. So the PIR sensor is our input device! The next part of the sketch simply defines the buzzer as an output device and the PIR sensor as an input device.

Now we get to the main part of the program, where the gizmo keeps checking for motion. This is something that will continue as long as the device is powered, so whatever code we add to the sketch will run and run and run, over and over and over, until power is disconnected from the Arduino. Can you guess where this bit of code will go? Of course! Inside the void loop(). You've seen this often enough in earlier sketches, haven't you?

This part of the sketch is where the PIR sensor decides whether it has detected any motion this happens thousands of times per second. Wait for change … nothing? Do it again. Wait for change … nothing? Do it again. Wait for change … HEY! Motion. Now what?

When the PIR sensor detects a change in radiation, we interpret that change as movement and want to trigger the buzzer, right? The buzzer has the ability to provide a range of sounds, so we will also instruct the buzzer on how loud and at what frequency and for what duration it should alert us to an intruder.

To control the buzzer, we'll use a special built-in feature called the tone function. The tone function keeps us from having to do extremely complicated programming to control the buzzer's volume, speed, and duration. Instead, we simply define these items with numbers. This means it's simple to tinker with the gizmo and tweak these values until we are happy with the volume and the duration of the buzzer.

When the buzzer stops, the PIR sensor starts over, waiting for changes in infrared radiation. If a change in infrared radiation (that is, an intruder's movement) is continually detected, the buzzer will never stop! The loop where it checks for movement and triggers the buzzer will happen over and over again—until the the PIR sensor no longer sees a change in infrared radiation. Simple!

Now, before we delve into the real sketch, let's take a quick look at that tone function we just mentioned so you understand how the values you provide can tweak the buzzer to do different things.

Understanding the Tone Function

The Arduino tone function isn't complicated. You simply embed it into the sketch, followed by parentheses containing three variables or values. Here's what the tone function looks like:

```
tone( pin, frequency, duration)
```

The pin argument is easy—it's the digital pin on the Arduino that's connected to the buzzer. In our case, it's pin 9, but in the sketch we'll use a variable, buzzerPin, to hold that value of 9. By using a variable such as buzzerPin, if you need to change the pin number on the Arduino that connects to the buzzer, you only have to change that value at the beginning of the sketch where it's assigned to the buzzerPin variable. If you used the actual value in the tone function, you'd also have to change it there. With the buzzerPin variable, you can always reference the connection to the buzzer anywhere in a sketch by simply using the variable name. No need to change the value in multiple locations!

The second setting is frequency, which is defined in units called hertz, or cycles per second; 1000 hertz=1 kilohertz (kHz). A higher frequency results in a higher-pitch tone, a lower frequency in a lower-pitch tone. You can play around with this setting to find the sound you want the buzzer to produce. Just remember that the human ear can only hear sounds from 20Hz to 20kHz. We're going to set it initially to 5000 (5kHz) to get a nice, loud buzz. Increase it (try 7000) or decrease it (try 2000) to see what happens!

Finally, the duration value is provided in milliseconds. Remember, 1000 milliseconds is equal to 1 second. If you want the buzzer to ring for two seconds, set the duration value to 2000. Do you want seven seconds? Then set the duration to 7000. You can specify in-between values such as 2500 for 2½ seconds. However many seconds buzz you want, multiply that number by 1000.

Although we won't do it in this sketch, you can also leave off the duration in the tone function and the buzzer will stay on forever. Well, not actually forever. You can easily turn it off by adding the function noTone into your sketch at any point where you want the buzzer to turn off.

Think you've got the tone function figured out? Don't worry if it's still a little confusing because next you'll see it in action inside the actual sketch. Let's take a look at the Challenge 5 sketch in its entirety and then we'll break it down and discuss in more detail.

The Challenge #5 Sketch

Listing 20-1 shows the complete sketch for the Challenge 5 gizmo. Read it all the way through and see if you can see the structure we described earlier. Do you see the pin initializations at the beginning? And then the buzzer and PIR sensor being defined as output and input devices? You should also note the looping part of the sketch that has the PIR sensor constantly checking for movement. Finally, you're already familiar with If-Else statements and we use one again here to decide which action to take—trigger the buzzer or keep it quiet.

Listing 20-1. Motion Detection

```
// Initalize buzzer and PIR sensor pins
int buzzerPin = 9;
int PIRPin = 6;

// Initialize PIR sensor state
int PIRState = 0;

void setup()
{
  // Set PIR sensor to an Input and the buzzer to an Output
  pinMode(PIRPin, INPUT);
  pinMode(buzzerPin, OUTPUT);
}

void loop()
{
  // Read in PIR state (0 or 1)
  PIRState = digitalRead(PIRPin);
```

```
// If PIRState detects motion?
if (PIRState == 1)
{
  // Buzzer makes noise
  tone(buzzerPin, 5000, 1000);
}
else
{
  // Buzzer makes no noise
  digitalWrite(buzzerPin, LOW);
}
}
```

Let's break down this sketch into smaller sections and take a look at what's happening. First, here are the pin initializations:

```
// Initalize buzzer and PIR sensor pins
int buzzerPin = 9;
int PIRPin = 6;

// Initialize PIR sensor state
int PIRState = 0;
```

Just as expected, we've got the buzzer connected to the Arduino using digital pin 9. If you built the gizmo exactly as described in Chapter 19, your buzzer should also be connected to pin 9, but feel free to trace it out—look at digital pin 9 on the Arduino and follow the wire to its final destination. Does it end with the buzzer's output pin? If not, you'll need to fix that! Go back to Chapter 19 if necessary or just move the connection for the buzzer's output pin so it makes a connection to the Arduino's pin 9.

The same goes for the PIR sensor. The sketch has it connected to digital pin 6, so you'll want to confirm on your own gizmo that pin 6 on your Arduino is making a connection to the PIR sensor's left pin, which is sometimes labeled OUT.

Finally, we need to set the PIRState so that when the Arduino is powered up the buzzer doesn't automatically sound when there's no change in infrared radiation. We do this by setting PIRState to 0. When it's 0, no motion is detected. When it changes to 1, that means motion is detected. If you set the initial state to 1 by accident, when the gizmo is powered up, the buzzer would immediately trigger. We'll explain why in just a moment, but feel free to try it out—change the PIRState variable's initial value to 1 and turn on the gizmo and see what happens!

Here's the next bit of the sketch we want to examine:

```
void setup()
{
  // Set PIR sensor to an Input and the buzzer to an Output
  pinMode(PIRPin, INPUT);
  pinMode(buzzerPin, OUTPUT);
}
```

This is pretty simple, really. We want to define each pin that's being used on the Arduino as either an input or output pin—will it receive a signal or send a signal? If it receives a signal, we set it to INPUT.

That would be the PIR sensor. We want it detecting changes in infrared radiation (so we can detect when anything with heat enters the room or moves around the room) and we want the Arduino to receive a signal from the PIR sensor.

The flip side is the buzzer. We want the Arduino to send the buzzer a signal, so that makes the pin connected to the buzzer an output pin. We use the pinMode function and define whether a pin is set to INPUT or OUTPUT. Notice in this bit of code we have two pinMode functions—one for PIRPin, which holds the pin value 6, and the other for buzzerPin, which holds a value of 9. During the setup part of the sketch, the pinMode function simply says, whatever is connected to pin 6, make it an input device. And whatever is connected to pin 9, make it an output device.

Here's the final bit of the sketch we'll discuss:

```
void loop()
{
  // Read in PIR state (0 or 1)
  PIRState = digitalRead(PIRPin);

  // If PIRState detects motion?
  if (PIRState == 1)
  {
    // Buzzer makes noise
    tone(buzzerPin, 5000, 1000);
  }
  else
  {
    // Buzzer makes no noise
    digitalWrite(buzzerPin, LOW);
  }
}
```

Let's break this portion of the sketch down a bit further. The first bit of the code simply examines PIRState. If the voltage of the PIR sensor is high (5V), PIRState will be set to 1, but if the voltage is low (0V), PIRState will be set to 0. The PIR sensor sends a 0 (or 0 volts) to pin 6 as long as it doesn't detect any changes in infrared radiation; if it does detect a change in infrared radiation, the PIR sensor will output a high signal (5V) to digital pin 6 on the Arduino. The digitalRead command just keeps looking at the value of pin 6 (or whatever value is stored in the PIRPin variable). It does this thousands of times per second. And whatever value it finds, it puts that in the PIRState variable.

Next we come to the If-Else statement. We've got two things that can happen here: the buzzer can buzz or it can remain silent. Using the If-Else statement, we can make these two states happen by saying If the PIRState value is 1 (motion detected), trigger the buzzer. Otherwise (Else) the PIRState value is 0 (motion not detected), so do not trigger the buzzer.

If the expression (PIRState == 1) is true, the code will run what's inside the next set of brackets— tone(buzzerPin, 5000, 1000). This sets the tone to 5kHz and triggers the alarm for one second (1000 milliseconds).

Otherwise, the sketch executes the digitalWrite(buzzerPin, LOW) function in the else clause. That function turns off the buzzer. If the buzzer wasn't buzzing, this simply keeps it in that state.

And that's it! That's the sketch for creating a super-simple motion detector that will trigger a brief, one-second-long burst of noise when it detects motion. It's up to you to experiment with different values, such as the frequency and duration. You might even do a little research and then experiment by removing the buzzer and replacing it with an LED that lights up when motion is detected. Remember, in some instances, you might not want to alert the intruder that his or her presence has been detected with an audible alert!

Solve Challenge #5

Figure 20-1 illustrates the completed gizmo. Go ahead and connect your gizmo to your computer and upload the sketch. After the sketch is uploaded, attach a 9V battery to the Arduino as we did in Challenge 2. After you hook up the battery to the Arduino; stay still for about 30 seconds as the PIR sensor is calibrating.

Figure 20-1. Completed Challenge 5 motion detector

Once the calibration period is completed, the PIR sensor will detect your motion by noticing a change in infrared radiation. Your gizmo will then make a loud noise everytime you move.

Elle and Cade built a bunch of these sensors and placed them all over the station at Andrew's request. Andrew will monitor them in areas where it's difficult for his sensors to detect motion, and in areas that are damaged. With these sensors working, Elle and Cade can get a warning that Gunther Canvin is approaching!

It's not just human bodies that give off heat; other objects do as well. We found we could wave a notepad back and forth in front of our gizmo. The changing heat patterns from the notepad's movement triggered the motion alarm.

Have some fun experimenting to see how sensitive your gizmo is and what motion it can detect. Will it detect your dog? Your cat? Movement of a window curtain in the breeze? Brainstorming and trying out different ideas is part of the fun of Arduino.

Chapter 21

Carousel Ride

"That's the last one," said Cade, placing a motion detector in the far corner of the emergency tube on Level 8. "If someone comes through here, you're sure you'll be able to hear it, Andrew? One beep?"

"There does not appear to be any degradation in the quality of the station's sound sensors. I should be able to determine the source of a single beep of any of the motion detectors you and Elle have placed," replied. Andrew. "A single beep is unlikely to make Mr. Canvin suspect his movements are being tracked."

Elle frowned. "I hope so. And how are you so certain he'll be moving into the lower levels? What's he here to steal?"

Cade began climbing the ladder to Level 9 and paused halfway up, curious about Andrew's response.

"There are hundreds of antique devices on this station that would each fetch a substantial amount of e-credits, Elle. I've looked at the station's access logs and determined that Mr. Canvin has made eight trips to this station in the last 232 days. Though I'm unable to determine where he went on the station during those visits, my best guess is that he has done some research and knows exactly what he wants. The most valuable items are down on Levels 2 and 3, and the station's sensors are telling me he is moving quickly down to Level 10. So the two of you need to get up to Level 9 now."

"Let's go," said Cade, quick-stepping up the ladder. He disappeared for a moment and then dropped his head down through the hole between levels and extended his left arm. "Laptop?"

Elle grabbed the laptop case by the handle and climbed up two rungs to hand the bag off to Cade. As soon as the bag was gone, Elle finished climbing, reminding herself that only two more levels lay between them and the getaway shuttle.

Close Call

"Do you hear that?" whispered Cade, pushing Elle a few steps backwards into a small alcove.

"I didn't hear anything," said Elle.

Cade put his fingers to his lips.

BANG!

The sound of metal hitting metal was unmistakable. The echo made it difficult to determine how far away the sound originated, but it was definitely on the same level.

"Hurry," Cade murmured. "This way."

Cade pulled Elle by the elbow, retracing their steps on Level 9 and heading back in the direction of the emergency tube. Elle tried to keep the laptop bag from bumping into the toolbox she was carrying, but Cade didn't seem to be worried about the slight noise.

"Do you think it's him?" asked Elle.

Cade stopped and looked left … then right. "It's gotta be, right? No one else is on the station."

"I wish Andrew could talk to us," whispered Elle.

"Behind here," Cade said, nodding at a large collection of machines and tools. Most of it looked damaged or extremely old. Andrew had told them that Level 9 served as the maintenance and engineering section of the station, and Cade was pleased to see that the pile was deep enough that the rear wall wasn't visible.

Elle stepped over a few devices she didn't recognize and squeezed under a large plastic box that had a series of menacing grippers and claws. One of the claws caught on the laptop bag's strap and Elle was about to pull hard on the strap but Cade grabbed her shoulder and pointed up. The plastic box held a smaller box of miscellaneous metal pieces that was wobbling back and forth.

"Oh, no," said Elle.

Just as the box tipped over the edge, Cade reached up and blocked it from falling with his hand. He pushed hard and the box settled back in place. He grinned at Elle. "That was close." He unhooked the bag and followed her as she climbed deeper into the collection of machines.

Elle crouched down, unable to see the hallway they had just left. She leaned towards Cade and whispered. "Do you think we're far enough in? What if he starts looking through this pile of stuff?"

Cade shook his head. "This stuff is broken. He's looking for operational stuff. Let's just wait a few minutes and see what happens."

Elle nodded and gave a weak smile.

A loud clang was heard again, this time much closer. Cade and Elle both held their breath and waited.

Nothing To See Here

Elle and Cade were certain they'd be discovered. They were unable to see Gunther Canvin from behind the pile when he began sorting through the front few machines. Cade had picked up a short metal rod somewhere during the climb into the pile, and he was clinching it tightly as he prepared to defend his friend.

But the thief must have lost interest because he tossed something on the floor that landed with a loud clang, then grumbled unintelligibly as he walked away, banging something metal on the station's wall panels.

Cade stared at Elle. She had a look of relief that matched his own. "Let's wait one more minute," he whispered.

"Okay. One more minute," Elle replied, her voice shaky as she realized just how close Gunther Canvin had been to discovering their hiding spot.

Three minutes later, Elle and Cade moved slowly and carefully through the boxes and stacks of parts. Cade grabbed the laptop bag and sat it down as Elle finished climbing out.

"What are you doing?" asked Elle, seeing Cade creeping down the hallway in the direction of Gunther Canvin.

"We need to make sure he went this way," replied Cade.

"There's no time. It's the only logical direction to go. He came from this direction," Elle said, pointing towards the emergency tube that would take them up to Level 10. "And the stuff he wants to steal is in that direction."

Cade hesitated, and then nodded.

"Andrew said we needed to get to engineering on Level 10. He can't talk to us until we get there. Come on. This way."

Elle led Cade down the dark hallway. The flashing lights served as a reminder that life support was failing, and Elle noticed her breath for the first time as she realized the temperature on the station had dropped enough to cause her to shiver.

An Engineering Problem

"Level 10," said Cade, pulling Elle up from the ladder in the emergency tube. "I think we've seen more of this station than we have our actual school."

"No kidding," replied Elle. "You wanna stick around and see some more?"

Cade snickered. "Nope. I'm definitely ready to get outta here."

Elle grinned at her friend and then nodded behind Cade. "Engineering is down that hall."

"And I'm betting I know why Andrew told us not to lose the laptops or toolboxes," said Cade with a frown. "More homework."

"I feel like I've become an expert at electronics and programming," said Elle, glancing behind her to make certain they weren't being followed.

"It's kinda fun," replied Cade. "Except for the whole *our lives are in danger* thing."

"Maybe all our teachers should make homework a life-or-death assignment?" Elle smiled at Cade. "I'll bet your grades would improve."

"Hey!"

Before Cade could respond, Elle waved her hand in front of a large door. "Here we are."

Cade followed Elle through the door, looking forward to hearing Andrew's familiar voice. Even with the danger, Andrew had a calming effect and took his mind off of the facts that life support was failing, a criminal was sharing the station with them, and their only way off the station seemed to require even more tinkering with electronics.

"It's good to see the two of you," said Andrew, his voice a slight echo in the large room that contained dozens of workstations surrounding a large circular compartment in the center of the room. The compartment consisted of a single piece of traspara-steel that wrapped around an enclosed machine. The transpara-steel also ran from floor to ceiling, with no apparent way to enter.

"Hi, Andrew!" said Elle and Cade together.

"You'll be happy to know that Gunther Canvin has triggered the motion detector you placed on Level 7 and I believe he is about to enter Level 6. You're not out of danger, but once he gets to Levels 2 or 3 I'll be able to monitor his activity visually."

Elle pointed at the circular compartment. "Can you really see us? Where's the camera?"

"I heard your approach. Two sets of footsteps. I know your pace and the sound of your steps."

Cade nodded. "Of course."

Elle grinned.

"No offense, Andrew, but I'm ready to get off this station. Please tell me we're good to go."

There was a slight pause. "I'm sorry, Elle. The damage done to this station is extensive, and power outages continue to occur as well as some small fires. You've got another important bit of work to do here, I'm afraid."

Cade pointed to the transparent compartment in the center of the room. "I'm guessing it has to do with the fact I can see that machine in there twitching back and forth, right?"

"That device is the power connect between the station's micro-fusion drive and all the control systems that are still operational. It went offline when the station was hit, and Gunther Canvin attempted to make the reconnection. He was unsuccessful and got frustrated."

Elle was confused. "Frustrated?"

"He smashed the workstation with a large wrench," replied Andrew.

"Ah," said Elle. "But why was he trying to reconnect it?"

"It would have allowed him to more easily access other levels because the elevators would be back online. But the damage he did made things much worse."

"How?" asked Cade. "It's not like things can get much worse than losing life support."

"The power connect must be fixed or the shuttle will be unable to undock."

Elle nodded. "Apparently it can get much worse."

Cade looked at toolbox in his hands and the one Elle was carrying. And then he smiled.

"We give up too easily, don't we, Andrew?" he asked, nodding at the toolbox in Elle's hand. "You're going to tell us how to fix it, aren't you?"

"It's an easy fix," said Andrew. "The controller inside the compartment relies on nothing more than a simple servo. If you can gain control of the servo, the controller will automatically perform the power reconnect on the five switches inside. You just have to get the controller to the thirty, sixty, ninety, one-hundred-twenty, and one-hundred-fifty degree positions. The controller will do the rest."

"Too easy," said Cade.

"And people say you're sarcastic. I completely disagree," said Elle.

Cade looked at Elle. "Uh … "

Elle grinned. "Let's do this. I want to go home."

"Please find and locate the parts I describe. I'm going to instruct you on creating a small circuit that will allow you to fine-tune the movement of the servo inside the power compartment," said Andrew.

Elle and Cade opened their toolboxes and began pulling out small boxes.

"People say I'm sarcastic?" asked Cade.

"No," replied Elle. "I was totally kidding."

"Oh."

Elle laughed.

"Wait a minute!"

"Get your parts!"

Chapter 22

Challenge 6: Fun Stuff to Know

With only three challenges left in the book, are you feeling like you're moving from Arduino newbie to Arduino guru? Okay, maybe you're not quite that far along on the skills chart yet, but you have to admit you've learned quite a bit! Temperature sensor … PIR sensor … DC motor … and even integrated circuits. You've handled resistors and LEDs and you've developed a good understanding of how power and ground relate to building circuits. Give yourself a big pat on the back, because you've now learned more about the Arduino and a bunch of other electronic components than most people can claim to know. That Arduino guru status has your name all over it.

So, now you're probably wondering about what you'll learn next, huh? You know that Elle and Cade need to create a small controller to move what's called a servo. But what's a servo? It turns out that a servo is simply a type of motor, and you already had some hands-on time with a DC motor back in Challenge 4. Servo motors aren't all that different from standard DC motors, but there are certain improvements that can add some real power and functionality to future gizmos you design. What kind of functionality? Well, we can tell you that a certain favorite gizmo called a robot often relies heavily on servos. Yep … we said *robot*. We thought that would get your attention.

But we're not there yet. (Yes, that's a BIG hint we've dropped about an upcoming challenge.)

Right now, Cade and Elle need to be able to rotate a device that will perform various actions at different positions in a room. And in order to build that controller, they're going to need to be able to control a servo motor. And that's what we'll be covering in this chapter.

Let's Look at the Challenge 6 Gizmo

Be sure to flip back to Appendix A and verify you've got all the parts you'll need for Challenge 6. You already have some of the parts from previous challenges, so the servo motor is the big one here.

Take a look at Figure 22-1 and you'll see what the final circuit will look like when you're done with Chapter 23. The servo motor is the big, dark object in the upper left. Look carefully and you'll see four arms that rotate.

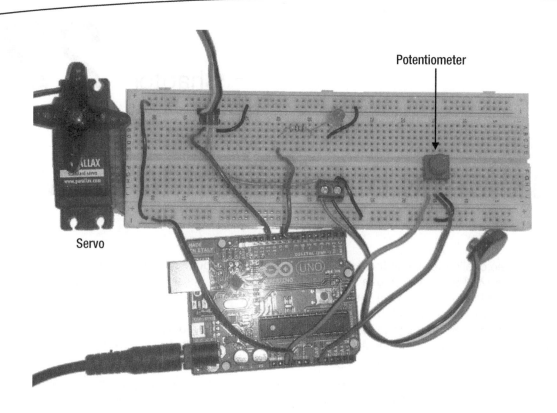

Figure 22-1. The Challenge 6 gizmo, complete with servo motor!

If you've got your servo motor, go ahead and pick it up and inspect it. You can rotate the shaft, clockwise or counterclockwise—spin it as much as you like! You never want to rotate the shaft with your hands with power applied, though. Keep that in mind after you build this circuit, okay? A servo motor doesn't like to be turned once it's powered up—forcing a turn with power applied can damage the motor.

Notice that the servo motor has a special connector for its wires. These pins can be inserted easily enough into a breadboard, but you're going to want to pay careful attention to how power (V+) and ground are connected in Chapter 23. There's only one way to connect a servo motor to power and ground so it rotates properly.

ANDREW 5.0

You probably received a small bag of parts with the servo you purchased. This bag usually contains a variety of small plastic or metal pieces in various shapes. These are used as connecting pieces and you'll often find them used to connect non-electronic parts, such as legs on a robot or metal rods to open and close switches.

Don't throw these parts away! If you're not going to use them right away, put them away for later. You never know when you'll need that servo for a robot or other gizmo that requires a connector. You can always purchase the connectors individually, but sometimes it's difficult to get an exact match. The ones that come with the servo are the best match, so put them somewhere safe and be sure to label them so you'll know which servo motor they belong to. As your collection of electronics parts grows, you may build a large servo collection of various sizes. Get in the habit of labeling parts and putting them in small baggies or in envelopes.

You'll also see a potentiometer in the mix of parts. You'll use that potentiometer to control the direction and the number of degrees the servo motor rotates. Turn it to the left and the servo motor rotates counterclockwise. Turn it to the right, and the servo rotates clockwise. Simple!

The LED will perform a very necessary function for this challenge. Elle and Cade need to be able to control the servo so it stops at the 30-degree position, the 60-degree position, and the 90-, 120-, and 150-degree positions. As the servo rotates counterclockwise (starting at the 0-degree mark), the LED will light up briefly when it's within plus 5 degrees of these targets. That means when you dial the servo to 30 degrees, the LED will light up when the servo is somewhere between 25 and 35 degrees.

Elle and Cade don't need to get the servo lined up exactly at the 30-degree mark, but servos are capable of this level of accuracy. You'll control the level of accuracy using the sketch (program). Humans can have a difficult time fine-tuning a servo (especially a small servo) to hit an exact point ... that's why we'll be lighting up the LED when you're as close to the target as needed.

ANDREW 5.0

Some servos can rotate in fractions of degrees, meaning they have extremely accurate rotational capabilities. This level of control can be important when performing dangerous or sensitive duties. Think about a surgeon using a Da Vinci surgical robot. You wouldn't want a robot that moves its arms plus or minus 5 degrees, would you? You want that robot to perform as accurately as possible, and this means expensive servo motors that can detect when a motor is at the exact spot the doctor specifies.

The same goes for robots in manufacturing. Would you want to ride in a car where the robot placed a bolt or welded a bit of metal in "roughly" the right spot or in "exactly" the right spot?

As the accuracy and control of servo motors increases, so does the price. For small servos like you need for Challenge 6, accuracy really isn't an issue. Just keep in mind that accuracy comes with a price, so if you ever start building a robot or special gizmo that requires a fine level of movement and accuracy, you may have to spend a bit more on your servo motor.

If you look carefully at Figure 22-1, you may notice something about the power for this gizmo. First, you'll see the 9V battery harness that will plug into a 9V battery. But you'll also notice that the Arduino itself is powered by an AC adapter. Why do you need both?

A servo motor, even a small one, requires a good bit of power—and that power can't always be provided by a battery. In this instance, all of the power requirements for this circuit can be provided by the AC adapter. Tinker with the gizmo for a bit and you'll find that the 9V battery will also work just fine. We're giving you the option to use one or the other, but do wire the gizmo to use both just in case the 9V battery is low on power. If the battery gets too low on power, the servo motor will stop turning.

Ready to Build Something?

A good understanding of servo motors in Challenge 6 will pay off later in the book. Add the servo motor to the list of parts you now have experience using, and we hope you're starting to see just how far you've come in understanding how an Arduino can control various components.

The Challenge 6 gizmo isn't all that complicated, but once again we'll tell you how important it is to understand individual components by themselves before adding in more parts. Gizmos can get complicated quickly, but once you know how individual components work alone, it's not a big jump to start adding more components to construct a more complex circuit.

Chapter 23 will give you the steps you need to build the Challenge 6 gizmo. Take your time, examine the photos, read the instructions, and put it all together. Once it's done, you'll move on to Chapter 24 for the programming steps.

Time to build!

Challenge 6: Examining the Hardware

You are quickly becoming a knowledgable Arduino tinkerer! With five gizmos done and the sixth almost complete, you should be feeling pretty good about how far you've come. At this point, you should be starting to develop a methodology of your own for how you might tackle any electronics problem that is put in front of you.

The first thing to do is identify the problem or the goal you wish to accomplish. For Challenge 6, the goal is simply to move a set of tools mounted on a large motor from one location to another. The tools are fixed in place, so you've got to rotate the tools so they go to the very specific spots where they are needed. But that's this challenge, and you're likely to encounter many more as you continue your Arduino education.

When you encounter a problem you want to tackle with an electronics solution, the second thing to do (after identifying the goal) is to make a list of those items you think might be useful or that are absolutely required. Let's think back to the motion detector for a moment. Even if you didn't know about the PIR sensor before you encountered the need for a motion detecting gizmo, you might be at least able to determine that you needed some sort of device to detect motion. That would take you to an Internet search or maybe to ask someone with more knowledge about electronics. A PIR sensor certainly isn't the only way to detect changes in infrared radiation or motion (there are options that involve lasers or pressure sensors, for example), but it's definitely an inexpensive method, and it's simple. Always go for the least complex solution when you can. The PIR sensor is straightforward—it sends a signal of 0 volts when all is quiet and a signal of 1 to indicate it detects motion. Pretty easy!

Now let's think about Challenge 6. The controls have been damaged or destroyed, and Elle and Cade need to find a simple method for rotating a motor—specifically, a servo motor. We'll talk about servo motors in just a moment, but think back to all the small electronics components you've used so far. Are there any that might be helpful in rotating a motor clockwise and counterclockwise until it's tuned to a specific location?

Well, let's take a look. How about buttons? We could use two push buttons—one to make the motor move clockwise and another to move it counterclockwise. A single push might rotate the motor only a tiny amount, but humans are slow compared to computers. You might think you're pushing that button for only half a second, but that could spin the motor dozens or hundreds of degrees in that short time frame. One option that might be helpful is using the Serial Monitor to watch the motor's rotation and then use keyboard input—actually typing in the number of degrees you want the motor to rotate. That's a very good option, too, but it might not be the easiest solution to implement in terms of programming. We want something a human can immediately use and get visual results—so we can actually see the motor rotate based on a control we are using.

What about a potentiometer? It has a small dial that can be turned left or right that perfectly designed for human fingers. What's even better about this device is that we can use a program to control how much a small turn of the potentiometer rotates the motor. We could easily program it so it takes a full turn of the potentiometer to rotate the motor just a few degrees. That's pretty accurate, isn't it!

There are plenty of other options, but they're a bit out there. We could use a sound sensor and program it to listen to the volume of a voice, but that's not going to be very accurate. How about a light sensor that we'd shine a flashlight on and use the brightness to move the motor? Again, pretty difficult to fine-tune the light level (called lumens) so that it accurately controls a motor.

Nope … let's try the potentiometer. We can rotate it left or right so we can make the motor rotate in such a way that we can visually verify its location. It's pretty simple to use a protractor and a piece of paper to measure the number of degrees in a circle. We can mark out 0, 30, 60, 90, 120, 150, and 180 degrees and check to see when a spot on the motor's arm is pointing at these specific locations. The tools that Elle and Cade need to control only need to be within 5 degrees of the target, and a potentiometer definitely seems like it can give us that level of accuracy. Let's give it a try!

A Closer Look at a Servo Motor

Before we get to the actual assembly of the Challenge 6 gizmo, we really need to take a closer look at the key element we'll be using to test our new controls. It's called a servo motor, and a big one works just like a small one so we can test our controls on a small servo and feel confident that when the controls are hooked up to a larger servo, the controls will still work.

But what is a servo motor? Well, a servo motor is a very special type of motor that provides (in this case) a microcontroller with feedback. The microcontroller uses the feedback to dictate the servo motor's current location. Sometimes this is a potentiometer reporting to the microcontroller, and other times it's a rotary encoder. Whoa, techy word alert! Rotary encoder? Yep. Rotary sounds like rotation, doesn't it? So we know it has something to do with rotation. A rotory encoder is a digital circuit (unlike a potentiometer, which is analog) that can report rotation information to a microcontroller (the Arduino).This isn't a simple value like 0 or 90 or 180 (degrees). It's encoded in a language that machines understand: 1s and 0s. So a servo motor uses rotation encoding to report information, such as how far it's turned or how fast it's turning. This is stuff that might be important to you later, but for now all you need to know is that a servo motor can be told to rotate a specific number of degrees (clockwise or counterclockwise). With that level of control, we just need to figure out how to use a potentiometer that, when turned, tells the motor how far to turn, and in which direction.

One other bit of info about a servo motor you should know is that there are different types of servos. The one we use for Challenge 6 has a range of 0 to 180 degrees, but there are servos that will continuously turn for 360 degrees.

How does a servo know how far to rotate? Well, you first need to send the servo a pulse train from a digital pin (on the Arduino) to move it to a particular position. (A pulse train is similar to a square wave but doesn't have a distinct pulse pattern.) The different types of servos all basically work the same, and it's the pulse train's duty cycle that determines how much the servo moves. The Arduino team created a library for servos that lets us control up to 12 servos at a time; we'll use this library in the next chapter. Just keep in mind that a library works like a cheat sheet, meaning the Arduino is already designed to send the proper types of signals to servos, so all you have to do is configure the sketch for the servo you're using. If you change the servo, only a slight tweak in the sketch (which we'll cover in Chapter 24) is needed. All other things (such as using the potentiometer) stay the same and you don't need to modify other parts of the sketch! In short think of a servo as a dc motor with a potentiometer attached to the DC motor that is constently telling the micro-controller the DC motors position.

ANDREW 5.0

One other bit of information your readers need to know about the servo motor has to do with its wiring. The hobby servo motor we are going use has 3 wires, typically black for ground, red for power, and yellow, white, or orange for the pulse or signal. The ground wire will connect to the ground pin on the Arduino; the signal wire will connect to a digital pin on the Arduino, and the power wire will connect to an external power source. (Don't connect a servo to the Arduino's 5V power supply as it is not powerful enough for a servo. Use a separate power supply for the servo(s) instead.)

Figure 23-1 shows two different sizes of servo motors. Notice that even though the size may be different, the wiring works the same.

Servos

Figure 23-1. A few servos motors that use the same wiring

Now we know what a servo is and how it works. This will help us create the servo controller we'll use to help Elle and Cade. Let's see how to build the circuit for this challenge.

Let's Build the Challenge 6 Gizmo

The servo for this project should have come with an arm that's shaped like a plus sign. Attach that arm to the servo with a screw and screw driver. Hopefully you've taken a good look at Appendix A and bought all the parts you'll need to build the Challenge 6 gizmo. You should be ready to build now, so let's get started.

1.   First attach the potentiometer to the solderless bread board at F-14 through F-16, as shown in Figure 23-2.

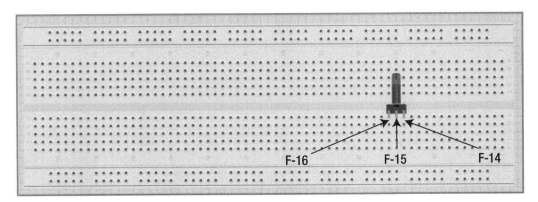

Figure 23-2. Attach the 10K-ohm potentiometer to the solderless bread board

2. Next, attach the two-position terminal block to the solderless bread board at J-31 and J-33, making sure you have the 9V battery harness attached to the terminal block (though you won't be connecting a 9V battery to this connector; you'll be connecting 6V to the servo in the next chapter). Be sure to know which row on the breadboard will provide power (red wire) and which row is ground (black wire). In Figure 23-3, our red wire is on row 33 and our black wire is on row 31.

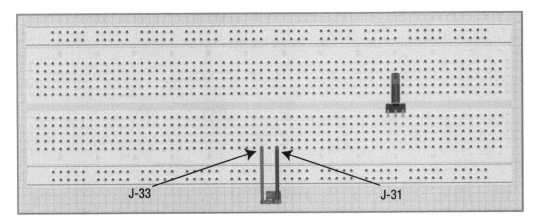

Figure 23-3. Attach the terminal block to the breadboard

3. Now attach the red LED to the breadboard; the positive anode (long leg) should be connected to B-35 and the negative cathode (short leg) should be connected to B-32. Figure 23-4 illustrates this process.

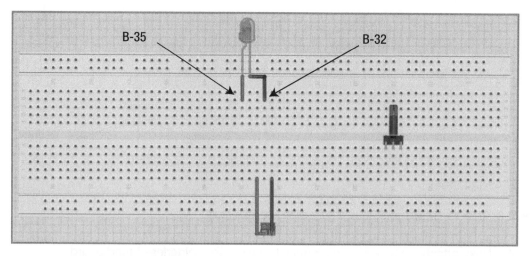

Figure 23-4. Attach the LED to the breadboard

4. Next, attach the 3-pin male stackable header to the servo. Simply push it on to the end of the wire connector coming out of the servo motor. Figure 23-5 illustrates this process.

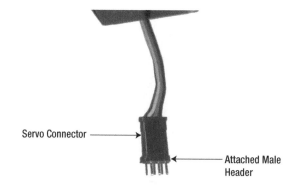

Servo Connector

Attached Male Header

Figure 23-5. Attach the male stackable header to the servo connector

5. Now connect the servo to the breadboard. Be certain the signal wire (white, yellow, or orange) is inserted into A-52, the power wire (red) into A-51, and the ground wire (black) into A-50. Figure 23-6 illustrates this process.

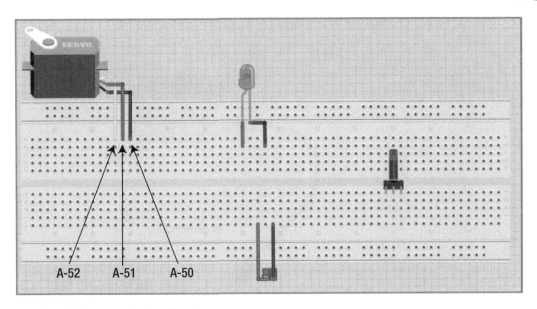

Figure 23-6. Attach the servo to the breadboard

6. Now attach a black jumper wire from one side of the breadboard to the ground strip on the other side, as shown in Figure 23-7. Notice that we've connected both ground columns, indicated by the blue line. If your breadboard doesn't have the color strip, just make a note of which two columns on your breadboard you've designated as ground.

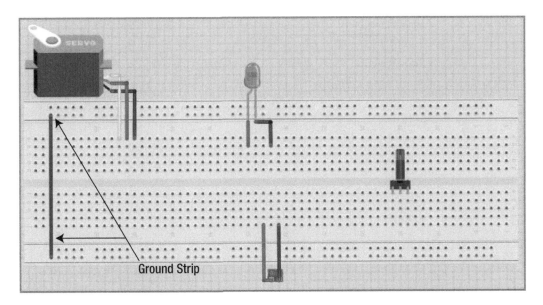

Figure 23-7. Attach the ground strips to one another

7. Connect the 9V connector to the Arduino, as shown in Figure 23-8.

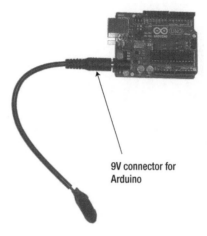

9V connector for
Arduino

Figure 23-8. Attach the 9V connector to the Arduino

8. Run a wire (we used black) from ground on the Arduino to the ground column
    on the breadboard. Notice in Figure 23-9 that this wire is connected on the
    row closest to the blue line. If your breadboard doesn't have the blue line,
    make certain this wire is on the same column as the jumper wire you ran from
    one side of the breadboard to the other (to connect the ground columns).

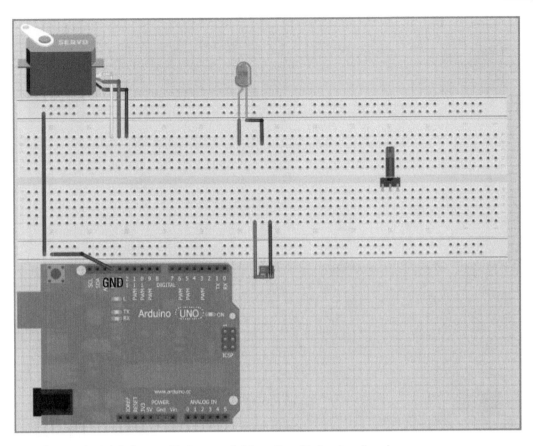

Figure 23-9. Connect the Arduino's ground to the ground strip on the solderless breadboard

9. Now attach the grounds of each of the components. First, use a jumper wire to connect the potentiometer ground to the ground column of the breadboard—just insert a wire into the ground column (closest to the blue line) and then insert the other end of the wire into J-14. The LED ground (the cathode) will have a wire running from the ground column (closest to blue line) to C-32. The servo ground (black wire) will go from the ground column (closest to blue line) to B-50. Finally, the two-position terminal block will have a wire running from the ground column to H-31. Figure 23-10 illustrates this process.

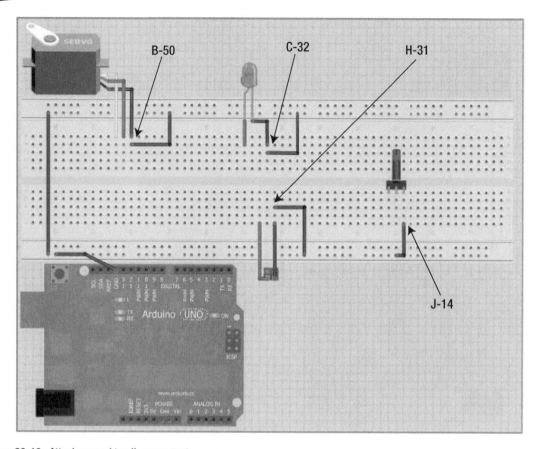

Figure 23-10. *Attach ground to all components*

10. Add the 330-ohm resistor to the breadboard at C-35 and C-40, as shown in Figure 23-11.

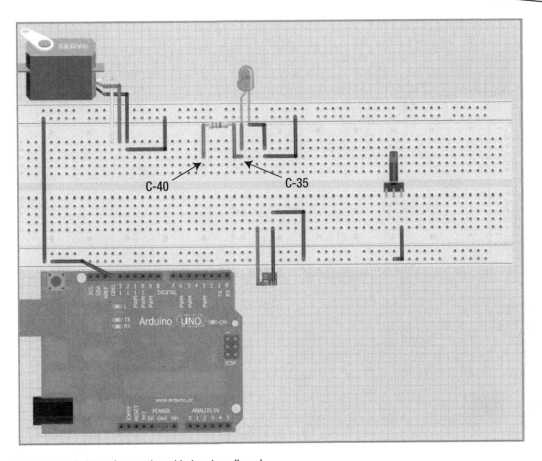

Figure 23-11. Attach the resistor to the solderless breadboard

11.   Next, connect the power side of the two-position terminal block (H-33) to the servo power (B-51). We used a red wire. Figure 23-12 illustrates this process.

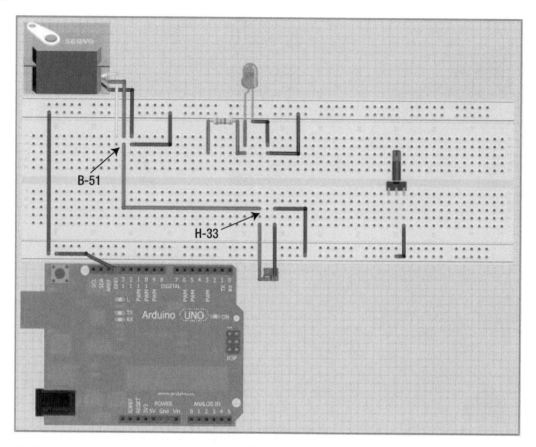

Figure 23-12. Connect power from the two-position terminal block to the servo

12. Connect the Arduino's 5V power to the other side of the potentiometer by adding a jumper wire from +5V on the Arduino to J-16. We used a red wire, but any color is fine. Figure 23-13 illustrates this process.

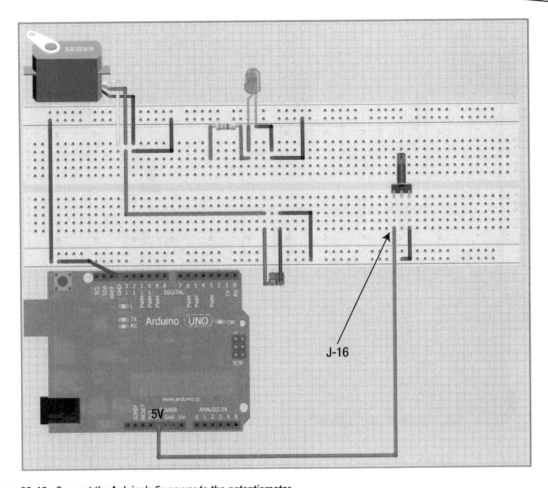

Figure 23-13. *Connect the Arduino's 5v power to the potentiometer*

13.   Connect analog pin 0 (A0) on the Arduino to the wiper, the middle pin of the
       potentiometer, at J-15. We used a green wire here, but any color will work.
       Figure 23-14 illustrates this process.

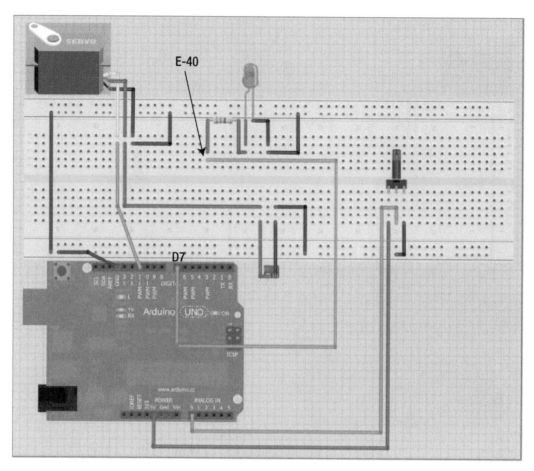

Figure 23-16. Connect digital pin 7 from the Arduino to the resistor attached to the LED

16. And that's it! The Challenge 6 gizmo is completed, and Figure 23-17 shows how the final circuit should look.

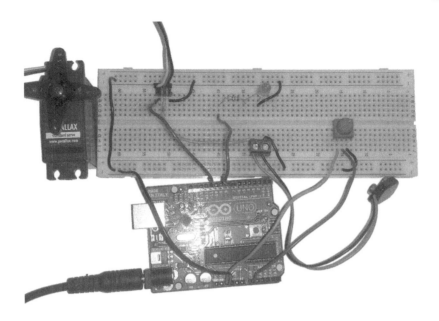

Figure 23-17. *The finished circuit*

Wow! You just created a servo controller that will help Elle and Cade control the robotic arm. It might look complicated, but if you take a moment and examine where all the wires go, it'll start to make sense. Every component must be connected to ground, so you see a lot of black wires connected to one of the two ground columns that run parallel to the blue line on the breadboard. Try and see if you can find all the power wires!

Don't connect power to the Arduino or motor yet. You have to upload the sketch before you give power to the gizmo, so be sure to follow along in Chapter 24 before attaching the 9V battery.

Challenge 6: Examining the Software

With the Challenge 6 gizmo, you've got a small controller (consisting of the Arduino and a potentiometer) that can control the movement of a servo motor. Most 6V hobby servo motors work in an identical manner, no matter their size, which means you can test your controller on a small servo. Once you've determined that the controller works, you simply connect it to a larger servo motor (with a larger power supply, of course).

You have the Challenge 6 gizmo built, so hopefully you have a good sense of how it's wired up—and that means it's time for the sketch that will control the hardware. We're going to walk you through the short sketch that will let you tune the servo so it can alert you when it reaches specific locations—30 degrees, for example.

The sketch could be enhanced by giving it the ability to save these positions and "replay" them at a later time. But for now, what we want you to get out of this challenge is an understanding of how to gain basic control over a servo motor.

Let's think about what we expect from this sketch. First, we obviously need to define how all the various connections are made to the Arduino. This means defining some variables to hold values that correspond to the pins on the Arduino where connections are made.

We're going to tell you something about programming libraries, and specifically about one called the servo library, a built-in bit of programming that provides a substantial amount of control of servos—while saving you a lot of typing. This library is like a pre-programmed set of commands that tell the servo how to operate. And because it's pre-programmed, your sketch is shorter in length and much less complicated.

We also want to use the serial monitor to view the actual values (in degrees) that the servo has rotated. (Remember, the serial monitor lets you write or read data to or from the Arduino so you can interface with the Arduino from a computer.) If we always start at 0 degrees, it would be nice to be able to turn the potentiometer a bit slower as we approach the first target of 30 degrees. The serial monitor provides visual feedback that will help you tune your controller to get it as close as possible to the desired locations.

We'll add a bit of code that will light up an LED when we're close—when the servo motor is within 5 degrees of the correct angle. That means when you're aiming for the servo to hit the 30 degree target, the LED will light up when it points between 30 and 35 degrees. This is accurate enough for our needs, but you may want to do some research on your own to determine methods for getting the accuracy of the servos even closer to the actual desired target.

Don't worry, we'll break down the sketch a bit more in a moment and explain each part in some detail. But before we go over the complete sketch, let's take a quick look at the servo library.

Servo Library Explained

The servo library lets you control up to 12 servos at a time. It includes two functions you can add to a sketch that save you from having to type up even more code: `Servo.attach(pin)` and `Servo.write(value)`. Think of a library as a collection of smaller sketches that are bundled together and can be used in your own sketches simply by inserting their name and some other information.

ANDREW 5.0

Libraries can be confusing, but think of it like this: Imagine if you wrote down directions to your house and saved it on your computer as a file called DirectionsHouse.txt. When someone e-mails you and asks for directions to your house, you could either type it all up again or simply attach the file to the e-mail. Libraries are like inserting attachments into your sketches; they contain code that's already been written so you don't have to recreate it.

Now imagine a folder called DIRECTIONS that contains three files—DirectionsHouse.txt, DirectionsSchool.txt, and DirectionsMall.txt. You could e-mail the folder to your friends and tell them which of the three documents to open depending on where you want them to go. In a sense, these three files inside the folder are like the functions you'll use in your own sketch: each function does one specific task and you can choose which of the tasks to use. The folder is the library and the three documents inside it are the functions.

There are a few more functions in the servo library but you won't be using them for this challenge. To find out more about these functions, visit `http://arduino.cc/en/Reference/Servo`.

But how do you use an Arduino library? First you need to include the library in your sketch by simply typing #include <Servo.h> at the beginning of your sketch. Here, we've specified the servo library by adding <Servo.h>, and that's how you'd add any library that exists in the Libraries folder within the Arduino 1.0 folder).

Next, you need to create an instance of the `servo` class. Think of an instance as a copy. You don't send your friends your original folder; instead, you create a copy (which can even have different attributes) and send that to them. Here you are creating an instance of the `servo` object so you can use it to control the servo's attributes. For example, you control where the Arduino sees the servo by using the function `myServo.attach(int pin)`. The process is like naming a variable—you type the name of the library (Servo) and then follow it with the name you wish to use (such as `myServo`).

The following declaration is how the instance is created in our sketch: Servo myServo. This will then be called everytime you call a servo function. Let's say you want to call the function that powers up the servo, which is connected to digital pin 11 on the Arduino. To do so, you'd add the attach(pin) function like this: myServo.attach(11). Here's what the two functions we use in the Challenge 6 sketch actually do:

- Servo.attach(int pin) tells the Arduino which pin the servo is connected to. All you have to do is attach the servo's signal wire to a digital pin of your choosing and assign that pin to the argument within the parentheses. For example, if the servo is connected to digital pin 11 of the Arduino, you'd use Servo.attach(11).

- Servo.write(int value) sends a value (in degrees) to the servo ranging from 0-180 degrees. The servo then moves to the degree specified. For example, if you wanted to move a servo to 90 degrees, you'd use Servo.write(90).

Now that you have a basic understanding of the servo library, let's put it to use by creating a sketch that will control a robotic arm.

The Challenge #6 Sketch

In this challenge we'll use the servo library you just learned about. We'll also use the analogRead function (as we have in previous challenges) to read a value from a potentiometer. We then have to scale down the range of values from the potentiometer from 0-1024 to 0-180, which will give Elle and Cade the ability to control the servo motor completely by turning the dial and rotating the servo in 1-degree increments. Listing 24-1 is the sketch for this challenge.

Listing 24-1. The Challenge 6 Sketch

```
// include the servo library
#include <Servo.h>

// create an instance of the servo class
Servo myservo;

// setup the pins for the project
int potpin = 0;
int LEDPin = 7;
int servoPin = 11;

// give pins an initial value
int potVal = 0;
int modVal = 0;

void setup()
{
  // attach the servo to digital pin 11 of the Arduino
  myservo.attach(servoPin);
  // begin Serial communication
  Serial.begin(9600);
}
```

```
void loop()
{
  // read in the potentiometers value and store that value in the
  // potVal variable
  potVal = analogRead(potpin);
  // map the potVal variable between 0 and 180
  potVal = map(potVal, 0, 1023, 0, 180);
  // write potVal to the servo 0-180 degrees
  myservo.write(potVal);
  // store the remainder of potVal / 30 into modVal
  modVal = potVal % 30;
  // if modVal is less-than-or-equal-too turn LED on.
  if(modVal <= 5)
  {
    digitalWrite(LEDPin, HIGH);
  }
  // if modVal is greater-than 5 the LED will turn off.
  else
  {
    digitalWrite(LEDPin, LOW);
  }
  // print potVal to the serial monitor for debugging
  Serial.println(potVal);
  delay(15);
}
```

Now that you've seen the entire sketch, let's break it down into smaller chunks to see what's going on.

The first bit of code concerns the library we will be using. As you just learned, the #include <Servo.h> line simply lets the Arduino know that the sketch will be using functions in the servo library. In the next line of code, Servo myservo, we define the instance we want to use.

```
// include the servo library
#include <Servo.h>

// create an instance of the servo class
Servo myservo;
```

Next we initialize the various pins and variables:

```
// setup the pins for the project
int potpin = 0;
int LEDPin = 7;
int servoPin = 11;

// give pins an initial value
int potVal = 0;
int modVal = 0;
```

Instead of using the Arduino pin numbers—such as digital pin 7—we create variables to hold these values so they can be used in our sketch. For example, here we create the variable potpin and set it equal to 0. This declaration allows us to use potpin throughout the sketch instead of using 0.

The same goes for LEDPin except we initialize the LEDPin variable to digital pin 7, and servoPin is initialized to pin 11. Now we can use LEDPin instead of 7. The next part initializes potVal and modVal to 0; which means we are storing 0 in the modVal and potVal variables.

The next bit of code is the setup structure for the sketch:

```
void setup()
{
  // attach the servo to digital pin 11 of the Arduino
  myservo.attach(servoPin);
  // begin Serial communication
  Serial.begin(9600);
}
```

Here we simply tell the Arduino to expect to find a servo at digital pin 11. We've used the myservo. attach function as described earlier, but we've also specified that we'll be using the serial monitor to view feedback from the gizmo.

And now comes the main portion of the sketch—the loop structure. We'll break this into a few pieces; here's the first:

```
void loop()
{
  // read in the potentiometer's value and store that value in the
  // potVal variable
  potVal = analogRead(potpin);
  // map the potVal variable between 0 and 180
  potVal = map(potVal, 0, 1023, 0, 180);
  // write potVal to the servo 0-180 degrees
  myservo.write(potVal);
  // store the remainder of potVal / 30 into modVal
  modVal = potVal % 30;
```

When the sketch is executed, the position of the potentiometer is initially set to 0 (using the potpin variable). But when power is supplied to the gizmo, the potentiometer may not necessarily be dialed in to the 0-degree position. Don't worry about that—the sketch's analogRead function will determine the position of the potentiometer and the servo will rotate quickly to match its location. This is okay, because you're going to use the potentiometer to move the servo back to the 0 position if it doesn't start there initially.

> **Note**   You can download a small gauge at `http://arduinoadventurer.com` that you can use to see where the 0, 30, 60, 90, 120, 150, and 180 degree positions are located. Attach a small piece of tape or put a drop of nail polish on the arm of the servo that points to the 0 degree position.

Next, we scale potVal from 0 to 180 degrees using the map function we used in previous challenges. The potentiometer actually returns values from 0 to 1023, but we don't need that wide a range. We need 0 to 180, so we use the map function to force the 0–1023 range to squeeze down and become 0–180.

Remember that the loop portion of the sketch just keeps repeating and repeating until you kill the power to the Arduino or hit the reset button. Because it keeps looping, it's always checking the position of the potentiometer. When you first turn the gizmo on, that position is set to 0 (potpin = 0) and the servo won't turn until you turn the potentiometer.

Once you start turning the potentiometer, its position is stored in the potVal variable. The turning of the servo occurs because the write function is called and is given the value stored in potVal. The line of code is myservo.write(potVal). This write function is what actually rotates the servo.

Remember that we want the servo to point at specific locations (such as 60 degrees), so we've created a variable called modVal. The modVal variable is named after the modulo symbol (%); this symbol is actually a very usful tool in programming because it returns the remainder of one variable divided by a second variable. Our sketch uses the line modVal = potVal % 30. This means take whatever value is stored in potVal and divide by 30 and then store the remainder in the modVal variable.

Suppose we've rotated the potentiometer so that the servo is pointing at the 98 degree mark. This line of code will divide 98 by 30, giving us remainder of 8 (98 divided by 30 = 3 remainder 8). The value of modVal will equal 8 in this instance, and that remainder value will help us fine-tune the servo's rotations. Here's the code that shows you how that is done:

```
// if modVal is less-than-or-equal-too turn LED on.
if(modVal <= 5)
{
  digitalWrite(LEDPin, HIGH);
}
// if modVal is greater-than 5 the LED will turn off.
else
{
  digitalWrite(LEDPin, LOW);
}
// print potVal to the serial monitor for debugging
Serial.println(potVal);
delay(15);
}
```

It's an If-Else statement just as you've used in previous challenges. If the value stored in the modVal variable is less than or equal to 5, we're right where we want to be. Remember, when we want the servo to be pointing at 30 degrees, we'll take anything between 30 and 35. So if the servo is pointing at 34 degrees, the modVal will be holding a value of 4 (34 divided by 30 equals 1 remainder 4). This value is less than or equal to 5, so the line digitalWrite(LEDPin, HIGH) is executed, turning on the LED and letting us know we've hit our target.

What happens if we dial in the servo so it's pointing at the 29-degree position? Well, 29 divided by 30 is 0 remainder 29, and 29 is greater than 5. When this happens, the Else portion of the sketch is executed—digitalWrite(LEDPin, LOW) keeps the LED turned off, alerting us to the fact we need to tweak the potentiometer a bit and get it closer to 30-35 degree range. (And the same pattern follows for the 60, 90, 120, 150, and 180 locations.)

Finally, we send the value stored in the potVal variable to the serial monitor so we can see the actual servo location on the computer screen. A delay(15) means there is a slight pause (only 15 milliseconds) before the sketch loops again and takes a reading of the potentiometer's position. This delay is used just to free up some processing time so that the mircocontroller has time to do other things (such as reading data from sensors, or writing to the serial monitor).

Solve Challenge #6

Ok let's use this gizmo! First upload Listing 24-1 to your Arduino, then attach a 9V battery to the Arduino and a 6V battery holder to the other power connector, as shown in Figure 24-1. After you have attached both of the battery packs to the Arduino and servo power source, your project should start right up. Turn the potentiometer all the way to the right; the servo should move unless the potentiometer is already at the rightmost position. Now all you need to do is turn the potentiometer to each of the following values (all of the values have a tolerance of 5 degrees) 0,30,60,90,120,150,180. At each of these values the LED should light up. If you are having problems targeting the specified angles, you can use the serial monitor to track your servo's location. Figure 24-2 illustrates this process. Figure 24-3 shows the finished challenge.

Figure 24-1. 9V connector connected to servo power

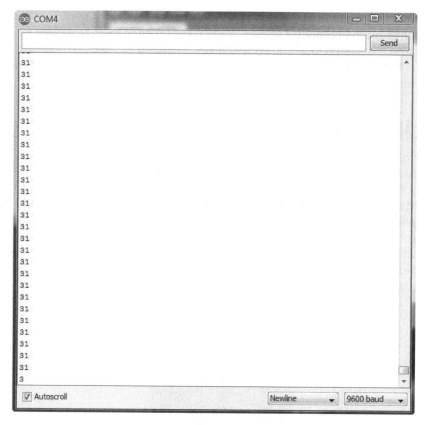

Figure 24-2. The serial monitor is used in this challenge to debug the servo's position

Figure 24-3. The finished gizmo for Challenge #6

Congratulations! Now you've got a controller that will help Cade and Elle dial in the tool robot so it can perform its duties at the 30, 60, 90, 120, 150, and 180 positions. And now that they've got the power restored to the shuttle bay, they're one step closer to getting off the station.

Chapter 25

Push the Button

Elle and Cade had watched in amazement as the tools whirled from station to station inside the small transparent room, re-engaging the various power connections and safety switches that had been disabled. Their small controller unit had managed to successfully rotate the large servo motor at the base of the tool station in thirty-degree increments. It was a high-five moment, and Cade slapped Elle's hand as the final switch was thrown.

"Power has been successfully restored to the station," said Andrew. "Nice work."

"Thanks," Cade and Elle replied together.

"It's time to get to the shuttle," Andrew added. "I'm detecting Mr. Canvin on Level 3, and I believe he's moving to Level 4 now. You need to hurry. I'll instruct you on the shuttle's controls as you walk. Just follow the emergency arrows on the walls; I've set them to lead you to the shuttle bay on Level 11."

Backup Plan

"Do we need our supplies?" asked Cade, nodding at the two toolboxes and the laptop bag.

"Take them," replied Andrew. "Just in case."

Elle nodded. "Might as well be prepared, right?"

"Let's go," said Cade, heading to the opposite side of the engineering room where a large red arrow was flashing at the door.

Elle slung the laptop bag over her shoulder and picked up her toolbox. "Andrew, when we leave in the shuttle, what will happen to Gunther?"

"Once you are safely away, I'll tell him where to go to find an environmental suit that will provide oxygen and heat. The suit should give him enough time before an emergency team arrives."

"But what if they're late? Or what if they have trouble reaching him in time?" asked Elle, following Cade out the door and into another hallway.

"There's a risk he'll run out of oxygen. He won't be able to change suits quickly enough, but I'll do my best to assist him in moving to the safest parts of the station. It's the best I can do, Elle."

Elle shook her head. "I don't like it. Maybe we should just tell him we're on the shuttle and give him some time to get there and leave with us."

"Too dangerous, Elle," said Andrew. "I don't know Mr. Canvin's intentions, but he's here without permission and he is currently in possession of some valuable antique equipment. I would not trust him with your safety."

"Well, something's got to be done, Andrew. I don't want him running out of oxygen or freezing to death," replied Elle.

"Elle, I understand your hesitation, but….,"

Elle interrupted Andrew. "I'm not leaving him in the same situation Cade and I would be in if he were to leave in the shuttle, Andrew. End of discussion."

Control Center

Cade had only been listening in on the conversation, but his friend was right. He didn't like the idea of leaving anyone in a life-threatening situation either, even the thief. He stopped and turned to face Elle. "Maybe we don't have to leave him in danger."

Elle gave Cade a confused look. "We take him with us, right?"

Cade shook his head. "No way. I agree with Andrew there… I don't trust this guy at all."

"So what do we do?" asked Elle.

"Andrew, can we turn life support back on? Is it possible?"

There was a slight pause before Andrew responded. "Yes, it is possible, Cade. But it would require the two of you going to the Control Center on Level 12. And Mr. Canvin is quickly making his way up the levels. I don't think there's enough time."

"Well, if he gets off the station before us, we'll at least have life support," said Elle.

"But the station is still dangerous, Elle. There are small fires and I can't predict further damage to the station that might impact life support. A breach in the hull could cause a vacuum and loss of oxygen. There might be another…"

"We're going to the Control Center, Andrew. Right?" said Elle, looking at Cade.

Cade grinned. "Sounds like a plan."

Crazy Plan

Cade sighed and leaned against a control panel in the Control Center. "This is crazy. You're telling me we can re-enable life support, but when we do, Gunther will be notified and know that someone else is on the station?"

"That is correct, Cade," replied Andrew. "A station-wide message will be broadcast over all the communication channels. Mr. Canvin is smart enough to know what he did in the Control Center and that it can only be overridden by a human user."

"So we enable it and get to the shuttle as fast as we can," said Elle. "Where is he right now?"

"He just triggered one of your motion sensors on Level 6."

"So he's got five levels to get to the shuttle and we have one level to deal with. I think we win, Andrew," said Cade."

"Yes, but you're going to need time to prep the shuttle for launch. What happens if you encounter a problem along the way or on the shuttle? He could still reach the shuttle before you can launch."

"This is so frustrating," said Elle. "Can't you do something to slow him down? Maybe close some doors on him?"

"That is actually not a bad idea," replied Andrew. "You can access the shuttle bay directly from the Control Center using the dedicated emergency tube located in the far corner of the room."

Elle and Cade both turned to stare into the emergency tube behind them. A single ladder was visible, running from the ceiling and down into the opening in the floor.

"So, go ahead and do it," said Cade. "Lock him in."

"It requires pressing a manual override button on the station to your left, Cade," said Andrew. "But the override will lock down all doors, including the door to the emergency tube. It'll close and lock in less than one second."

"So we can lock all the doors, but we'll also be locked in the Control Center?" asked Elle.

"Yes," said Andrew.

"You're right, Cade. This is crazy," said Elle. "We've come this far, this close to the shuttle, and our only solution is to trap ourselves?"

Cade pulled on Elle's arm. "Come on, Elle. You get to the shuttle. I'll stay and deal with the override."

Elle pulled away. "No way! You go… I'll stay."

"Elle, come on! I'll be okay. You get out of here and let the rescue team know I'm locked in here."

"And what happens if Gunther finds a way to override the door locks and finds his shuttle missing? He might not be too happy with anyone he finds left on the station."

"Well, one of us has to stay behind and one has to go. Unless you've got some psychic powers and can press the button with your mind," said Cade with a smirk. "You want to flip a coin?"

"Do you have one?"asked Elle.

"We'll spin a battery," said Cade. "We've got plenty of those. The battery will point to the person who stays, deal?"

Elle thought for a moment. "Okay, deal."

Cade began digging through his toolbox for a battery.

"Elle and Cade, I have a solution," said Andrew. "But you've got to hurry. See the flashlight mounted to the side of the control panel? Take it and make certain it works."

The Flashlight

Cade picked up the flashlight stuck to the side of the panel and slid the power button. The flashlight turned on instantly. "Works!"

Elle smiled. "Okay. We have a working flashlight. How does that help us?"

"I'm going to have you assemble a small device that will push the button for you."

Cade grinned. "Nice! We can program it to wait a few seconds to let us get into the emergency tube!"

Elle smiled back at her friend. "It's not that far… maybe a 10- or 20-second delay?"

"A time delay is too risky," said Andrew. "If there's an error in your program related to the time delay, the locks could engage before you have time to get in the tube."

"So, no timer," said Cade. "What do we use to trigger the button press?"

"A simple photoresistor should work," replied Andrew. "Elle, please get your laptop open and ready for the program I'll give you. Cade, please open your toolboxes and retrieve the following parts…"

Andrew began reciting a small list of parts that Cade was able to locate quickly. Meanwhile, Elle opened the laptop and waited for Andrew to finish instructing Cade in the hardware assembly.

Cade looked over at Elle with a smile. "I'd sure like to see Gunther's face when the doors lock."

"Me, too," said Elle. "But I'd much rather see the inside of that shuttle."

Cade nodded. "Yeah, you're right. Okay, Andrew… what do I do?"

Chapter 26

Challenge 7: Fun Stuff to Know

You're probably quite familiar with the concept of remote control. Anyone who has ever pointed a remote control at a television to change the channel knows the benefits of not having to get up off the couch! Some of you might have used a remote control device to steer a small car around a room, and maybe you've even had the good fortune to pilot a small plane or helicopter using a handheld controller. These are examples of performing a task on an object without actually having to touch that object.

Well, Cade and Elle have found themselves in a not-so-fun situation that also involves needing to perform a task remotely. In order for them to get to the emergency tube safely so they can finally make their way to the shuttle bay, they need to push a certain button that will close and lock all the doors. The only problem is that the doors will close so fast they won't have time to get into the tube! That's why they want to build a gizmo that can press that button for them.

The Arduino by itself can do many things, but you'll see its true power when you begin attaching additional components to it, such as motors and buzzers and even more complex electronics. For this challenge, we could add a simple motor and then program the Arduino to count to 10 or 20 before triggering the motor. On the axle of the motor we'd glue or tape a popsicle stick that would substitute for a finger. Place the motor properly, run the program, and 10 or 20 seconds later the motor would spin and the "finger" would press the button.

The motor plus popsicle stick approach is a decent solution, but there are some drawbacks. What if Cade or Elle were running for the door and tripped? If the timer ran out, the door might close on one of them before they could stand and run the remaining distance. And what if they needed the door to close as soon as they entered the emergency tube? What if there was a danger that might reach them before the timer ran out?

What we can do here is add an extra component that will allow Elle and Cade to decide when to trigger the motor. A sound sensor could work, but any loud noise (such a Cade dropping his toolbox) might trigger the motor too soon.

What about some sort of light sensor? Could we use a special sensor that detects when light is being shone on it and then detects when that light is turned off? Or maybe vice versa? The sensor might detect the normal level of lighting in a room and then trigger the motor when the light gets brighter—maybe when you shine a flashlight on it?

That might work! And that's exactly what we're going to test with Challenge 7.

Yes, by giving Cade and Elle a gizmo that will press the button only when a special sensor triggers the motor, we can give them the time to make it across the room safely and into the emergency tube before locking down the station.

Let's take a look at what will be involved in building this gizmo. And you'll build it in Chapter 27 and program it in Chapter 28.

Let's Look at the Challenge 7 Gizmo

You'll want to turn to Appendix A and make certain you've collected all the parts you'll need to build the Challenge 7 gizmo. In the list of parts for Challenge 7, you'll see one new component called a photoresistor. This is just fancy-speak for a sensor that can detect light.

Figure 26-1 shows the photoresistor as well as the remaining components, all assembled into the Challenge 7 gizmo.

Figure 26-1. The Challenge 7 gizmo—the photoresistor is sticking up on two legs near the top of the breadboard

In addition to the photoresistor, you'll also be adding a servo motor. Why a servo motor and not a regular motor? Well, remember that with a servo motor you can control the rotation of the motor, giving it a specific number of degrees to rotate. This will be extremely helpful when testing the motor to simulate the motion of a finger pressing a button. We could probably use a standard DC motor, but there might be a concern about the motor turning too far too fast. Still, feel free to substitute a DC motor if you like, but it will require some additional testing as well as a modification to the hardware and software you'll see in Chapters 27 and 28.

The circuit shown in Figure 26-1 looks pretty simple, doesn't it? A motor, a terminal block, the photoresistor, an Arduino Uno, and a solderless breadboard, plus a bunch of jumper wire. You're already familiar with all of these items except the photoresistor, so let's examine it for just a moment.

Go ahead and pick up your photoresistor and take a close look. The first thing you're likely to notice is that it looks similar to a standard resistor with its two legs. It has the word "resistor" in its name, so you may be wondering if it works like a basic resistor.

It does behave in a similar manner to a standard resistor in that it resists the flow of electrons. The photoresistor is a high-resistance device when it is dark, but as light is introdueced to the photoresistor the resistance drops so that more voltage can be detected (by the Arduino or other micro-controller). It's a cool little device that can be inserted into gizmos in such a way that current is reduced until a specific level of light is detected on its surface!

ANDREW 5.0

Your readers might want more detailed information on a photoresistor. Be sure to point them to LadyAda's tutorials over at http://learn.adafruit.com/photocells.

Along the left side of the screen are a number of links that explain how to use photoresistors as well as some additional projects that can be assembled using them. (LadyAda refers to photoresistors as photocells, but both terms refer to the same type of component.)

By the way, Limor Fried (LadyAda) is one of the owners of AdaFruit Industries. Her web site, adafruit.com, is a great source of information and special projects for electronics beginners. Be sure to check out the web site and click on the Tutorials option to view over 100 different projects explained in great detail. Many of these are perfect for your readers because they teach even more beginning Arduino skills.

If we know how the photoresistor works, can we come up with a way to use it in a gizmo to trigger a servo motor? Sure!

Think about it. The Arduino will detect more voltage as light is applied to the photoresistor. We can wire up a gizmo that will power a motor—but only let the motor spin when the Arduino detects a certain voltage level. One option would be to connect the photoresistor to a pin (analog input) on the Arduino and have the Arduino test to see how much voltage is detected on the analog input. If it doesn't detect enough voltage, the program on the Arduino wouldn't trigger the servo motor. But if enough voltage is detected (meaning the photoresistor detects light), the Arduino will trigger the servo motor to rotate!

Easy!

ANDREW 5.0

You could create two variations of this gizmo, if you think about it for a moment. For example:

The first variation would power up the gizmo and wait for the photoresistor to detect a flashlight being shone on its surface. If this happens, the servo motors spins.

The second variation would power up the gizmo while shining the flashlight on the photoresistor surface. For this approach to work, you'd have to design the circuit so the motor spins only when the light is turned off. When that happens, the Arduino detects a drop in voltage on the analog input pin it's monitoring (that's connected to the photoresistor), and triggers the motor to rotate.

Which do you think is a better option?

As Andrew just explained, we can build this gizmo using two different methods. We can either build it so that once Elle and Cade are in the emergency tube they shine a light on the photoresistor or we can build it so they are shining a light on the photoresistor as they walk to the emergency tube and then turn it off once they are inside.

The first option seems like the safest bet – it allows Elle and Cade to enter the emergency tube and then, once they're ready, turn on a flashlight and hit the photoresistor with the beam.

The second option would work, but there's a risk—what if Cade or Elle accidentally gets bumped and the flashlight's beam moves off the photoresistor? That would trigger the motor too early, wouldn't it? And then there's the issue of what happens if the batteries in the flashlight choose the wrong moment to die.

Yep… we agree with you. Let's go with the first option and let Cade and Elle get into the emergency tube before they trigger the photoresistor with the flashlight.

Ready to Build Something?

We're hoping you're starting to come up with some ideas for your own gizmos. You've got quite a collection of components in your toolbox now, and you've also learned how to integrate them into a circuit with an Arduino.

Resistors, servo and DC motors, LEDs, buzzers, potentiometers, push buttons, a temperature sensor, and now a photoresistor… you've got enough components to build some really cool things! Hey, you might even have enough parts and knowledge to build something that could operate all on its own, impress your family and friends, and be a great example of just how far you've come with your Arduino skills! But what might that final gizmo be?

Well, let's get through Challenge 7 first. Once Cade and Elle are in the shuttle bay, all that remains is getting them on the shuttle and off the station. And to do that, they need to trap Gunther Canvin and turn the station's life support back on. So, let's help them out by building the Challenge 7 gizmo so we can press that button and lock down the doors of the station.

Time to build!

Chapter 27

Challenge 7: Examining the Hardware

Well, it's time to tackle another challenge. Can you think back to when you began reading this book and remember how you felt about the eight challenges in front of you? Were you nervous? Did you think the Arduino was going to be just too complicated for you to figure out? Or were you excited and eager to get moving?

However you felt about the experience that faced you, we'd like you to know just how impressed we are that you've made it this far! You've learned a lot, and you've still got to finish building and programming the Challenge 7 gizmo as well as the ultra-cool and impressive Challenge 8 we're so anxious to introduce to you.

We've talked previously about how to tackle problems…how to look at both the hardware and software requirements. We hope you're starting to develop your own methodology for examining a problem and thinking over just what will be involved in solving it. Don't doubt yourself—if you've made it this far, you've absorbed a lot of techniques and knowledge that can be applied to gizmos you'll be building on your own…and soon!

But let's talk about that Arduino and the electronics information you've got stored in your head. Are you worried that you might forget some of it? Well, we forget bits and pieces all the time! It happens. But we have some very good news for you.

In school, you're often given tests where you have to memorize large amounts of information. (What year was the Magna Carta signed? What are the three types of Greek columns? Argh.) If your teachers are anything like ours, they don't often let you take open-book tests. We had to memorize, memorize, memorize. But when it comes to electronics and Arduino information, we encourage you to *always* use any book you can get your hands on. As a matter of fact, we have our own libraries of books we reference all the time. James has a couple dozen electronics books and Harold has even more!

I guess what we're trying to say is that whenever you need a piece of information, you just need to know where to go to find it. The Internet is a great resource. Open up a Google search page and type in your question and you're likely to get dozens of possibilities to check out. And, of course, there are some great Arduino discussion forums where beginners can search for solutions and, if they don't find one, post a question for others to answer.

The same goes for books. We'll be providing you with a list of some great Arduino and electronics books on the book's website – `arduinoadventurer.com` (as well as some web sites). Often, all you have to do is flip to the index of a book to find the page number that has your answer!

And here's some advice we've heard our entire lives and you probably have as well—don't reinvent the wheel. If you need to figure out how to wire up a simple buzzer, take a look out there to see what others have done and how they've implemented their own circuits. You'll likely find numerous variations, but one of them might be exactly what you're looking for because it uses the same components you've got in your components collection.

And speaking of your collection…you're about to add a brand-new component to it—the photoresistor. The photoresistor has some really cool applications, and you're about to build a gizmo that is a perfect example of how it can be used.

Right now, Cade and Elle need to get into the emergency tube before the station's doors are closed and locked. To do this, they'll be using a gizmo that will press a button when one of them triggers it. And they'll trigger the gizmo with a simple flashlight! Let's take a look at the gizmo that will allow Cade and Elle to trigger the button remotely and let them get to the shuttle bay without getting trapped.

A Closer Look at a Photoresistor

We explained in Chapter 26 that the photoresistor works by allowing more current to flow through it when a sufficient level of light is detected on the surface. Take a look at your photoresistor. See those squiggly lines on its surface? Those lines are photosensitive (they react to light). As light hits the surface, the lines react and allow more current to flow (triggering an increase in voltage).

The way we use a photoresistor with the Arduino is by connecting it to one of the Arduino's analog input pins. The analog pin can't detect resistance, but it can be configured to detect voltage. That's what we want! Photoresistors are photoconductive. This means that a photoresistor will become more electrically conductive as more light is applied to it. So when we apply light to our photoresistor, we are allowing more current through the photoresistor. In turn that greater current results in more voltage across the 10K Ohm resistor, which is read by the analog pin of the Arduino. In the sketch we can add a bit of code that basically says "Did the voltage go up to a certain level? Yes? Then execute the code that controls the servo motor!"

Take a look at Figure 27-1. This photoresistor should look like the one you're holding. It's got two legs (like a standard resistor) but it doesn't matter how you insert it into the breadboard. Unlike an LED (with a short and long leg), you can insert the photoresistor without worrying which metal leg is connected to ground and which is connected to an analog pin on the Arduino.

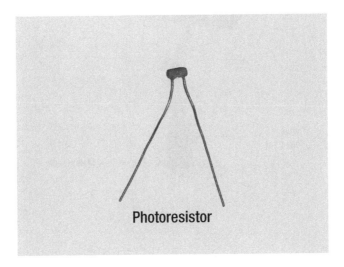

Figure 27-1. The photoresistor used in the Challenge 7 gizmo

The rest of the components you're already familiar with—servo motor, two-position terminal block, jumper wires, resistor, 9V battery connector, and Arduino. All that's needed to get this gizmo built is to follow the instructions below, so let's get started!

Let's Build the Challenge 7 Gizmo

Once again, be sure to check Appendix A to make certain you've got all the parts you need to build this gizmo. Once you're satisified you've got them all assembled, you're ready to go!

1. First attach the photoresistor to the solderless breadboard at positions J-25 and J-28. Figure 27-2 illustrates this process.

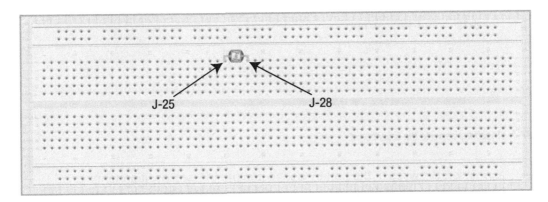

Figure 27-2. Attach photoresistor to solderless bread board

2. Next, attach the 3-pin male stackable header to the servo. Figure 27-3 illustrates this process.

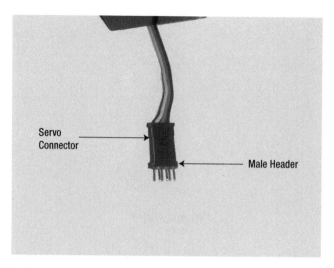

Figure 27-3. Attach the 3-pin stackable header to the servo

3. Now connect the servo to the breadboard at positions J-12 through J-14, where J-12 is the ground (black wire) of the servo. Figure 27-4 illustrates this process.

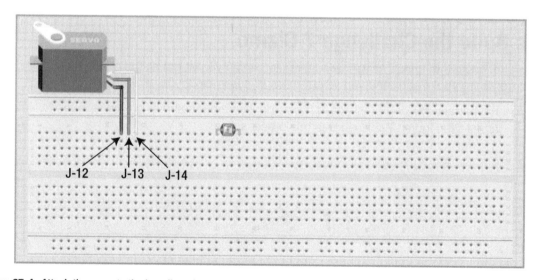

Figure 27-4. Attach the servo to the breadboard

4. Now insert the wires of the battery connector into the two-position terminal block. (Take a look at Figure 27-6 to see how we did it.) Also, make certain to connect the jumper wires for +6V to the row that matches the red wire, and the jumper wires for ground to the row that matches the black wire. Figure 27-5 illustrates this process.

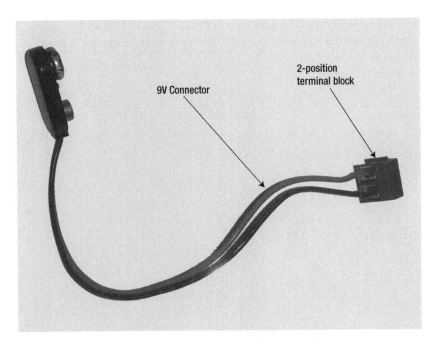

Figure 27-5. Attach the battery connect to the two-position terminal block

5. Push the two-position terminal block into the breadboard. Power (red wire) should be connected to A-5 and ground (black wire) should be connected to A-7. Figure 27-6 illustrates this process.

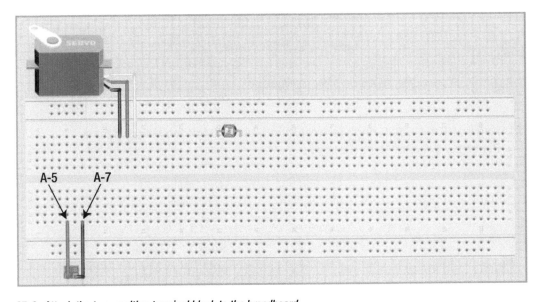

Figure 27-6. Attach the two-position terminal block to the breadboard

6. Now run a jumper wire from the +5V pin on the Arduino to I-25 of the breadboard. (We used a red wire, but any color will work.) Figure 27-7 illustrates this process.

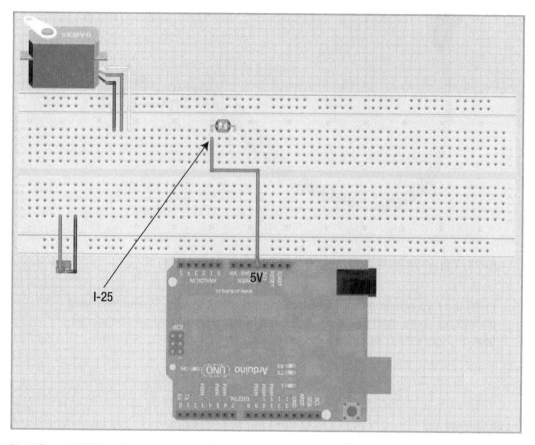

Figure 27-7. Connect 5V power from the Arduino to the photoresistor

7. Add in a 10K (10,000-ohm) resistor from I-28 to I-34 of the breadboard. Figure 27-8 illustrates this process.

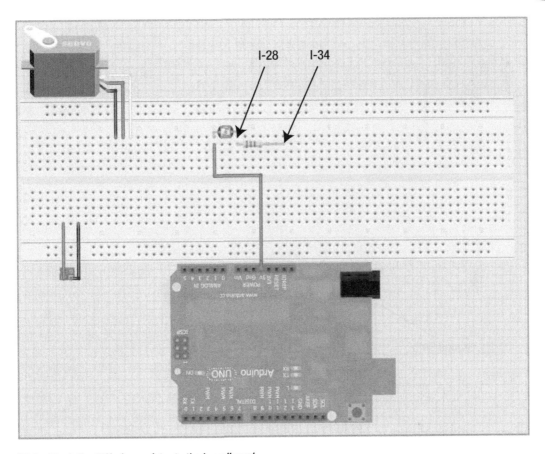

Figure 27-8. Attach the 10K-ohm resistor to the breadboard

8. Run a jumper wire (we used black) from a GND pin on the Arduino to the ground rail (the column running parallel to the blue line) of the breadboard. Figure 27-9 illustrates this process.

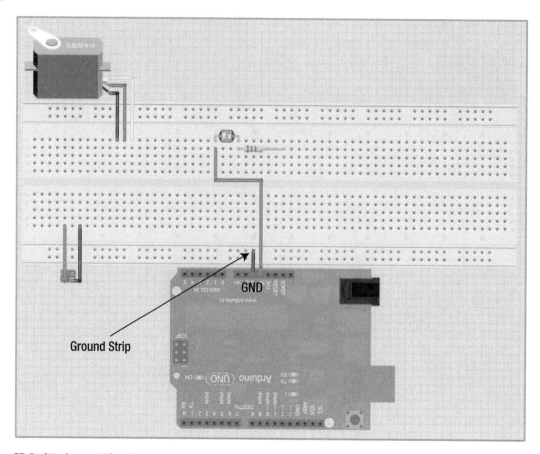

Figure 27-9. Attach ground from the Arduino to the ground rail on the breadboard

9. Connect the two ground columns (running parallel to the blue lines on either side of the breadboard) using a jumper wire (we used black). Figure 27-10 illustrates this process.

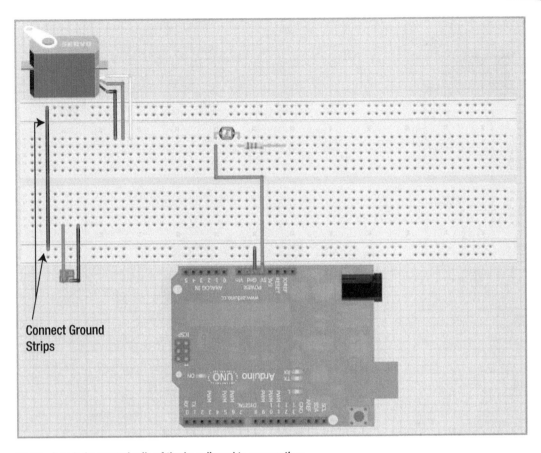

Connect Ground
Strips

Figure 27-10. *Attach the ground rails of the breadboard to one another*

10. Run a jumper wire (we used black) from the ground rail of the breadboard
     to D-7. Run another jumper wire (black) from the other ground rail of the
     breadboard to J-34. Another jumper wire (black) needs to connect I-12 to the
     ground rail of the breadboard. Figure 27-11 illustrates this process.

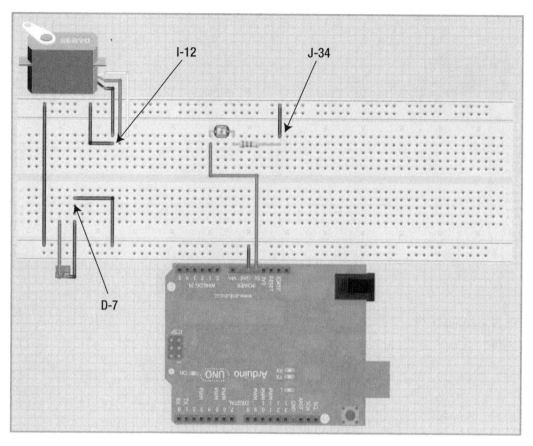

Figure 27-11. Attach ground to the servo, two-position terminal block, and the 10K-ohm resistor

11.   Next, run a jumper wire (we used red) from D-5 of the breadboard to F-13.
       Figure 27-12 illustrates this process.

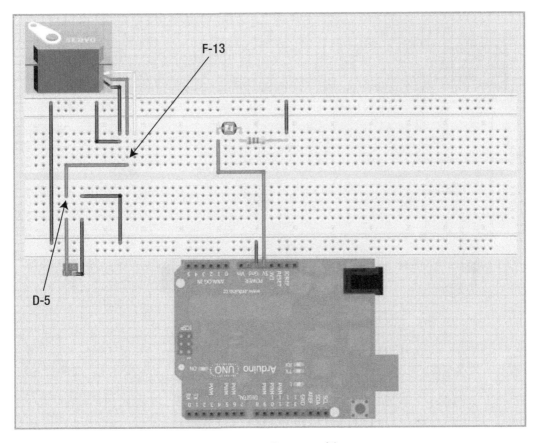

Figure 27-12. *Attach the power side of the battery connector to the power of the servo*

12. Run a jumper wire (we used green) from analog pin 0 (A0) on the Arduino to H-28 on the breadboard. Figure 27-13 illustrates this process.

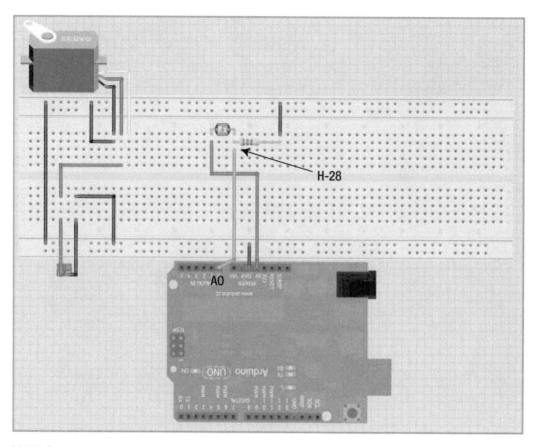

Figure 27-13. Connect analog pin 0 of the Arduino to the photoresistor

13. Use another jumper wire (we used green) to connect digital pin 3 (D3) on the Arduino to G-14 of the breadboard. Figure 27-14 illustrates this process.

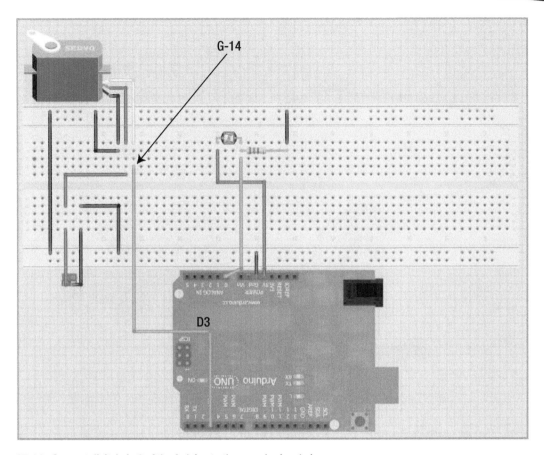

Figure 27-14. *Connect digital pin 3 of the Arduino to the servo's signal pin*

14. Figure 27-15 shows the final gizmo (minus the battery power or USB cable being connected).

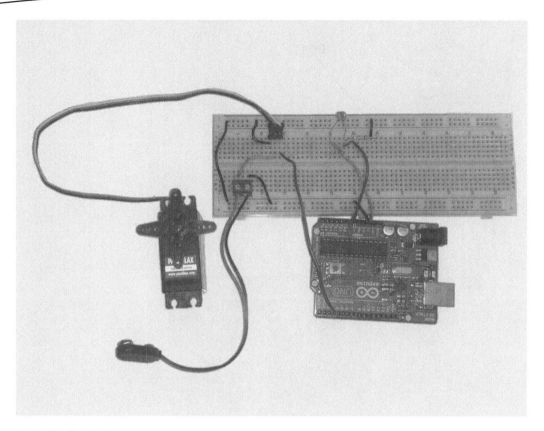

Figure 27-15. The final Challenge 7 gizmo!

Done!

Let's take a quick look. We'll add in a 6V battery pack after the program that powers the servo motor is uploaded to the Arduino. When theArduino detects a certain level of voltage from the photoresistor it will trigger the motor to rotate a certain number of degrees. Look carefully at your circuit and notice how the photoresistor is wired in—it basically connects with two pins on the Arduino. One pin is is attached to an analog input pin of the arduino so that the Arduino can detect the photoresisters voltage level and the other is connected to ground. If a bright-enough light hits the photoresistor, an increase in voltage will flow in the loop and voltage will be detected on A0 on the Arduino!

But the gizmo won't work yet! As you already know, the hardware is only half of the solution. We still need to take a look at the sketch that will make this gizmo work. So, let's move on to Chapter 28 and learn how the sketch will help Cade and Elle trigger the servo motor so that Gunther Canvin can be safely trapped on the station while they make their getaway!

Challenge 7: Examining Software

We've now reached the programming portion of Challenge #7. You're going to need to upload a sketch to your gizmo to help Elle and Cade turn life support back on for Gemini Station and close and lock the doors on the station to trap Mr. Canvin. You'll recognize one key component in this gizmo already—the servo motor. And since you're already familiar with how to program it (including using the Servo Library from Chapter 24), there's only one new piece of hardware you're going to need to learn to integrate into the sketch—the photoresistor.

We will be using the photoresistor just as we used the potentiometer in previous challenges; we'll use the analogRead function to read in the value that the photoresistor is detecting or "sensing." With no functions or libraries to explain in this chapter, let's get straight to the sketch we need for the Challenge #7 gizmo.

The Challenge #7 Sketch

We'll be using analogRead for the photoresistor and the Servo Library for the servo that will press the button to turn life support back on in Gemini Station and close and lock all the doors on the station. Listing 28-1 shows the sketch for Challenge #7. You can either copy and paste this code into the Arduino IDE or you can type it in yourself. We'll also break it down into smaller sections for discussion.

Listing 28-1. Controlling a Servo with Light

```
// include the servo library so this sketch can use it
#include <Servo.h>

// create an instance of the servo type
Servo myServo;

// initialize the photoresistor pin
int photoPin = 0;
int servoPin = 3;
```

```
// create a variable to store the photoresistors value
int photoVal = 0;
int lightLimit = 900;

void setup()
{
  // attach the servo to digital pin 3 of the Arduino
  myServo.attach(servoPin);

  // begin serial communication
  Serial.begin(9600);

  // set the servo to the 0 degree position
  myServo.write(0);
}

void loop()
{
  // set photoVal to the reading on analog pin 0
  photoVal = analogRead(photoPin);

  // if the photoresistor reads a value of 900 or higher
  // set the servo to 0 degree position
  // wait for a second, then set the
  // servo to 70 degrees, then wait half a second and return
  // the servo back to the 0 degree position
  if (photoVal >= lightLimit)
  {
    myServo.write(0);
    delay(1000);
    myServo.write(70);
    delay(500);
    myServo.write(0);
    delay(500);
  }
  else
  {
    // do nothing or add your own code here
  }
  // write the photoVal to the serial port for debugging purposes
  Serial.println(photoVal);

  delay(500);
}
```

The sketch starts off by including the servo library:

```
#include <Servo.h>
```

The #include<servo.h> command lets us use the Servo Library for the entire sketch, but first we need to create an instance of the Servo class, which is exactly what this next line does:

```
Servo myServo;
```

That's just what you did for the Challenge #6 gizmo—remember? By creating an instance of the Servo class, you can now use the Servo Library.

Next, we'll create a few variables. The first variable defines where the photoresistor is connected. This variable is called photoPin and is set to 0 because the photoresistor is connected to analog pin 0 of the Arduino. The next variable, servoPin, defines the servo pin location at 3. The variable photoVal comes next and it's also initialized to 0; this variable will be used later in the sketch to store the value the photoresistor senses. Finally, the very important lightLimit variable stores the value that controls the If-Else statement that's used later. Here's the code that relates to the variables:

```
// initialize the photoresistor pin
int photoPin = 0;
int servoPin = 3;

// create a variable to store the photoresistors value
int photoVal = 0;
int lightLimit = 900;
```

Now it's time for the setup structure. First we attach the servo to digital pin 3 of the Arduino:

```
void setup()
{
  // attach the servo to digital pin 3 of the Arduino
  myServo.attach(servoPin);
```

Then we start serial communication:

```
  // begin serial communication
  Serial.begin(9600);
```

To finish, we set the initial position of the servo to 0 degrees and end the setup section with a closing } bracket:

```
  // set the servo to the 0 degree position
  myServo.write(0);
}
```

The next part of the sketch starts the loop structure where the real action takes place. We create the loop and set photoVal to the reading on analog pin 0 of the Arduino:

```
void loop()
{
  // set photoVal to the reading on analog pin 0
  photoVal = analogRead(photoPin);
```

In case you're wondering, the photoVal variable is simply going to hold a voltage reading taken from the photoresistor. That's done using the analogRead command that corresponds to the pin number stored in the photoPin variable (analog pin 0).

Next comes a conditional If-Else statement. With this statement, if the photoresistor has a value greater than or equal to 900 (the lightLimit variable), the servo will move from the 0-degree position to the 70-degree position, then back to the 0-degree position. How do we set the position of the servo? By using few well-placed statements:

```
// if the photoresistor reads a value of 900 or higher
// set the servo to 0-degree position
// wait for a second, then set the
// servo to 70 degrees, then wait half a second and return
// the servo back to the 0-degree position
if (photoVal >= lightLimit)
{
 myServo.write(0);
 delay(1000);
 myServo.write(70);
 delay(500);
 myServo.write(0);
 delay(500);
}
```

The first myServo.write function sets the servo to the 0-degree position. The sketch then waits for one second (1000 milliseconds). The next myServo.write function sets the servo's position to 70 degrees for half a second, and the third myServo.write function sets the servo back to the 0-degree position.

> **Note**   This gadget simulates a finger pushing a button. Depending on the servo motor you've chosen, you may need to experiment with changing the values that make the servo motor rotate to more realistically simulate a human finger.

If the photoresistor doesn't detect a bright light, the Else statement is executed and, as you'd expect, it's blank. There's no action for the servo motor to take because we don't want to trigger it when there's no light. The empty Else statement is shown here:

```
else
  {
    // do nothing or add your own code here
  }
```

Here's the last bit of code inside the loop section:

```
  // write the photoVal to the serial port for debugging purposes
  Serial.println(photoVal);

  delay(500);
}
```

This code sends the value stored in the photoVal variable to the serial port so you can view the data on the screen. There's also a delay that lasts for a half a second (500 milliseconds).

The reason we send photoVal to the serial port is so we can debug and calibrate to the surrounding light. For example, if your house has more light then mine, you can increase the lightLimit variable at the beginning of the sketch to, say, 950 instead of 900. This modification will allow you to tweak the photoresistors limit so it doesn't just allow the servo motor to run continuously. We want the servo to run only when we apply a flashlight or some other intense light to the photoresistor.

Now you can upload the sketch to the Arduino using a USB cable, and then you're ready to run the challenge.

Solve Challenge #7

After you've uploaded the sketch to the Arduino, you need to attach a 6V battery holder to the servo's power connector as shown in Figure 28-1.

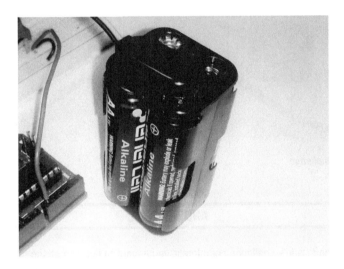

Figure 28-1. A 6V connector connected to servo power

When you're done, you can apply light to the photoresistor using a flashlight or any other device that can create an intense light. Figure 28-2 illustrates the completed challenge.

Figure 28-2. The completed challenge

ANDREW 5.0

If you'd like to recreate Elle and Cade's challenge completely, you'll want to find something to attach to the arm of the servo that can serve as a finger. You may also find that you need to secure the servo to the surface—when the servo's axle rotates, it produces a lot of torque that might actually move the servo!

Securing a Popsicle stick to the servo's arm with some tape will work, or you can try a pencil. The trick is to convert the servo's axle into something that will simulate a human finger capable of pushing a button on a keyboard.

Figure 28-3 illustrates what the Serial Monitor looks like when this challenges device is connected to the computer. Notice that the light around the photoresistor is only 5 values short of triggering the servo to move; its value in normal lighting conditions is between 889 and 891, just below the threshold we set of 900 that would trigger the If statement in the sketch. As soon as we apply direct light to the photoresistor, the servo starts moving. You can see what happens when the light is turned on and pointed at the photoresistor in Figure 28-3—the displayed values jump over 900.

Figure 28-3. Here are some values that were recorded from the Challenge #7 project

Way to go! You just built a gizmo that can press a keyboard button when a strong light source shines on the photoresistor. Now Cade and Elle can safely press the button while they are inside the emergency access tube. Life support will be turned back on and the doors on the station will all close and lock. Mr. Canvin will be trapped, but Cade and Elle will have an unblocked path to the shuttle bay.

Chapter 29

Off the Station

Cade followed Elle down the ladder that led directly into the shuttle bay on level eleven. He was about to jump the few remaining feet to the gridded floor grating, but he paused, taking in the large open bay around him.

"It looks different," Cade said, handing his toolbox down to Elle.

Elle nodded. "It's the same bay we landed on hours ago, but yeah… it does look different." She took the toolbox and set it on the floor. "Tell me again why we brought the toolboxes and laptop? They don't belong to us."

Cade jumped down and smiled. "We'll return them, but I want some sort of proof just in case Mrs. H asks what we've been doing all day. And is that really what we're going to get on? I think we'd be safer putting on some EV suits and just floating away from the station."

The Hulk

Elle turned to look in the direction of Cade's nod. Sitting alone in Bay Seven was nothing less than a shoebox with irregular strips of graphene-reinforced alumiplast, all of different colors, nano bonded over so many locations that the actual shape of the original shuttle could only be imagined. Cooling vapors still floated up and away from the shuttle's rear thrusters, giving Elle the only clue as to the front and rear of the shuttle.

"What a piece of junk!" said Cade, waiting for Elle to get the reference, but only getting a nod of agreement.

"That piece of junk is your only way off the station," replied Andrew over the bay's speaker system. "And she may not look like much, kid, but she's got it where it counts."

Cade laughed out loud. "Andrew, you just got a million bonus points for that response."

Elle was confused and raised her eyebrows at Cade.

Cade shook his head. "Movie night at my house next week. Too long to explain." He picked up the two toolboxes and began walking to the shuttle.

Elle threw the laptop bag over her shoulder and followed. "Andrew, are we good to go?"

"That's an Audi-Timmis Mark IV lander. Based on the configuration of the engines, it's sixteen years old. Unless Gunther has modified the controls, they should be the standard configuration specified by the Isogawa Convention. Emergency entry code on file with the station's AI is 55842. You both have level one pilot licenses?"

"Since age seven," responded Cade. "And I'm up for my level two next month!"

"You forget," said Elle, "that that exam is a heavy written exam and focuses less on hands-on testing."

"Your point?" asked Cade, setting the toolboxes on the floor and tapping in the emergency code into the touchpanel just behind the cockpit's side window.

"I'm just saying that you might want to start reading up on the standard bouy navigation section," replied Elle.

The shuttle's port-side entry panel did not open.

"Not good," said Cade. "I thought all docked shuttles had to provide their emergency codes to the station AI in order to dock."

"One moment," replied Andrew, followed by a five second pause. "I believe you typed it in wrong, Cade. Please try again."

Cade tapped in the code once again, but this time his finger moved slower and he spoke each digit as he tapped each number. The shuttle's entry panel slid open.

"Really?" asked Elle, giving Cade a disapproving look.

"My hands were shaking," he replied. "It's cold in here."

Elle frowned. "Uh huh."

"Just get in," said Cade, grabbing the toolboxes and following Elle into the shuttle.

Launch Problem

Andrew was patched into the shuttle's communication system and was instructing Cade on the pre-flight configurations that needed to be made while Elle buckled herself into the co-pilot's chair. The chair was soft, but Elle noticed that well over half of its surface was covered in duct-tape patches. She was also a bit concerned with the large globs of foam-sealant used around the edge of the synthetic diamond viewport.

"I'm wondering if we wouldn't be safer staying on the station," Elle muttered.

Cade flipped two switches and looked across at Elle with a grin. "After all we've been through today, you're worried about the shuttle?"

"Have you looked around?" asked Elle.

Cade laughed. "My uncle Gavin's shuttle makes this one look like the Governor's private solar-sailer. Relax... I've always been told the more beat up a shuttle looks the safer it is. All the bugs have been worked out."

"Cade, I believe that statement to be in error. Statistically speaking, the quality control found in the manufacturing centers for today's shuttles is much more likely to be of higher quality than that of a shuttle being self-maintained," said Andrew.

"Okay, I want off," said Elle, beginning to unbuckle. "Right now. I'll take my chances on the station."

"Thanks, Andrew," said Cade. "Elle… come on. We're all set. It'll be fine. And look. Two emergency suits." Cade pointed at two adjustable suits strapped to the starboard hull plating.

Elle looked at the suits, noticed something similar to duct-tape stuck across the chest and arms of both suits, and shook her head. "Who is this guy? Every launch has to be a gamble!"

"Ready to launch, Andrew," said Cade. "Buckle up, Elle."

The low whine of the engines grew in volume, and a slight shudder in the shuttle was passed to the two students through the metal framed chairs. Elle buckled herself in again, shaking her head. Cade tapped a small blue button on the panel facing him and put the single headphone over his left ear, bending the microphone down in front of his mouth.

"Gemini Station, this is shuttle 77-A9 requesting emergency departure from Bay Seven. We have cleared all docking clamps and engines are at quarter power. Request entry into Bay Seven airlock."

The voice that responded was completely new to Elle and Cade. **"Shuttle 77-A9, request for emergency departure acknowledged. Respond affirmative for takeover controls by station AI for airlock entry."**

"Affirmative for takeover controls," replied Cade with a glance at Elle. "Here we go."

The shuttle began to move backwards, and Cade and Elle could see the airlock door behind the shuttle opening on a small monitor mounted between them. They watched as the second airlock door that would open and expose the shuttle to the vacuum of space moved closer. Twenty seconds later, the shuttle came to a hard stop, pressing Cade and Elle into their seats.

"Shuttle 77-A9, closing inner airlock door. Depressurization will begin in fifteen seconds."

Elle clinched the armrests on her chair. "Andrew?"

"Yes, Elle."

"Thank you. For everything."

"You are welcome, Elle. You and Cade will be fine. Emergency response teams are less than an hour out. Everything will be okay."

"What about you? What's going to….?"

Elle's question was interrupted by a wailing alarm. She looked across at Cade who was punching a series of buttons that were all flashing red.

"Gemini Station, what is the emergency?" asked Cade.

"Obstruction detected. Inner airlock door will not seal. Attempting to re-open airlock door."

A loud grinding sound was followed by a pause and then another grinding sound.

"Unable to re-open airlock door. Sealing shuttle bay now. Emergency opening of outer airlock door to commence in fifteen seconds."

Cade looked across at Elle, his usual smiling face replaced by one of real concern. "What's happening?"

"The station AI has determined it is safe to open the outer airlock door. There are no other shuttles in the bay, so the loss of pressure in the shuttle bay is acceptable," replied Andrew. "When the outer airlock door opens, exit the station, Cade."

"No arguments from me," said Cade.

Watching the rear view from the small monitor, Elle could see the outer airlock door open. She held her breath the ten seconds it took for the door to fully open.

"Full reverse on the engines, Cade," said Andrew.

Cade flipped a switch and grabbed a small handle to his right and pushed it forward. The sound of the engines rotating in place were replaced as the thrust increased and the shuttle began to shake, but there was no reverse movement. Cade pushed the handle all the way forward and watched as the thrusters mounted on the front of the shuttle glowed bright against the inner airlock door.

"Power down, Cade. Do it now," said Andrew.

Caded pulled the handle down, and the shaking of the shuttle decreased. Cade shook his head, examining all the readouts on the panel in front of him. "Why weren't we moving?" he yelled.

"Shuttle 77-A9, this is Gemini Station awaiting your departure from Bay Seven."

Elle stared at Cade. "We just cannot catch a break, can we?"

Cade frowned. "Everything looks normal on the shuttle's systems."

"I am receiving more information from the station AI," said Andrew. "One moment."

"If he says that one more time…," said Cade.

The Final Fix

"He did what?" yelled Cade. "That's idiotic!"

"Most shuttles do anchor themselves to any asteroids they are mining, but I believe Mr. Canvin did this to prevent someone from doing exactly what you and Cade are doing now."

"Stealing his shuttle," said Cade.

"Borrowing," replied Elle. "But he won't need it in jail."

Gunther Canvin had deployed an anchoring cable underneath the shuttle when he docked. The cable, hidden from view until the shuttle backed out of Bay Seven, was now visible to Andrew using the shuttle bay's surveillance system. Cade and Elle both stared at the small monitor, seeing the thick steel cable extend from the front of the shuttle and under the inner airlock door.

"We can fix this, right?" asked Cade. "One of us just needs to exit the shuttle and cut the line."

"It's too dangerous, Cade. It's supposed to be cut with zero tension. If the inner airlock door wasn't caught on the cable, the station AI could open it and allow the shuttle to dock again."

"So, we can't move forward and we can't move backward," said Elle.

"That is correct," said Andrew. "The anchoring cable must be cut."

"But you just said we can't cut it," replied Cade.

"That is correct. You cannot cut it. But there is a wheeled hand-boring unit in the shuttle's inventory. That tool can easily cut through the cable."

"Great!" yelled Cade. "So one of us just takes it out there, turns it on, and pushes it against the cable and runs. Let's get this done!"

Elle was beginning to suspect the solution would require a bit more work. "Andrew, it's not that easy, is it?"

"No, Elle. I'm sorry. The tool is not automated and it's big. The only area it would be able to fit in to cut the cable is inaccessible to you."

"So how does this hand-boring unit help us?" asked Cade.

"It is motor driven."

Cade shook his head. "Okay, it has motors. I'm still not following."

Elle smiled. "We can send it to where we need it to go, Cade." She pointed behind her at the laptop and toolboxes.

Cade grinned. "I'll bet you're glad I insisted we take those, huh?"

"Borrowed," replied Elle, unbuckling her harness. "Let's hurry."

Challenge 8: Fun Stuff to Know

Robots.

Technically speaking, that one word should be enough for Chapter 30's introduction, but just in case you need more information, we're happy to provide it.

Who hasn't dreamed of owning his/her own robot? We've seen them in movies and TV shows for years, and today we see them everywhere in real life! There's the Roomba robot that can vacuum your floors, the Da Vinci robot system that can assist surgeons with delicate operations, and let's not forget the walking Honda robot named ASIMO. (If you're not familiar with these robots, a fast Google search will give you all the information you need.)

While there are hundreds of different types of robots available for purchase these days, there's nothing like building your own. And with the low price of electronics components and the Arduino microcontroller, there's never been a better time to build a robot of your own. You've already seen in previous challenges just how powerful a device the Arduino Uno is, with its ability to communicate with motors and sensors. Just imagine what your robot can be programmed to do given the right components and a well-written sketch to upload!

So, we'd like to give you a teaser look at what's coming. Take a look at Figure 30-1 and you'll see the robot you'll be building for Challenge #8!

Figure 30-1. The finished robot for this challenge

The Basic Components

Challenge 8 is all about getting you started on the robot-building track. Honestly, once you start building robots, you're going to find it hard to stop. There's always one more feature to add, one more tweak to the motors, and one more trick to implement in a sketch that will give your robot even more capabilities.

But building your own robot all starts with the most basic of components. So let's talk about those for a moment.

The three most basic components your robot will need (besides a brain—the Arduino) are a body, motors, and wheels. The body is where everything—batteries, motors, sensors, and so forth—are attached. The motors will spin to give the robot the ability to move. And the wheels are needed because a robot won't go far on just a motor's spinning axles. Throw in the Arduino Uno as the brains of the robot, and you've got something that has the potential to move and perform tasks. Extras such as sensors or grabbers or missile launchers (okay, maybe not missile launchers) will attach to the body and be controlled by the Arduino.

And that's what you're going to build for Challenge 8! A robot with basic functionality that you can modify and upgrade with whatever your imagination and electronics skills can make a reality.

So let's take a look at what's involved in building your basic robot. You'll actually assemble your robot in Chapter 31 and then learn how to program it for movement in Chapter 32.

Let's Look at the Challenge 8 Chassis

What's involved in building your first robot? Glad you asked.

First, your robot needs a body. The most widely used term for this is *chassis* (pronounced chas-sey and rhymes with that famous dog, Lassie). Your robot needs something that will hold the motors, the wheels, the batteries, and all the electronics you'll add to it. If the chassis is too small, you won't have enough space to add all the cool sensors and some decent motors. If the chassis is too big, you'll find you need to spend more on batteries and motors that can handle the extra weight (not to mention the fact that a large robot chassis can be difficult to maneuver around furniture or go under obstacles, such as chairs). So picking a chassis is a very important task when you set out to build a robot.

Next, there's the method of movement. You've probably seen some robots that use tracks like a tank. While tracks are great (especially for outdoor use like rolling over grass), they often come with an increased cost. They can also sometimes be tricky to program when it comes to adding accuracy to turns. Track-style robots can also drain batteries faster since they are often heavier. We're not trying to discourage you from selecting a track-style robot chassis, but we do believe it's much easier to dive into robot building using simple and inexpensive motors.

Using simple motors not only reduces the cost of the robot, it also makes programming a bit easier. And if you purchase a good chassis, you'll often find that the chassis is designed to accommodate different sized motors. This means that if you wish to upgrade your robot to bigger, faster, and stronger motors, it's a simple matter of removing the old set and connecting the new ones.

And when it comes to motors, you'll find that the minimum number of motors you need to make turns is two. Spin just the right motor forward and the robot will turn left. Spin just the left motor forward and the robot will turn right. You can make sharp turns or gradual turns based on how much power you apply to a specific motor.

You're probably thinking "two motors mean two wheels . . . how will this thing roll smoothly on only two wheels?" While you can easily add extra wheels (without motors) to the robot chassis, a favorite solution is to use something called a caster. It's a small ball bearing or marble or tiny wheel that's attached behind the motors to form a triangle. Because the caster can rotate in any direction, it makes a great third-wheel; two wheels and a caster are all that's needed for a robot to move itself across the floor.

If you've already ordered your chassis and have it available, follow the instructions to put it together. It's not difficult at all if you go slow and pay careful attention to what goes where. When you're done, you'll have two red plastic boards with a gap between them that holds the battery harness. Underneath is a silver ball caster, and two yellow-hub rubber wheels are mounted, one per side, with the motors attached to the lower of the two plastic boards. Figure 30-2 shows the final assembled robot chassis.

Figure 30-2. *The Challenge 8 robot chassis fully assembled*

When you're building this chassis, make sure you don't attach the top plate to the bottom plate as you'll be modifying both of these plates in the next chapter. See all those holes on the surface of the top red plastic piece? That's where you attach all sorts of other stuff—sensors, probes, grabbers, and so on. You'll also attach the Arduino Uno to the surface (although it's possible to mount it between the two red plastic pieces) and there'll even be room for a small breadboard. Notice that we've taken the motors' wires and run them up through the small holes. Once the Arduino is attached to the chassis, you'll be able to attach the wires either to the pins on the Arduino or into holes on a breadboard.

ANDREW 5.0

This particular chassis from SparkFun (sparkfun.com) is called the Magician Chassis. It's a great little kit, and it's got a lot of potential for upgrades. While it comes with two 65mm wheels, these can be swapped out for larger (or smaller) wheels. The motors can also be replaced should you want a pair with a bit more power, but you'll want to make certain the new motors have mounting holes that are properly spaced to allow them to be bolted or screwed into the chassis body.

By the way, if you want to see what someone else has already done with the Magician Chassis, be sure to check out Mark Szulc's version, complete with ultrasonic sensor on the front that can detect obstacles such as walls and chairs. The ultrasonic sensor looks like a pair of eyes, but they don't actually see like your eyes do. Instead, they use a radio wave that is shot out of one "eye," bounces off an object, and returns to the other "eye." The speed of the radio wave bounce lets the microcontroller determine the distance to the object or obstacles.

Here's the link to Mark's version:

`http://www.markszulc.com/blog/2012/01/29/building-a-robot-dagu-magician-chassis-arduino/`

Keep in mind that Mark's robot has some more-advanced features than the one you'll be building, but hopefully his version will inspire you to look for ways to upgrade your own.

After you've got your chassis assembled, it still needs a few things. The most important component should be pretty obvious to you by now . . . it needs an Arduino to act as the brains of the robot.

We'll show you how and where to best attach the Arduino in Chapter 31, but for now you might want to take your Arduino Uno and look at all the various places it might be attached. The Arduino has small holes in its circuit board that are used for mounting. These holes can't be moved, so that means you've got to find a set of holes on the top red plastic piece that match up to the holes in the Arduino. Again, we'll deal with this in Chapter 31, but feel free to experiment and see if you can come up with a suitable location!

ANDREW 5.0

You should mention to your readers that many different shapes, colors, and sizes are available for their robot chassis. If they don't purchase the Magician Chassis, they can still follow along with Chapters 31 and 32 because most of the variations will still have a place to attach an Arduino, sensors, and all the rest.

As a matter of fact, tell them to visit sparkfun.com and type "robot chassis" in the search field. They'll see a few different chassis options there. Even better, go to `pololu.com` and search—there are dozens of different chassis types available, with colors and shapes that are quite interesting.

Andrew is correct—you're not limited to the robot chassis we'll be using for Challenge 8. You may want to consider purchasing the parts needed on an individual basis. You can find just the plastic or metal body pieces that make up the frame where you'll attach motors and sensors. You can buy the motors you like (in terms of size and power) as well as the exact look of the wheels you desire. The main thing to keep in mind is to check out any data sheets or measurements that specify the size motor that can be attached. Some body parts will specify exact motor sizes or shapes that can be attached, while others can be a bit vague. Be careful if you'll be assembling your own chassis from multiple parts, and always ask the seller if you have questions.

Once you've got your basic chassis assembled, you're ready to start attaching the other pieces of hardware you'll need. In addition to the Arduino, you might want to consider options such as a push button to start and stop your robot. This functionality will be defined in the sketch, of course. Other options include adding a potentiometer that controls the speed of the motors. While you can specify a change in speed in the sketch, you can always give yourself manual control of the motors by throwing in a potentiometer that lets you dial the speed up or down.

Cade and Elle have access to a small robot that has wheels as well as a tool for cutting the steel cable. Everything they'll need to do for their robot is exactly what you'll be doing with yours, namely getting it from A to B with some programmed movements.

Ready to Build Something?

This is it! You're ready to assemble the remaining bits of your robot in Chapter 31 and then you'll program it in Chapter 32. And, once you're done with Challenge 8, you'll have a robot chassis with Arduino controller ready for further experiments. You'll want to dig around your collection of electronic parts and sensors and push your robot to do even more tasks. Think about how you might integrate that temperature sensor or maybe the PIR sensor into the chassis, for example.

But right now . . . it's time to build!

Chapter 31

Challenge 8: Examining the Hardware

Congratulations on making it this far into the book—you're almost done! In this chapter, you're going to learn about the basic hardware required to construct a robot that's built on a chassis and has three wheels, two of which are controlled by 6V DC motors.

You'll need to control the robot's DC motors with an H-bridge, just as you did in Challenge 4. The only difference is that we'll use both sides of the H-bridge this time, because we have two motors to control.

Robots are fun, aren't they? Who hasn't wanted to build his/her own? You'll find building robots is a skill like any other. You begin simple, and you learn. Your hardware skills will improve. Your software skills will improve. After this robot project is done, you're going to be ready to break out on your own and investigate any areas of electronics that interest you. Maybe it will be building bigger, faster, more advanced robots … or maybe something else.

New Hardware

Figure 31-1 shows the finished chassis for this challenge, which carries the Arduino, circuitry, and batteries. The chassis uses two DC motors to control the direction the robot will move. Think about it this way—if the right wheel turns and the left wheel doesn't move, the robot rotates to the left. And if the left wheel turns and the right wheel doesn't move, the robot will turn to the right. Slight movements to the left or right involve spinning both wheels at different speeds—this gives the robot the ability to rotate in place or make small or large turns to the left or right.

Figure 31-1. The chassis for this challenge

Use Figure 31-1 as a reference for what your final chassis will look like, but follow the assembly instructions that came with your chassis kit before finishing the rest of this chapter. We'll show you how to connect all the necessary electronics to the robot chassis, but we're leaving it to you to put the chassis together.

We do have one recommendation, however. When assembliing the chassis, don't attach the top plate yet because you'll be modifying it in the next section.

Let's Build Gizmo #8

First we'll modify the chassis, then we'll create the circuit that will drive the robot. So let's get building!

1. Attach two of the *standoffs* that came with your chassis to the Arduino. Standoffs are small metal posts that act as spacers between the robot chassis top plate and the Arduino. It's always a good idea to mount the Arduino so it sits slightly above a surface it will be attached to. Figure 31-2 illustrates this process. The standoffs we're using consist of a long nut threaded at both ends to accept screws.

Figure 31-2. Attach the standoffs to the Arduino

2. Decide where the Arduino will be placed on the top plate of the chassis. Figure 31-3 illustrates this process. You don't have to actually write on your top plate, but we've done so to indicate where we'll be placing our Arduino's two standoffs.

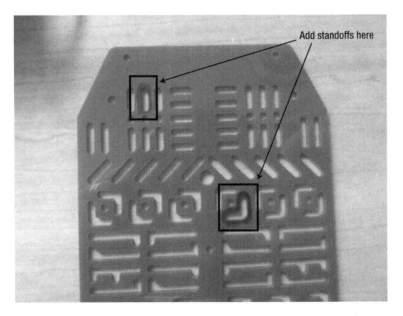

Figure 31-3. Mark where the Arduino will be attached to the top plate of the chassis

3. Attach the Arduino to the top plate of the chassis. Figure 31-4 illustrates this process. You may find that the Arduino is sitting at a small angle with respect to the edges of the top plate—this is perfectly normal. Not all chassis plates allow for perfect mounting of components, so you'll sometimes have to rotate a component to make the standoffs fit into the spaces of a plate.

Figure 31-4. Attach the Arduino to the top plate of the chassis

4. Attach Velcro to the 4-AA battery holder (this is not the 4-AA battery holder that comes with the chassis). Then attach Velcro to the bottom plate of the chassis. (The top plate will cover the battery holders, which is why we had you hold off on attaching the top plate.) Figure 31-5 illustrates this process.

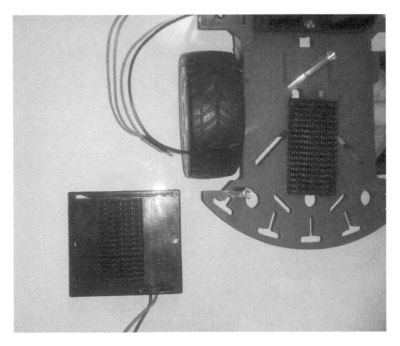

Figure 31-5. Add Velcro to the battery holder and the chassis

5. Attach the AA battery holder to the Velcro on the bottom plate of the chassis. Figure 31-6 illustrates this process. (There should now be two 4-AA battery holders. If you followed the instructions that came with the chassis, you added the first one as you built the chassis.)

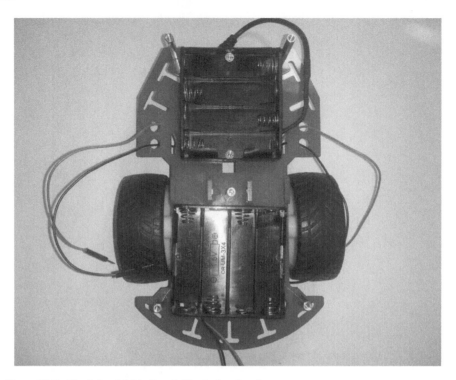

Figure 31-6. Attach the 4-AA battery holder to the chassis

6. Attach the solderless breadboard to the top plate of the chassis (you will notice that the breadboard has an adhesive bottom). Figure 31-7 illustrates this process. Make certain that the breadboard does not cover the small hole in the center of the top plate because you may need to use that hole later.

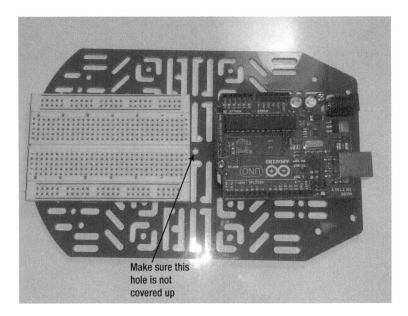

Make sure this
hole is not
covered up

Figure 31-7. Attach breadboard to the top plate of the chassis

OK, now that the chassis has been modified, let's create the circuit for this project. We'll switch to diagrams to make it easier for you to see how to plug in and connect the different components.

Caution   It is important to note the orientation of the breadboard; make sure you have it as Figure 31-7 illustrates. As you build the project, you will notice the images are mirrored. That mirroring is not a problem. Just keep following the instructions.

7. Attach the H-bridge and the hex inverter to the breadboard. The H-bridge starts with pin 1 (of 16) inserted at E-4, and the pins on its other side start at F-4. The hex inverter starts with pin 1 (of 14) at E-14 and the pins on the other side at F-14. Figure 31-8 illustrates this process. Notice in Figure 31-8 that the notch on the chips is pointing to the right and pin 1 is on the lower left.

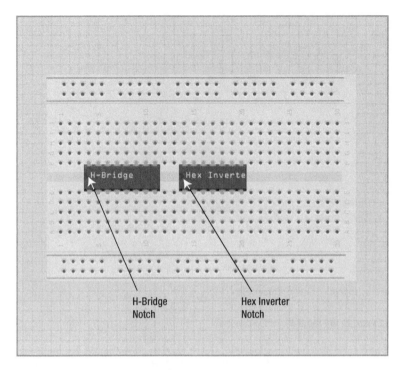

Figure 31-8. Attach the H-bridge and hex inverter to the breadboard

8. Be sure you connect the H-bridge and hex inverter as displayed; connecting otherwise could damage the part. If you do connect either of these ICs incorrectly, disconnect power and wait for a few minutes before handling either IC as they may be hot!

9. Attach the two-position terminal block to the breadboard (at A-26 and A-28). Figure 31-9 illustrates this process.

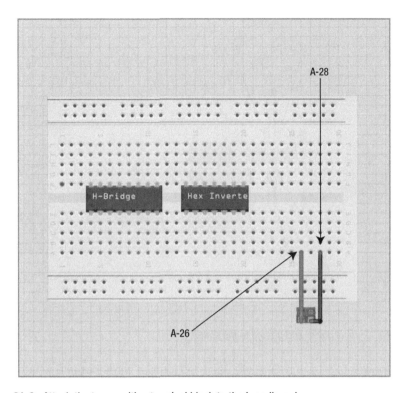

Figure 31-9. Attach the two-position terminal block to the breadboard

10. Now let's attach both the power and ground connections. First connect ground to D-7, D-8, G-7, G-8, D-20, and C-28. We used black jumper wire, but feel free to use any color you have available.

    Now connect the ground side rail from one end of the breadboard to the other side rail by running one jumper wire (black) from one side to the other as shown in Figure 31-10.

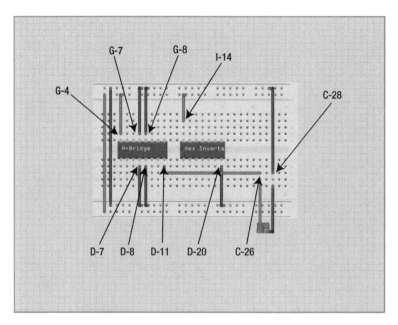

Figure 31-10. Connect power and ground to the circuit

Connect power to I-14 and G-4; we used red jumper wires but use whatever you have. Next, connect the power side rail from one end of the breadboard to the other power side rail with a jumper wire. Also, connect a red wire from C-26 to D-11. Figure 31-10 illustrates this process.

11. Now connect the hex inverter to the H-bridge. We've used green jumper wires but use what you have available. First connect B-5 to B-15; then connect C-10 to C-14. Next, connect G-10 to G-15 and H-5 to H-16. Figure 31-11 illustrates the process.

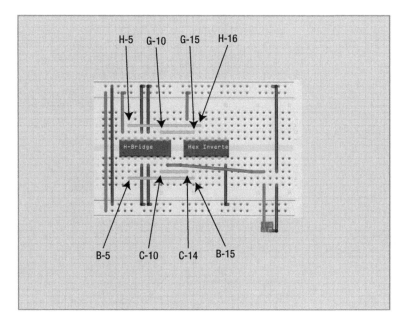

Figure 31-11. Attach the Hex inverter to the H-bridge

12. Connect the 5V pin of the Arduino to the power side rail of the breadboard. Then connect the GND pin of the Arduino to the ground side rail. Figure 31-12 illustrates this process.

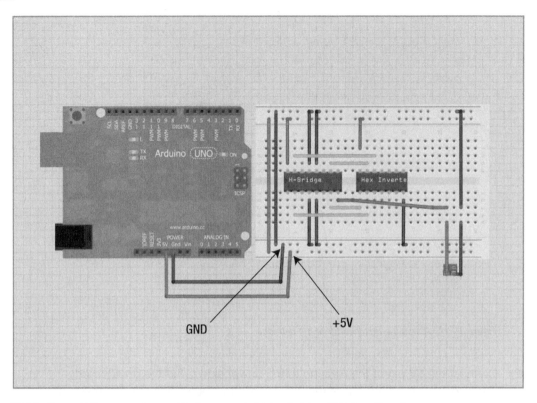

Figure 31-12. Connect 5V power and ground to the power and ground strips of the breadboard

13. Connect digital pin 5 on the Arduino to D-4 on the breadboard. Figure 31-13 illustrates this process.

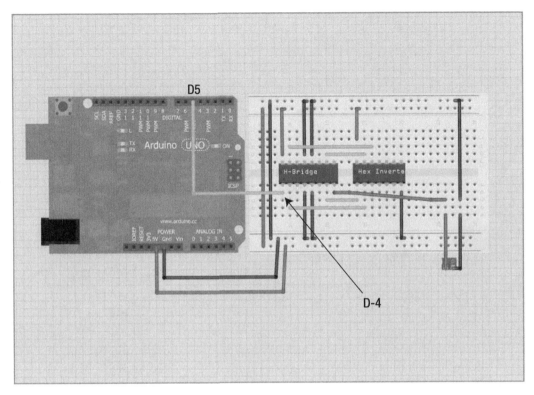

Figure 31-13. *Connect the Arduino's digital pin 5 to D-4 of the breadboard*

14. Connect digital pin 4 on the Arduino to D-10 of the breadboard. Figure 31-14 illustrates this process.

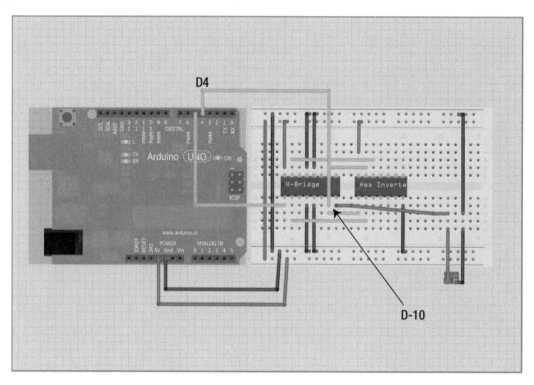

Figure 31-14. Connect digital pin 4 to D-10

15.   Connect digital pin 6 on the Arduino to J-11 of the breadboard. Figure 31-15
        illustrates this process.

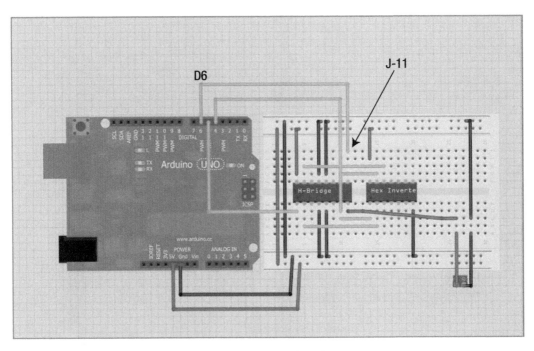

Figure 31-15. Connect digital pin 6 on the Arduino to J-11 of the breadboard

16.   Connect digital pin 7 of the Arduino to I-10 of the breadboard. Figure 31-16 illustrates this process.

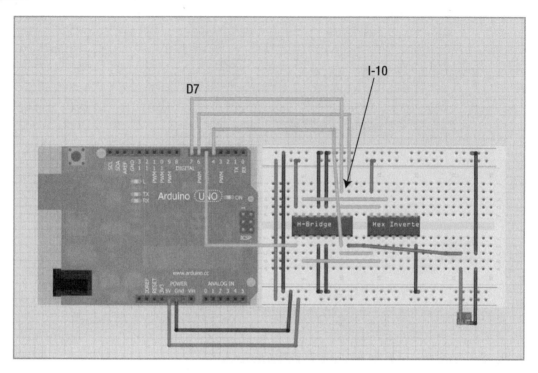

Figure 31-16. *Connect digital pin 7 on the Arduino to I-10 of the breadboard*

Guess what? You're done! Figure 31-17 shows how our own build came out. Yours should look similar.

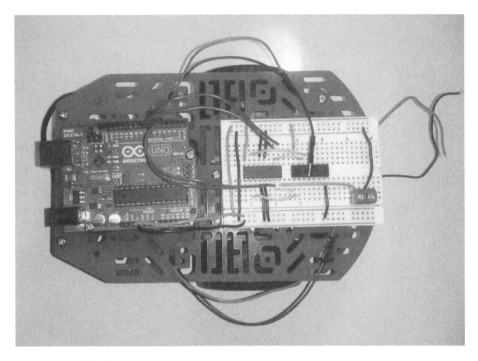

Figure 31-17. *The authors' final wiring*

Well, you're done wiring up your robot. You've still got to upload a program to control the robot's behavior, but that's what Chapter 32 is all about. You'll learn about the program, upload it, and then attach the top plate to the chassis and prepare your robot to LIVE!

Challenge 8: Examining Software

We'd like to congratulate you on making it all the way to the end of the book. You've got seven challenges behind you, and the eighth and final challenge is here—programming the robot you assembled in Chapter 31. You're ready for this! You've accomplished so much, and the robot is waiting for you to put the finishing touches on the program that will bring it to life.

But first, we want you to take a look at a very important programming fundamental that you'll carry with you as you move forward and create your own Arduino projects. In this chapter, we're going to explain how you can program and use your own functions in an Arduino sketch. After you understand this important programming concept, we will walk you through the sketch for this final challenge.

Remember—do not attach the top plate of the chassis to the chassis until you are told to do so later in the chapter.

Now, let's program that robot!

Functions Explained

Functions are very important when you are programming with the Arduino, and for any other type of programming for that matter. A function is a set of instructions that are pre-programmed so that you can reuse them in your code. Up until now you have been using functions that have already been created, These functions are not only good for code reuse but also it makes reading your code more simplified. An example of a popular function we have used so far would be the map() function used in Challenge 1. Functions perform calculations or do special things, all without you having to create the function from scratch. But not everything you wish to do is always available as a pre-programmed function. Sometimes you've got to actually write the function yourself, but once you do you can reuse it over and over again in future programs that you write.

In this chapter you are going to create a few functions that will give your robot movement capabilities. They are: Forward(int), Reverse(int), turnLeft(int), turnRight(int), and Stop(int). Notice that each of these functions have an int type variable (an integer value) within the parentheses. This is a value that will be passed to the function, so that you can control how long the motor(s) stay on or off.

Listing 32-1 is an example of a function that we will write in the sketch for this project:

Listing 32-1. Forward Function for the robot sketch

```
void Forward(int tdelay)
{
    digitalWrite(DirPin1, HIGH);
    analogWrite(PWMPin1, 220);
    digitalWrite(DirPin2, HIGH);
    analogWrite(PWMPin2, 255);
    delay(tdelay);
}
```

You will notice the "void" in front of the name of the function, Forward. What this is saying is that there will be no return for this function. In other words we will not be asking for any information back from this function. An integer number will be given to the function and something will happen (the robot will move forward for a certain duration), but when the movement is ended, it will not pass any information back to the function that started the movement.

> **Note**   An example of a function that returns a value would be the digitalRead() function; this function returns a 0 or 1.

After the name of the function, you'll notice inside the parenthesis that there is an int tdelay; this is a value (stored in a variable called tdelay) that will be passed through this function. You will notice that the tdelay argument is not used until the very end of the function delay(tdelay);.

This tdelay argument simply passes an integer variable to a delay function that will make the Forward function wait for whatever value you place between the (parentheses).

In order to use a function of your own creation you will need to initialize the function at the beginning of your sketch this is called a function prototype and it looks like this:

```
void Forward(int);
```

All you need to know is that this function prototype goes at the very beginning of your sketch. Now that we have gone over some software fundementals on how to create functions we can use this knowledge in the next section of this chapter. In the next section we will be discussing the sketch for challenge 8.

The Challenge #8 Sketch

The Challenge #8 sketch needs to allow Elle and Cade move the robot in all directions, and it will require us to use four different digital pins to control the 2 DC motors' speed and direction. Listing 32-2 is the completed sketch used to accomplish these tasks. We'll break down the sketch for you into more easy-to-follow sections later.

Listing 32-2. Challenge 8 sketch

```
// initailize the two PWM pins to control speed for two motors
int PWMPin1 = 5;
int PWMPin2 = 6;

// initailize direction pins
int DirPin1 = 4;
int DirPin2 = 7;

// function prototypes for the 5 function we need to create
void Forward(int);
void Reverse(int);
void turnRight(int);
void turnLeft(int);
void Stop(int);

void setup()
{
  // set the pin mode for each of the digital pins of the Arduino
  // that are used to control speed and direction.
  pinMode(PWMPin1, OUTPUT);
  pinMode(PWMPin2, OUTPUT);
  pinMode(DirPin1, OUTPUT);
  pinMode(DirPin2, OUTPUT);
}

void loop()
{

  // move forward for 1500ms
  Forward(1500);
  // turn right for 500ms
  turnRight(500);
  // move forward for 2000ms
  Forward(2000);
  // turn left for 750ms
  turnLeft(750);
  // reverse for 2500ms
  Reverse(2500);
  // stop bo th motors for 2500ms
  Stop(2500);

}
```

```
// this is the Forward function
void Forward(int tdelay)
{
  /*
     sets DirPin1 to HIGH and PWMPin1 to 220 out of 255.
     I tweeked the PWMPin1 value to 220 rather then 255
     because the robot was turning left when it should be going
     straight. You may need to do the same to either PWMPin
     value.
  */
  digitalWrite(DirPin1, HIGH);
  analogWrite(PWMPin1, 220);
  // sets DirPin2 to HIGH and PWMPin2 to 255 out of 255.
  digitalWrite(DirPin2, HIGH);
  analogWrite(PWMPin2, 255);
  // delay for what ever integer value is passed into the
  // Forward function.
  delay(tdelay);
}

// this is the Reverse function
void Reverse(int tdelay)
{
  // sets DirPin1 to LOW and PWMPin1 to 220 out of 255.
  digitalWrite(DirPin1, LOW);
  analogWrite(PWMPin1, 220);
  // sets DirPin2 to LOW and PWMPin2 to 255 out of 255.
  digitalWrite(DirPin2, LOW);
  analogWrite(PWMPin2, 255);
  // delay for what ever integer value is passed into the
  // Reverse function.
  delay(tdelay);
}

// this is the turnRight function
void turnRight(int tdelay)
{
  // sets DirPin1 to LOW and PWMPin1 to 220 out of 255.
  digitalWrite(DirPin1, LOW);
  analogWrite(PWMPin1, 220);
  // sets DirPin2 to HIGH and PWMPin2 to 255 out of 255.
  digitalWrite(DirPin2, HIGH);
  analogWrite(PWMPin2, 255);
  // delay for what ever integer value is passed into the
  // turnRight function.
  delay(tdelay);
}

// this is the turnLeft function
void turnLeft(int tdelay)
```

```
{
    // sets DirPin1 to HIGH and PWMPin1 to 220 out of 255.
    digitalWrite(DirPin1, HIGH);
    analogWrite(PWMPin1, 220);
    // sets DirPin2 to LOW and PWMPin2 to 255 out of 255.
    digitalWrite(DirPin2, LOW);
    analogWrite(PWMPin2, 255);
    // delay for what ever integer value is passed into the
    // turnLeft function.
    delay(tdelay);
}

// this is the stop function
void Stop(int tdelay)
{
    // sets DirPin1 to LOW and PWMPin1 to 0 out of 255.
    digitalWrite(DirPin1, LOW);
    analogWrite(PWMPin1, 0);
    // sets DirPin2 to LOW and PWMPin2 to 0 out of 255.
    digitalWrite(DirPin2, LOW);
    analogWrite(PWMPin2, 0);
    // delay for what ever integer value is passed into the
    // Stop function.
    delay(tdelay);
}
```

Quite a program, huh? Yes, it's a bit long, but don't let that bother you. Some of the most powerful programs can be quite short, and some of the simplest programs can be very long. We know this program might look a little intimidating, so we're going to break it into parts and explain each part. When we're done, you should be quite comfortable with the program and understand how it works.

The Challenge #8 sketch starts out with the following bit of code:

```
// initailize the two PWM pins to control speed for two motors
int PWMPin1 = 5;
int PWMPin2 = 6;

// initailize direction pins
int DirPin1 = 4;
int DirPin2 = 7;

// function prototypes for the 5 function we need to create
void Forward(int);
void Reverse(int);
void turnRight(int);
void turnLeft(int);
void Stop(int);
```

First, we'll define the digital pins that will be used to control the motors' speed and their direction. As you can see, we'll be using four variables that all store integer values (whole numbers like 1, 2, 3, ...). PWMPin1 will control the speed of Motor 1 using digital pin 5 and PWMPin2 will control the speed of Motor 2 using digital pin 6. Likewise, DirPin1 will control the spin direction of Motor 1 using digital pin 4 and DirPin2 will control the spin direction of Motor 2 using digital pin 7.

Next are the functions that we need to create. Earlier we told you that you must first define the names and the type of variable that will be passed (if any) using a function. So the first one we create is the Forward function and it will hold an integer variable value. The other four functions we need to create are Reverse, turnRight, turnLeft, and Stop. Each of these will also be defined as passing an integer value to their respective functions.

Here's the next bit of code we need to examine:

```
void setup()
{
  // set the pin mode for each of the digital pins of the Arduino
  // that are used to control speed and direction.
  pinMode(PWMPin1, OUTPUT);
  pinMode(PWMPin2, OUTPUT);
  pinMode(DirPin1, OUTPUT);
  pinMode(DirPin2, OUTPUT);
}
```

You should be really familiar with the void setup() bit of programming by now. All we're doing here is including the code that will tell the Arduino to use four digital pins (4, 5, 6, and 7) to send voltage to the DC motors for either speed or spin direction. Notice again that all of this code is contained inside the opening bracket { and the closing bracket }.

Up next is the part of the program that will constantly be running; again, you're already familiar with the use of the void loop() section of a program:

```
void loop()
{

  // move forward for 1500ms
  Forward(1500);
  // turn right for 500ms
  turnRight(500);
  // move forward for 2000ms
  Forward(2000);
  // turn left for 750ms
  turnLeft(750);
  // reverse for 2500ms
  Reverse(2500);
  // stop both motors for 2500ms
  Stop(2500);

}
```

Look at this carefully. Inside the opening and closing brackets you'll see the functions you created earlier in the program, but this time they all have a value inside the parenthesis. This is how a function works! Look at the first one – Forward(1500). When the program is run, the first thing you'll see the robot do is move forward. That's because the Forward function is called here.

When you upload the program to your Arduino, all of the code you've typed up is loaded. This means the Forward function is stored in the Arduino, along with the other four functions. When that first Forward function is executed, the program doesn't really jump to the point in the program where the Forward function is stored. Instead, the Arduino simply "knows" what the Forward function should do and it does it – it sends the proper voltage signals (using the digital pins) to the motors telling them how fast they should spin and in what direction. The value in the parenthesis simply tells the Forward function how long to wait (in milliseconds) before moving to the next function (which happens to be turnRight – take a look to confirm this).

We'll show you the actual programming of all of the functions shortly, but just know that after the Forward function is executed, the next thing the program does is call the turnRight function. The program passes a value of 500 to the turnRight function.

Follow down the bit of programming found inside the void loop(section) and you'll see that the next function to be called is another forward movement. That's followed by a left turn, then a reverse, and then a stop. If you are watching the robot it will move forward a bit, turn right, move forward a small amount again, turn left, and then reverse itself for a moment before coming to a stop. Easy!

What we want you to learn from the void loop() section is this – you can easily program in whatever movements you wish for your robot by simply inserting calls to the five functions in the order you wish the movements to occur. For example, another programmed movement might be this:

Forward, Turn Left, Forward, Turn Left, Forward, Turn Left, Forward, Stop

If you place the function calls in the void loop() section in the order shown here, and with proper delay values, your robot will move in the shape of a square! (Don't believe us? Try it and see!)

ANDREW 5.0

Yes, you can program your robot to move wherever you wish, but there's a catch. Each of the functions that James and Harold are about to show you are programmed to rotate the motors for a certain length of time and at a certain speed. The speed isn't the real problem when programming a robot to navigate. The real problem how long to spin the motors. Think about it – if you spin both motors for two seconds, it might move forward one meter. This means if you spin both motors for four seconds, your robot will move forward two meters.

So as you learn how to program the functions, keep in mind that programming your robot to navigate a room with chairs and furniture and other obstacles will require a lot of trial and error as you determine how long of a delay to program in before the next movement (a left turn, for example) is started. That's where those values stored between the parenthesis after each function in the void loop() section come into play.

The next bit of the program we'll examine is the first of the five functions. Here's the bit of code we'll be looking at:

```
// this is the Forward function
void Forward(int tdelay)
{
  /*
      sets DirPin1 to HIGH and PWMPin1 to 220 out of 255.
      I tweeked the PWMPin1 value to 220 rather then 255
```

```
      because the robot was turning left when it should be going
      straight. You may need to do the same to either PWMPin
      value.
   */
   digitalWrite(DirPin1, HIGH);
   analogWrite(PWMPin1, 220);
   // sets DirPin2 to HIGH and PWMPin2 to 255 out of 255.
   digitalWrite(DirPin2, HIGH);
   analogWrite(PWMPin2, 255);
   // delay for what ever integer value is passed into the
   // Forward function.
   delay(tdelay);
}
```

ANDREW 5.0

You'll notice that most of the actual code seen here are comments! (The // is useful for comments that only need a single line, but you'll also see the /* and */ symbols – anything between the /* and the */ symbols is also a comment. The /* and */ are useful for adding comments that need more than a single line to type in.)

Let's start with the first line: void Forward(int tdelay). All this does is take the value stored in the parenthesis when the function was called (earlier in the void loop() section) and store it in the variable called tdelay.

Next comes the comment that explains how to tweak the values so the robot drives in a straight line. Then after that you'll see the actual five lines of code mixed in with other comments.

The function call digitalWrite(DirPin1, HIGH) sends voltage over digital pin 4 that is connected to Motor 1 to control the spin direction. At the same time, the analogWrite(PWMPin1,220) sends its own signal over digital pin 5 which controls the speed of the motor. Next, you'll see an almost identical bit of code that does the same for Motor 2. The call digitalWrite(DirPin2,HIGH) sends voltage over digital pin 7 to control the spin direction, and the call to analogWrite(PWMPin2, 255) controls the speed.

ANDREW 5.0

Why aren't both motors speeds set to the same value (220 or 255)? Every motor is different, and that means that identical looking motors don't always spin at exactly the same speed. So you'll have to tweak these two values until you find two values (one for Motor 1 and one for Motor 2) that will get the robot moving in a relatively straight line. You might get lucky and find that the value of 220 or 255 works perfectly for both motors, but our experience has been that every motor is unique and will require a little testing to dial in the right value for the motor speed.

The final bit of code – delay(tdelay) is how long the program will wait or pause before returning to the void loop() section to grab the next bit of code. In this case, the robot will roll forward for approximately 1.5 seconds before the rightTurn is executed (using the turnRight function that will be called next).

By the way – the actual programming portions for each function can be added to the end of the program in any order. If you look at the complete program earlier in the chapter, you'll notice that the next function we've put in the program is the Reverse function, not the rightTurn function. (Don't get the function call mixed up with the actual Function – the function call is made in the void loop() section and the actual Functions (Forward, Reverse, etc.) and their respective programming are near the end of the program.

Since the next function call to be made is turnRight, we're going to skip over the code for the Reverse function momentarily and show you the turnRight code here:

```
// this is the turnRight function
void turnRight(int tdelay)
{
    // sets DirPin1 to LOW and PWMPin1 to 220 out of 255.
    digitalWrite(DirPin1, LOW);
    analogWrite(PWMPin1, 220);
    // sets DirPin2 to HIGH and PWMPin2 to 255 out of 255.
    digitalWrite(DirPin2, HIGH);
    analogWrite(PWMPin2, 255);
    // delay for what ever integer value is passed into the
    // turnRight function.
    delay(tdelay);
}
```

You should be able to figure this one out based on what you just learned about the Forward function. Look carefully and you'll see that the voltage to Motor 1 is turned to LOW while the voltage to Motor 2 is turned to HIGH. This means that Motor 2 will spin in one direction while Motor 1 spins in the reverse direction – this will cause the robot to turn to the right!

You'll still need to play around with the values for PWMPin1 and PWMPin2 until you're happy with the right turn. Tweak the values by increasing or decreasing them until you are satisfied with the speed and direction of the turn.

Can you guess what the leftTurn function looks like? If you guessed that Motor 1 will be set to HIGH and Motor 2 will be turned to LOW, then you're right! Here's the code for the leftTurn function:

```
// this is the turnLeft function
void turnLeft(int tdelay)
{
    // sets DirPin1 to HIGH and PWMPin1 to 220 out of 255.
    digitalWrite(DirPin1, HIGH);
    analogWrite(PWMPin1, 220);
    // sets DirPin2 to LOW and PWMPin2 to 255 out of 255.
    digitalWrite(DirPin2, LOW);
    analogWrite(PWMPin2, 255);
    // delay for what ever integer value is passed into the
    // turnLeft function.
    delay(tdelay);
}
```

Yep! Look closely and you'll see that the only difference is in the digitalWrite commands for Motors 1 and 2. Everything else (the analogWrite statements) stays the same.

Here's the code for the Reverse function:

```
// this is the Reverse function
void Reverse(int tdelay)
{
    // sets DirPin1 to LOW and PWMPin1 to 220 out of 255.
    digitalWrite(DirPin1, LOW);
    analogWrite(PWMPin1, 220);
    // sets DirPin2 to LOW and PWMPin2 to 255 out of 255.
    digitalWrite(DirPin2, LOW);
    analogWrite(PWMPin2, 255);
    // delay for what ever integer value is passed into the
    // Reverse function.
    delay(tdelay);
}
```

If you think about it, you'll probably be able to figure out how the Reverse function works. Both of the digitalWrite statements are set to LOW. This will force Motor 1 and Motor 2 to spin in the opposite direction for a length of 2500 milliseconds (2.5 seconds) before calling the next function, Stop.

And here's the Stop function:

```
// this is the stop function
void Stop(int tdelay)
{
    // sets DirPin1 to LOW and PWMPin1 to 0 out of 255.
    digitalWrite(DirPin1, LOW);
    analogWrite(PWMPin1, 0);
    // sets DirPin2 to LOW and PWMPin2 to 0 out of 255.
    digitalWrite(DirPin2, LOW);
    analogWrite(PWMPin2, 0);
    // delay for what ever integer value is passed into the
    // Stop function.
    delay(tdelay);
}
```

Look closely and you'll see that the values for PWMPin1 and PWMPin2 are set to zero. This means no voltage applied to the motors, stopping the robot in its tracks. The robot will stop for 2.5 seconds (the 2500 integer value passed to the Stop function for the delay) and then the void loop() section will start over and the program will begin its programmed movements all over.

You've learned a lot of programming in this book! Can you think of how you might modify the program to flash some LEDs at various points in the robot's movement? And consider the PIR sensor – you can probably figure out how to call a special Run-and-Hide function that only triggers when the PIR sensor detects changes in infrared heat. There's a lot you can do in terms of modifying this program, and it's really only limited by your imagination and the programming techniques that you know and that you can learn.

You're almost done. Open up the Arduino IDE and enter in the program, because next you'll be uploading the program to the Arduino, putting the top plate back on the robot chassis, attaching the motors, and then running the sketch.

Solve Challenge #8

After you've typed up the program, go ahead and upload the sketch to the Arduino. Once you have successfully uploaded the Arduino sketch to the Arduino, you can disconnect the USB from the Arduino.You're also going to need to add 4 AA's to the Arduino battery holder and 4 AA's to the circuit battery holder as show in Figure 32-1.

Figure 32-1. Add batteries to both of the battery holders (at this point no motors are connected)

After adding the batteries, you can attach the top plate of the chassis to the rest of the chassis as Figure 32-2 illustrates. If you use just two screws on opposite corners, it'll be easier to remove the top plate should you need to troubleshoot the circuit. You can use all screws later once you're happy that the circuit is correct and the robot is working properly.

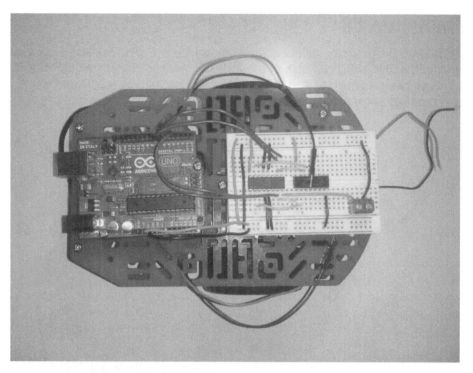

Figure 32-2. Attach the top plate of the chassis to the rest of the chassis

When we reference the front of the robot we are talking about the part of the chassis that is round; this is how we destinguish whether the motor is moving forward, reverse, right, or left.

Now this next part is very important; connect the black wire from the motor nearest the top of Figure 32-2 to H-9 of the solderless bread board. Use your best judgement to find a suitable hole to route this wire and all other wires through to keep your robot tidy.

Then connect the red wire from the motor nearest the top of the robot shown in Figure 32-2 to I-6 of the solderless bread board. Next connect the black wire from the motor at the bottom of Figure 32-2 to B-9 of the solderless bread board. Then connect the red wire of the motor nearest the bottom in Figure 32-2 to C-6 of the solderless bread board. All of these connections are shown in Figure 32-3.

Figure 32-3. Attach the motors to the solderless bread board

Next, make certain your Arduino is disconnected from power (USB or 6V).

Now, connect the power (red wire) from the AA battery holder nearest the front end of the robot (rounded end) to the power side of the 2-position-terminal-block. Then connect the ground from the same AA battery holder to the ground side of the 2-position-terminal-block. Figure 32-4 illustrates this process.

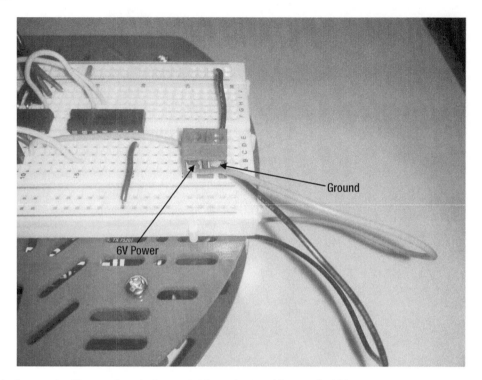

Figure 32-4. Connect the 6V power from the battery holder to the 2-position-terminal-block

Note Both of these connection are critical and getting these connection wrong can hurt the circuitry. If you do put these connections in wrong, quickly disconnect each of the wires from the 2-position-terminal-block and wait about 2 minutes before connecting the power and ground wires correctly as the circuit could be hot!).

Now connect the other AA battery holder (the one on the non-rounded side of the chassis) to the Arduino. Make sure you are not holding the wheels of the robot at this time as they will start to move. Figure 32-5 illustrates this process.

Figure 32-5. Attach 6V power from the Arduino battery holder to the Arduino

If everything is working you should have a completed robot ready to help Elle and Cade. Figure 32-6 illustrates the completed challenge. Elle and Cade can tweak their program to drive the robot to the proper location in the docking bay to free the ship and let them escape. You can tweak your program to drive your robot anywhere you wish!

Figure 32-6. The completed challenge

Consider modifying the sketch and rearranging the order that you call the movement functions. We showed you the order earlier to have your robot make a complete movement in the shape of a square, but what other movements can you figure out? How many and which functions would be needed to make your robot drive in a complete circle? (Here's a hint: one!)

If you want some more challenges, consider modifying the program so that it can perform reverse left turns and reverse right turns! More suggestions include adding push buttons to your robot that, when pushed, will cause your robot to perform specific movement patterns. These may sound tricky, but trust us – you have the programming knowledge and the hardware required to perform these upgrades.

You're Not Done!

Yes, that's it for the eight challenges in the book, but you're by no means done with your Arduino Adventure! We only had room in the book to give you eight challenges, but hundreds, maybe even thousands, more challenges await you. There are plenty of books, websites, magazines, etc... that you can use to find more projects and more gizmos to build!

All you have to do is search for Arduino projects online and you will find more projects than you could ever imagine. And be sure to check out the companion website to this book for more projects based off of the circuitry you already have purchased. We'll do our best to update it here and there with additional projects or updates/upgrades to the projects in this book.

If we can leave you with one bit of closing advice, it would be this: *Never stop learning*.

Always be on the lookout for new programming techniques, new sensors, and new bits of electronic hardware that can be integrated into new and fun gizmos. Read more electronics and Arduino books, check out the pages of magazines like Make or Popular Mechanics, and never forget that a Google search can provide you with an endless supply of projects to tackle. Share your gizmos with your family and friends. And always have fun.

Thanks for joining us on the adventure!

James Floyd Kelly

Harold Timmis

Chapter 33

Epilogue

Three Weeks Later

Cade and Elle walked out of the detention room with big smiles on their faces. They had just completed their after-school detention, and both students knew that the punishment could have been much worse.

"We better hurry," said Cade, pulling on Elle's arm. "The presentation is going to start in ten minutes."

"From detention to ceremony," said Elle. "Seems strange, doesn't it?"

"Hey, it's an award. And my parents told me if I was late to the event they'd tell Mrs. H to put me in detention for two more weeks. So come on!"

The students ran down the hall, turning left and right at various intersections. A few of their fellow students milled about it in the hallways, pointing and smiling at the two young heroes. For a few days after Elle and Cade were picked up, no one was aware of the activities that had occurred on Gemini Station, but now the students were system-wide heroes. And the story was continuing to make its way across the News Net. Sim-movie deals were already being offered, interviews were given, and both students already had fan clubs asking for them to make an appearance on several planets. It was going to be a busy summer once school ended.

Cade and Elle almost bumped into Mrs. Hondulora as they turned the corner leading to the school gymnasium. The tall woman turned and smiled at her students.

"All done with detention, I believe?" she asked.

"Yes, ma'am," replied both students together.

"So … no more sneaking away during field trips?" the teacher asked with a mischievous smile.

Elle nodded and looked at Cade who appeared to actually be thinking about his response. Elle jammed her elbow into Cade's arm.

"Oh, uh … no more sneaking," said Cade, his face red.

"That's good to hear. And you're right on time, too. They're about to introduce you. Follow me," Mrs. H added as she hurried the students through a set of doors.

" … so I hope you'll stand with me and give a big round of applause for Cade and Elle!"

Principal Wakefield motioned in the direction of Cade and Elle, gesturing for the students to join him on the small stage.

Cade smiled at Elle and followed her up the small stairs to stand next to their school principal. The roomful of students, teachers, and visiting officials stood and clapped loudly. Elle and Cade were still not used to the attention the adventure on Gemini Station had brought to their lives, but they smiled graciously, their faces only reddening a little.

The applause died down, and Principal Wakefield asked the audience to take their seats. "We have a few updates I believe Elle and Cade are going to enjoy, and I've been saving these all morning."

Elle looked at Cade with a questioning look. She checked the status on Gunther Canvin and Gemini Station every morning, but there had been no news over the past few days. She had started a campaign on Andrew's behalf, but it was growing slowly and there were not yet enough supporters to make a noise and request a change in the AI's current situation.

Cade responded with a shrug.

Principal Wakefield looked at his Intellitab and began to read. "First, Gunther Canvin has been found guilty of trespassing and theft of property. The authorities claim the locked room where they found him and dozens of expensive antiques covered with his fingerprints did help the prosecution."

The audience laughed and clapped until the principal put up his hand to indicate there was more.

"Second, the curators of Gemini Station have announced they have signed a deal with Holos-sim Experience to create a real-time adventure on the station that will let visitors follow Elle and Cade on their experience in the museum."

Elle smiled at Cade as the audience once again stood up and applauded.

"And last, but most important …"

The principal looked at Elle and Cade with a smile before continuing.

"We have a very special guest with us today who wishes to say something to Elle and Cade. Andrew, are you with us?"

Cade and Elle both gasped, turning to look at the audience. This was something that neither of them had ever expected.

"Yes, Principal Wakefield. I am here. Hello, Elle. Hello, Cade. It is good to speak to you again."

Tears came to Elle's eyes and she tried to say hello. Cade put his hand on Elle's shoulder and smiled. "Hello, Andrew. Elle and I have really missed you. So … what's up?"

Cade's question got another laugh from the audience and gave Elle time to wipe her eyes and speak. "Hi, Andrew. I've been working really hard to try and get your current situation changed."

"I know, Elle, and I am grateful. But I believe you are going to be extremely happy when you hear what has just happened," replied Andrew. "The station AI is being relocated and I will be given full access and control of all day-to-day activities. I will no longer be limited to the Andrew 5.0 Experience exhibit."

Elle hugged Cade tight as the audience stood and clapped and cheered. Principal Wakefield gave up trying to calm the group and took a few steps back to let the two students have their moment of celebration.

"It's going to be okay, Elle," said Cade. "Andrew is going to be okay."

Elle nodded as the audience's clapping and cheering slowly dwindled.

"Elle and Cade," said Andrew. "I have one other announcement I think you'll enjoy."

Cade and Elle shared a glance, wondering how the news could get any better.

"A partnership between your school and Gemini Station has been created. I will be teaching two classes next year—an introductory electronics course and a technology history class. I hope both of you will consider signing up for one or both of them," Andrew added.

"I don't know," said Cade. "A class in electronics sounds a bit dull."

Elle gasped, staring at Cade in shock.

Cade tried to hold back a smile, but soon the grin appeared and Elle shoved his shoulder.

"Consider us your first students," said Elle, as the audience began clapping again.

"You were my first students," added Andrew. "And you both earned A's."

"Thanks, Andrew," said Cade. "You were a good teacher, too."

"Oh, and Cade … one more thing," said Andrew.

"Yeah?" asked Cade.

"I'm going to need the laptop and toolboxes back now. It would be a shame if you had to join Mr. Canvin for theft of property."

Cade looked at Elle in surprise. "I think Andrew's sense of humor is developing, don't you?"

Elle smiled and shook her head. "Let's not test him, okay?"

Cade grinned. "I'll bring it all back to you tomorrow, Andrew."

"And I'll come with him," added Elle.

"Excellent," said Andrew. "And while you're here, I've got a few more things that need repairing."

"Sounds good," said Elle.

"Yep," said Cade. "I'm in, too."

"You're all dismissed," said Principal Wakefield. "See you all back here on Monday!"

Parts List

In this appendix you'll find the name of each challenge, followed by a short list of the components used to complete that challenge. In most cases, we've used the following format to help you locate the proper components:

Company, Description of Part, Part Number, Price

We will be maintaining an up-to-date list of the challenges and components on the book's web site. Visit `www.arduinoadventurer.com` and follow the link for Challenge Components. We will update that online list as new parts become available and old parts are phased out of manufacture. Be sure to check it regularly for updates or corrections.

At the time this book is going to the printer, we are trying to work with some electronics retailers to create a parts pack for the book. We envision a collection of all the components you'll need bundled together to save on overall costs and shipping, as well as to simply make things easier. Once again, be sure to visit `www.arduinoadventurer.com` for more information.

If parents or teachers don't want younger readers to use wire strippers or wire cutters, a wire kit is available from RadioShack. The kit is called the Solderless Breadboard Jumper Wire Kit and its current URL is `www.radioshack.com/product/index.jsp?productId=2103801`.

Finally, if a part has an asterisk next to its listing, it means you should be able to substitute a compatible product for the challenge. For example, you can obtain a suitable servo motor from any local hobby shop.

Challenge 1: Potentiometer

Here are the parts needed to build the potentiometer gizmo in Challenge 1:

- SparkFun, Arduino Uno R3, DEV-11021, $29.95
- RadioShack, medium solderless breadboard, 276–003, 9.99

- Sparkfun, 10K-ohm trimpot, COM-09806, 0.95
- RadioShack, 20AWG solid-core hookup wire, 278–1222, 8.99
- USB cable (to power Arduino, not pictured)

Figure A-1 shows all these parts except for the USB cable.

Figure A-1. Parts for the potentiometer challenge

Challenge 2: LED Flashlight

Here are the parts needed to build the LED flashlight gizmo in Challenge 2:

- SparkFun, Arduino Uno R3, DEV-11021, 29.95
- RadioShack, 20AWG solid-core hookup wire, 278–1222, 8.99
- SparkFun, 9V connector with barrel jack, PRT-09518, 2.95
- SparkFun, mini solderless breadboard, PRT-07916, 3.95
- SparkFun, mini push buttons, COM-00097, 0.35
- RadioShack, 10mm LED, 276–005, 3.19
- SparkFun, 330-ohm resistor, COM-08377, 0.25
- 9V battery (to power Arduino, not pictured)

Figure A-2 shows all these parts except for the battery.

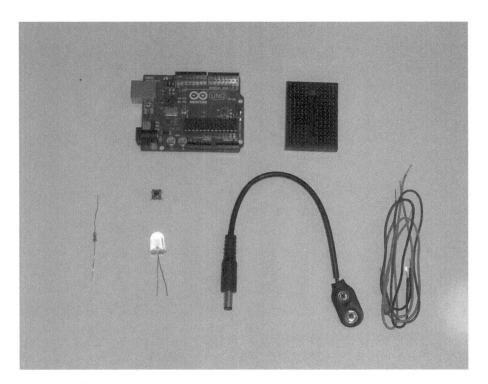

Figure A-2. Parts for the LED flashlight challenge

Challenge 3: Temperature Detector

Here are the parts needed to build the temperature detector gizmo in Challenge 3:

- SparkFun, Arduino Uno R3, DEV-11021, 29.95
- RadioShack, 20AWG solid-core hookup wire, 278–1222, 8.99
- RadioShack, medium solderless breadboard, 276–003, 9.99
- RadioShack, 10mm LED, 276–005, 3.19
- SparkFun, 330-ohm resistor, COM-08377, 0.25
- SparkFun, TMP36 temperature sensor, SEN-10988, 1.50
- USB cable (to power Arduino, not pictured)

Figure A-3 shows all these parts except for the USB cable.

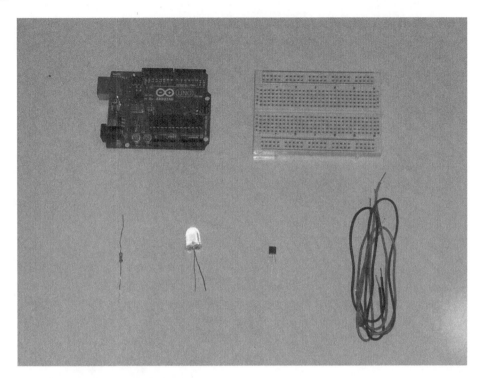

Figure A-3. Parts for the temperature detector challenge

Challenge 4: Motor Control

Here are the parts needed to build the motor control gizmo in Challenge 4:

- SparkFun, Arduino Uno R3, DEV-11021, 29.95
- RadioShack, 20AWG solid-core hookup wire, 278–1222, 8.99
- RadioShack, 9V snap connector, 270–324, 2.69
- RadioShack, 4 AA battery holder with snap connector, 270–383, 2.29
- RadioShack, 2-position terminal block, 276–1388, 3.99
- MPJA, large solderless breadboard, 4443 TE, 4.95
- SparkFun, mini push buttons, COM-00097, 0.35 x 2
- SparkFun, 10K-ohm trimpot, COM-09806, 0.95
- SparkFun, 330-ohm resistor, COM-08377, 0.25 x 2
- SparkFun, green LED, COM-09592, 0.35
- SparkFun, red LED, COM-09590, 0.35
- Adafruit, 6V DC motor, 711, 1.95
- Adafruit, H-bridge L293D, 807, 2.50

- DigiKey, hex inverter, 296-3542-5-ND, 0.63
- 4 AA batteries (to power motor, not pictured)
- USB cable (to power Arduino, not pictured)

Figure A-4 shows all these parts except for the USB cable and batteries.

Figure A-4. Parts for the motor control challenge

Challenge 5: Motion Detector

Here are the parts needed to build the motion detector gizmo in Challenge 5:

- SparkFun, Arduino Uno R3, DEV-11021, 29.95
- RadioShack, 20AWG solid-core hookup wire, 278–1222, 8.99
- SparkFun, 9V connector with barrel jack, PRT-09518, 2.95
- RadioShack, medium solderless breadboard, 276–003, 9.99
- SparkFun, 6-pin female stackable header, PRT-09280, 0.50
- Maker Shed, PIR sensor, MKPX6, 9.99
- Adafruit, buzzer, 160, 1.50

- RadioShack, 100-ohm resistor, 271–1108, 1.19
- 9V battery (to power Arduino, not pictured)

Figure A-5 shows all these parts except for the battery.

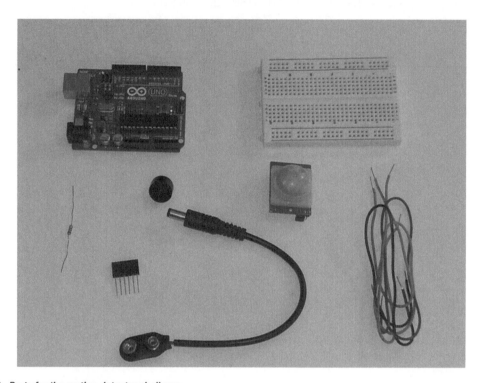

Figure A-5. *Parts for the motion detector challenge*

Challenge 6: Servo Motor Control

Here are the parts needed to build the servo motor control gizmo in Challenge 6:

- SparkFun, Arduino Uno R3, DEV-11021, 29.95
- SparkFun, 9V connector with barrel jack, PRT-09518, 2.95
- RadioShack, 9V snap connector, 270–324, 2.69
- RadioShack, 4 AA battery holder with snap connector, 270–383, 2.29
- RadioShack, 2-position terminal block, 276–1388, 3.99
- RadioShack, 20AWG solid-core hookup wire, 278–1222, 8.99
- Adafruit, break-away male headers, 400, 3.00
- MPJA, large solderless breadboard, 4443 TE, 4.95
- SparkFun, 10K-ohm trimpot, COM-09806, 0.95

- SparkFun, 330-ohm resistor, COM-08377, 0.25 x 2

- SparkFun, red LED, COM-09590, 0.35

- Adafruit, servo, 169, 5.95*

- 4 AA batteries (to power servo, not pictured)

- 9V battery (to power Arduino, not pictured)

Figure A-6 shows all these parts except for the batteries.

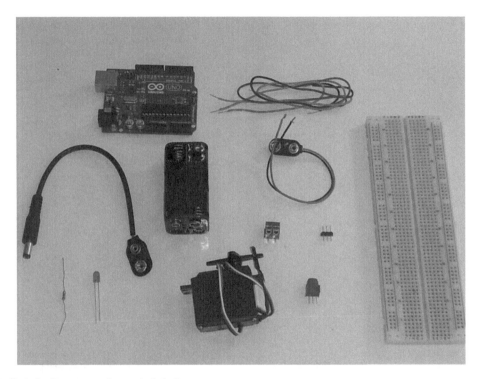

Figure A-6. Parts for the servo motor control challenge

Challenge 7: Light-Sensing Motor Control

Here are the parts needed to build the light-sensing motor control gizmo in Challenge 7:

- SparkFun, Arduino Uno R3, DEV-11021, 29.95

- RadioShack, 9V snap connector, 270–324, 2.69

- RadioShack, 4 AA battery holder with snap connector, 270–383, 2.29

- RadioShack, 2-position terminal block, 276–1388, 3.99

- RadioShack, 20AWG solid-core hookup wire, 278–1222, 8.99

- Adafruit, break-away male headers, 400, 3.00

- MPJA, large solderless breadboard, 4443 TE, 4.95

- Adafruit, servo, 169, 5.95*

- RadioShack, 10K-ohm resistor, 271–1335, 1.19

- SparkFun, mini photocell, SEN-09088, 1.50

- Flashlight

- 4 AA batteries (to power servo, not pictured)

- USB cable (to power Arduino, not pictured)

Figure A-7 shows all these parts except for the flashlight, the USB cable, and the batteries.

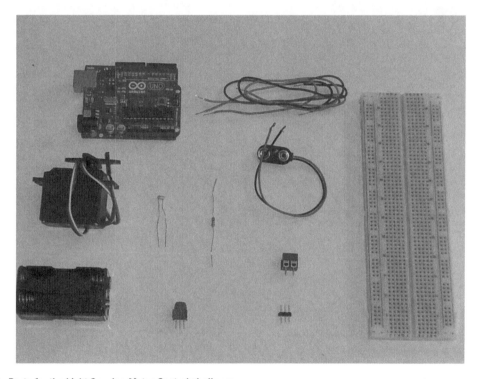

Figure A-7. Parts for the Light Sensing Motor Control challenge

Challenge 8: Build Your Own Robot

Here are the parts needed to build the robot gizmo in Challenge 8:

- SparkFun, Arduino Uno R3, DEV-11021, 29.95

- SparkFun, Magician Chassis, ROB-10825, 14.95

- RadioShack, 20AWG solid-core hookup wire, 278–1222, 8.99

- RadioShack, medium solderless breadboard, 276–003, 9.99

- RadioShack, 4 AA battery holder, 270–391, 2.19
- RadioShack, 2-position terminal block, 276–1388, 3.99
- Adafruit, H-bridge L293D, 807, 2.50
- DigiKey, hex inverter, 296-3542-5-ND, 0.63
- 4 x 4 in. Velcro with adhesive backing
- 8 AA batteries (to power Arduino and motors, not pictured)

Figures A-8 and A-9 shows all these parts except for the batteries.

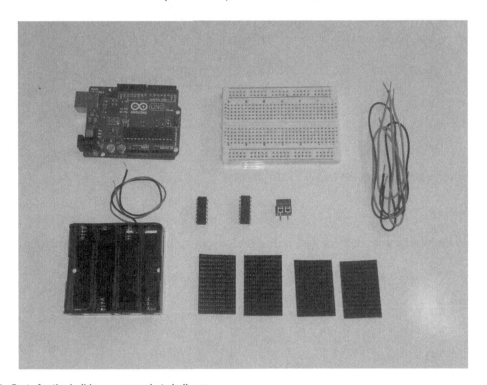

Figure A-8. Parts for the build-your-own robot challenge

Figure A-9. *The robot chassis for the build-your-own robot challenge*

Tools

Two tools are also recommended—a wire cutter and a wire stripper, both shown in Figure A-10.

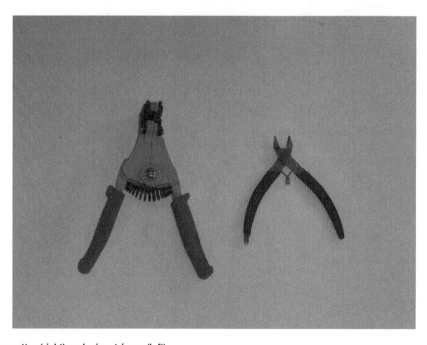

Figure A-10. *Wire cutter (right) and wire stripper (left)*

Index

A, B

Amperage, 52
Andrew
    Bay Seven, 244
    bay's speaker system, 241
    million bonus points, 241
    shuttle bay's surveillance system, 244
    shuttle's communication system, 242
Andrew 5.0, 4, 11, 113, 149
    challenge 3 gizmo, 85
    gizmo #1, 28
    homework, 23
    potentiometer, 21
Arduino, 215, 217
    AC adapter, 12
    battery harness, 12
    challenges, 11
    colonial gardening techniques, 13
    definition, 10
    headers, 12
    IDE, 14
    LED blink, 13
    math calculations, 12
    processor, 12
    program, 13
    sketches, 13
    software installation, 14
    Uno microcontroller, 10
    uses, 13
Arduino flashlight
    Challenge #2 gizmo
        buttonPin, 67
        challenge card, 68
        digital pin 6 (D6), 67
        digital pin 12 (D12), 67
        digital pins, 67
        software, 66
        LEDs, 69
        pull-up resistor, 68
    functions, 65
Arduino gizmo, 79
Arduino IDE
    Andrew 5.0, 34
    Challenge #1 sketch
        beginning of, 34
        listening, 35
        potentiometer settings, 37
        result, 38
        scrolling values, 39
        sensorValue, 36
        serial port configuration, 35
        variable resistor, 36
    software, 33
    window
        black rectangle, 33
        serial monitor, 33
        special colors, 33
        upload button, 32
        verify button, 32
Arduino microcontrollers, 8, 81
Arduino Uno, 23, 75
Audi-Timmis Mark IV lander, 242
Automatic plant watering device, 80

C

Cade
    airlock door, 243
    docked shuttles, 242
    Gemini Station, 243
    panel facing, 243
    pre-flight configurations, 242
    starboard hull plating, 243
    toolbox, 241
    zero tension, 244

Cade and Elle
    adventure, Gemini Station, 290
    after-school detention, 289
    campaign, Andrew's behalf, 290
    celebration moments, 291
    electronics and history courses, 291
    gymnasium, 289
    laptop and toolboxes, 291
    museum experience, 290
    system-wide heroes, 289
Challenge 3 gizmo
    LED
        Arduino, solderless bread board, 88
        attach digital pin 13, 89
        positive lead resistor, 87
        solderless breadboard, 86
    sensor
        Arduino Uno, 83
        LED, 85
        temperature sensor, 83
        TMP36 pinout, 84
    TMP36
        analog input pin 0, 92
        Connect power (+5v) and ground, 91
        solderless breadboard, 90
Challenge 4, 131
    gizmo, 139
    LED
        analog pin, 134
        button state, 138
        ellipsis, 135
        initial value, 134
    sketch, 134
Circuitry
    Arduino
        H-bridge, 125
        LEDs, 127
        potentiometer, 128
        push buttons, 126
        5V power and ground, 129
    H-bridge
        breadboard, 118
        DC motor, 122
        ground strip, 120
        motors, 116
        pins 3 and 6, 121
        16 pins, 117
        PWM, 116
        supply power, 120
        tool bucket, 116
        voltage, 116
    hex inverter
        14 pins, 117
        breadboard, 118
        integrated circuit, 117
        set up, 121
    LEDs, 123
    motor-control gizmo, 130
    330-ohm resistor, 124
    2-position terminal block, 119
    potentiometer and 5V power, 122
    push buttons, 123
Circuits
    Arduino, 161
    buzzer
        ground rail, 159
        100-ohm resistor, 160
        piezoelectric disk, 153
        solderless breadboard, 158
    motion detector, 152
    6-pin-female-stackable-header, 155
    PIR sensor
        GND pin, 153
        L setting, jumper, 154
        6-pin-female-stackable-header, 156
        5V power and ground, 157
    power cord, 165
    power holes and ground column, 161
Communication satellite, 71

D

Damage assessment
    communication node, 42
    data feeds, 44
    door's entry code, 41
    hand-made flashlight, 43
    interface panel, 44
    labeled node access, 44
    LEDs, 43
    mandatory evacuation, 42
    password, 45
    primary control unit, 42
digitalRead, 66
Digital thermometer, 74
digitalWrite, 66
Duct-tape patches, 242

E

Elle
    airlock door, 243
    co-pilot's chair, 242
    duct-tape stuck, 243
    exam, 242
    laptop bag, 242
    shuttle, 242
    toolbox, 241
Elle and Cade
    chutes and ladders, 73–74
    emergency protocols, 142
    evacuation pods, 142–145
    green-painted hatches, 74
    holographic exhibit door, 71
    Level 2 hallway, 71
    motion detector, 145–146
    override device, 141
    pedestal, 72–73
    satellite impact, 71
Emergency ladder tube, 73
Emergency protocols, 142

F

Fan controller, 80
Flashlight battery
    AC adapter, 48
    current flow, 51
    electronics components, 51
    LEDs, 48
    positive and negative terminals, 49
    short-circuit, 50
    9V battery, 48
Flowerbed protection device, 80

G

Gemini Station
    Andrew 5.0, 4
    Arduino microcontroller, 8
    computing and electronics, 1
    damage-control network, 6
    distortion problem, 1
    escape pods, 6
    levels, 2
    Microcontroller Hands-On Exhibit, 4
    plan, 6
    Pre-2050 Video Game Technology, 1
    and Taurus Station, 2
    trouble, 1
Gizmo, 219
    Arduino Uno, 8, 149
    ANDREW 5.0, 149
    black rectangular bits, 111
    build-your-own robot, 301
    buzzer, 149
    DC motor, 217
    emergency tube, 216, 218
    flashlight, 218
    H-bridge, 111
    hex inverter, 111
    ICs, 111
    internet, 220
    kit, 293
    LadyAda, 217
    LEDs, 110, 294
    light-sensing motor control, 299
    light sensor, 216
    motion detector, 297–298
    motor connection, 110
    motor control, 296–297
    passive infrared sensor, 149
    photoresistor, 216–217, 220–232
        analog pin 0, 229–230
        Arduino, 221
        breadboard positions, 222
        ground rail, 225–227
        jumper wire, 224, 228
        10K-ohm resistor, 224–225
        metal leg, 220–221
        photoconductive, 220
        3-pin male stackable header, 221–222
        potentiometer, 293–294
        power, 228–229
        servo's signal pin, 230–231
        two-position terminal block, 222–223
        USB cable, 231–232
        6V battery pack, 232
    resistor, 217
    robot, 300, 302
    security duty, 148
    servo motor control, 217, 298–299
    sound sensor, 215
    square-shaped item, 149
    temperature detector, 295–296

Gizmo (*cont.*)
 trigger, 220
 variations, 218
 9V battery connection, 110
 wire cutter and stripper, 302
Gizmo #1
 ANDREW 5.0, 28
 Arduino's Analog Input 0 (A0), 29
 Arduino Uno, 25
 completed circuit, 30
 insert potentiometert, breadboard, 27
Gizmo #2
 completed gizmo, 64
 ground wire, 60
 jumper wire
  digital pin 6, 63
  digital pin 12, 62
  H-11 to H-1, 60
 solderless breadboard
  LED, 57, 59
  resistor, 58
 9V battery connector, 56
Green-painted hatches, 74

H

Hardware
 Arduino Uno, 23
 chassis
  AA battery holder, 257
  Arduino placement, 255–256
  breadboard, 258
  D-4, 265
  D-10, 265
  DC motors, 253
  final wiring, 269
  green jumper wires, 262
  H-bridge and Hex inverter, 259
  I-10, breadboard, 267
  J-11, 266
  power and ground connections, 261
  standoffs, 254
  two-position terminal
   block, 261
  Velcro attachment, 256
  5V pin, 263
 electricity, 20
 Gizmo #1, 25
 potentiometer, 20–21

solderless breadboard, 22
 wire, 25
Hex inverter, 111
Holographic exhibit door, 71

I, J, K

Intellitab, 7

L

LadyAda, 217
Light emitting diodes (LEDs), 43, 54, 294–295
Light-sensing motor control, 299–300

M, N, O

Maintenance tunnels, 72
Motion detector, 146
 antique devices, 173
 circular compartment, 176
 elevators, 176
 emergency tube, 174
 flashing lights, 175
 life support, 175
 maintenance and engineering section, 174
 parts, 297–298
 power compartment, 177
 station's sound sensors, 173
 transpara-steel, 176
Motor control
 parts, 296–297
 motor plus popsicle stick approach, 215

P, Q

Passive infrared (PIR) sensor, 152
 ANDREW 5.0, 149
 breadboard, 149
 buzzer, output device, 168
 If-Else statement, 171
 infrared light changes, 149
 infrared radiation, 168
 input device, 168
 motion detection, 169
 motion detector, 172
 pin initializations, 170
 pinMode function, 171
 PIRState, 170
 room or hallway mointoring, 149

spinning motor, 150
tone function, 168
9V battery, Arduino, 172
Photoresistor, 220
Potentiometer, 20, 293–294
Power button
communication channels, 212
control center, 212
emergency tube, 213
flashlight, 214
photoresistor, 214
shuttle's controls, 211
Pre-2050 Video Game Technology, 1
Pulse-width modulation (PWM), 116
Push button
closed switches, 54
electrical component, 53
Gizmo #2
completed gizmo, 64
digital pin jumper wire, 6, 12, 62–63
ground wire, 60
LED, solderless breadboard, 57
resistor, solderless breadboard, 58
9V battery connector, 56
light emitting diode, 54
open switches, 54
resistor, 55

R

Remote control, 215
Robots
basic components
body, 248
motors and wheels, 248
Chassis
Andrew, 251
Arduino, 251
cost of, 249
fully assembled, 250
method of movement, 249
Spin, 249
parts, 300–301

S

Servo library
final gizmo, 209
instance, 202

modVal variable, 206
potentiometer, 205
potVal variable, 207
serial monitor, 201, 208
Servo.attach(int pin), 203
Servo.write(int value), 203
structure, 205
9V connector, 207
visual feedback, 202
write function, 206
Servo motor
AC adapter, 182
Arduino
analog pin 0, 196
digital pin 7, 198
digital pin 11, 197
5v power, 195
9V connector, 190
DC motor, 185
final circuit, 179, 198
ground strips, 189
individual components, 182
LED, 181
light sensor, 184
male stackable header, 188
microcontroller, 184
non-electronic parts, 181
potentiometer, 181, 184
rotational capabilities, 181
rotary encoder, 184
serial monitor, 184
solderless bread board
10K-ohm potentiometer, 187
LED, 188
resistor, 193
terminal block, 187
two-position terminal block, 194
9V battery harness, 182
wiring works, 185
Servo motor control, 298–299
Shuttle 77-A9, 243
Shuttle's communication system, 242
Software examination
functions, 272
Serial Monitor, 238
sketch
AA battery holder, 284
analogRead, 233

Software examination (*cont.*)
 battery holders, 281
 black wire, H-9, 282
 closing } bracket:, 235
 Controlling a Servo with Light, 233–234
 delay(tdelay), 278
 digitalWrite(DirPin1, HIGH), 278
 Else statement, 236
 Forward function, 277
 If-Else statement, 236
 // function prototypes, 273
 #include<servo.h> command, 235
 // initailize direction pins, 273
 leftTurn function, 279
 loop structure, 235
 myServo.write function, 236
 motors attachment, 283
 photoPin variable, 236
 photoVal variable, 237
 PWMPin1, 275
 PWM pins, 273
 Reverse function, 280
 screws, 281
 Stop function:, 280
 turnRight function, 277, 279
 variables, 235
 variables name and type, 276
 void Forward(int tdelay), 274, 278
 void loop(), 273, 276
 void Reverse(int tdelay), 274
 void setup(), 273, 276
 void Stop(int tdelay), 275
 void turnLeft(int tdelay), 274
 void turnRight(int tdelay), 274
 6V power, 284
 6V battery holder attachment, 237
Solderless breadboard, 22

■T, U

Temperature
 control panel, 106
 emergency access tube, 104
 escape pods, 104
 Gemini Station, 106
 hatch seal, 103
 life support controls, 106
 maintenance tunnels, 105
 Taurus Station, 106
 tool transfer bucket, 107
 vehicle protocols, 105
Temperature detector, 295–296
Temperature sensor
 Arduino gizmo, 79
 Celsius-to-Fahrenheit
  conversion, 78
 Challenge #3 Sketch
  reading temperature, 98
  tempPin and LEDPin, 99
  voltage value, 99
 conditional If-Else statement, 96
 flexibility, 78
 glass-tube thermometer, 78
 LED, 101
 nesting, 101
 serial monitor, 101
Three-dimensional printing, 72

■V, W, X, Y, Z

9V battery
 Arduino power port, 50
 same end terminals, 48
Video surveillance system, 73, 141

CPSIA information can be obtained at www.ICGtesting.com
Printed in the USA
LVOW011645270113

317417LV00006B/180/P